WHEN·THE·
PRISØNERS
RAN·WALPØLE

a true story in the movement

for prison abolition

dedications

Jamie Bissonette
For William and Bertha Bissonette;
Emily and Erika, who taught me to dare.

Robert Dellelo
For all the men who put their lives on the line in this struggle, and held fast regardless of what came at them: those who died inside, those still living within those walls, those who are finally out. There are too many to name.

Ralph Hamm
First and foremost, I want to make mention of my ancestors, those kidnapped, murdered, and brutalized men and women who faced the terror and barbarity of the African Diaspora here in AmeriK.K.K.a. To the survivors, I owe my inheritance of courage and perseverance in the face of inhumanity and insurmountable odds.

To my mother, Margaret, who instilled within me the concept of strength and freedom through education and knowledge that was passed on to her through her mother—my grandmother.

Also to those men and women throughout the his-story of this country who surrendered their sanity and often their lives in the struggle for the abolition of the prison industrial complex.

Ed Rodman
In memory of Dyche Freeman, who went beyond the call of duty in his last days on this earth.

WHEN·THE·
PRISØNERS
RAN·WALPØLE

a true story in the movement

for prison abolition

JAMIE
BISSONETTE

with Ralph Hamm, Robert Dellelo,
and Edward Rodman

South End Press · Cambridge, Massachusetts · Read · Write · Revolt

Discounted bulk quantities of this book are available for organizing, educational, or fundraising purposes. Please contact South End Press for more information.

Design and production by Asha Tall, South End Press collective
Cover illustration by Darrell Gane-McCalla

All royalties from this book are placed in a trust to support the vision of those Massachusetts prisoners who dared to chance resistance. If you would like to donate to this fund directly as well, please make checks out to "When the Prisoners Ran Walpole" Fund and send them to Criminal Justice Program, American Friends Service Committee, 2161 Massachusetts Avenue, Cambridge, MA 02140.

Library of Congress Cataloging-in-Publication Data
Bissonette, Jamie.
  When the prisoners ran Walpole : a true story in the movement for prison
  abolition / by Jamie Bissonette.
    p. cm.
  Includes bibliographical references and index.
  ISBN 978-0-89608-770-5
  1. Prisoners--Massachusetts. 2. Massachusetts Correctional Institution,
    Walpole--History--20th century. 3. Labor unions--Massachusetts. I. Title.
  HV9306.W342M372 2008
  365'.97447--dc22

2008006161

Printed by union workers in Canada on recycled, acid-free paper.

12 11 10 09 08   1 2 3 4 5

contents

acknowledgments

The process of writing this book began in the fall of 2003. It has been a long and amazing journey supported by many people. I thank all of you for your love, patience, and support. Most importantly, I want to thank Denise and Brian Altvater—and Diahnie and Gavin—for giving me the spiritual and physical space to do my writing. This book was written in your sun-filled kitchen while you were at work and Diahnie and Gavin were at school. Woliwan.

I also want to thank my co-authors—from the bottom of my heart—you dared to let me into your lives and you trusted me with your brilliant story and the agony that came with it. Ralph, Ed, and Bobby—there are no words that are big enough to encompass the love and respect I have for you men. You have prayed and you have sacrificed for the people and we are stronger because of it.

Next is Bob Heard, our reliable ancestor; you nurtured this project, and without your guidance and memories it would have been much less. And Phyllis Ryan, whom I never met, thank you for your notes, the bottomless trove of newspaper articles, your passion, and for all those late nights when I felt you pushing me to get this done. I thank John Osler for introducing us and making sure I really understood how important and how beautiful you were. Additionally, thanks to Bill Owens, Jack Backman, Obalaji Rust, Doug Butler, and Sunny Robinson. Special thanks Donna Finn and Ruth McCambridge, whose dedicated work in CARCAP was a crucial support to the NPRA.

John Boone, you show all of us what could be. You blazed a trail and marked it well. If we have the courage to follow it, we will have, in your words, "made a difference." Jim Isenberg, thank you for taking the time out of your life to make sure this was done well, for all the careful reading you have done of the many drafts, and for never failing to take my calls or answer my questions. Additional thanks go to Robert Bell and Arnold Jaffe.

Ralph Hamm thanks the board of BANTU, who took the chance to make a difference: Jack Harris, Donald Robertson, James Flowers, Henry Cribbs, Solomon Brown, Robert Penrose, Charles 2X McDonald, Alfonse Pinckney, and Floyd Hamilton.

Thanks to Staughton and Alice Lynd for telling me that I could write this book and standing by me while I did.

There were many "friends in the media" that I would like to thank who made sure "The Wall" was not a barrier.

And at the American Friends Service Committee, I want to give special thanks to Phyllis Cohen-Gately, who carefully proofread my work and was gentle with me, Claudia Wilson, who believed in me, and Keith Harvey, who recognized the importance of this project. I also want to thank Mary Norris for opening the door to this work and Joyce Miller for refusing to allow it to be shut. I would also like to thank Willie Brown, Linda Thurston, John Ramos, Dave Collins, Patricia Watson, Gerda Conant, and Barbara Moffit for taking the time to mentor and empower, and John Boughner for maintaining communication.

And then there are the friends who suffer the late nights and moments of doubt and times of brilliant clarity, my sisters and brothers in the struggle: Judith Roderick, Bonnie Kerness, Eve Lyman, Tina Chery, Annette Newell, Plansowes Dana, Mary Bassett, Daureen Stevens, Viola Francis, Pat Phillips-Doyle, Tiffany Wade, Elizabeth Eliades, Kazi Toure, Chuck Turner, John McGrath, Jack McCambridge, Russ Carmichael, Aaron Tanaka, Paul Thibeault, and Toussaint Losier. And Patricia Walden and Jarvis Chen for teaching balance.

Special thanks to Randall Conrad and Calliope Films for generously allowing the brilliant documentary, *Three Thousand Years and Life,* to be re-released with this book.

I thank South End Press for taking a risk with this project and with me. Asha Tall, my editor, you pushed me to write better and harder than I ever thought I could. You believed in me and in all of us and never wavered in your insistence that this huge story would fit between the covers of a book. Thanks also to the many interns who provided support in the production of this book, to Erich Strom and Jessica Hoffmann, and to the union workers in Canada who printed the actual volumes.

And Emily and Erika—my brilliant daughters, who acted as midwives to this birth. I can never thank you enough for your patience in reading and your willingness to pick up the pieces when all I could do was write. And Newell, who made the final steps of this process much easier to bear.

A FINAL WORD

by ralph hamm

I WAS ONE WHO DARED. I DID NOT DARE FOR GOOD-TIME CREDITS, a furlough, or a parole. I did not dare to detract from the severity of the crimes that I was convicted for. But what I did dare to do has profoundly changed my life, and the lives of many others, for the better.

Recently, my prison caseworker said to me, "You've had a rough life." I shook my head, looked him in the eyes, and said, "Not as rough as [the person] who has had to live as a victim of my crimes." In a way, this sums up my achievements within the National Prisoners Reform Association between 1972 and 1973. Life would be far more difficult for Massachusetts prisoners now had we not taken on the powers-that-be directly, and struggled for prison reform. The sacrifices we may have made were worth the lives that we ultimately saved—including our own.

When I entered Walpole State Prison in June of 1969, it was clear that I would have to devise a strategy for survival. The firebombing of my cell led to my confrontation with the guards in Isolation Block 9, which in turn led to the early retirement of Officer Joe Devlin. Joe Devlin was the leader of the "goon squad," a gang of guards who celebrated using excessive force to subdue prisoners. When I beat Joe Devlin, and thus the image of the goon squad, I made a reputation for myself as a fearless fighter who would stand up to repressive guards. I later used this persona to protect myself from attacks from both guards and prisoners, as well as to quell potentially explosive race riots in the prison when the NPRA was in control—the prisoners were afraid of the myth that surrounded me from the block incident, and I used it to my advantage.

The myth also proved to be a formidable, even if contrived, mechanism for saving lives and gaining collective-bargaining concessions during that turbulent and exciting period. However, I did not and do not want to rest upon such laurels as a reputation of reactionary violence for the remainder of my life. I have grown and moved on, spurred by the experiences and relationships I had during that great experiment—now over 30 years ago.

My participation in the development and maintenance of the NPRA (the experiment) brought me into contact with many dedicated people in professional and government life who did not live a myth—or at least not the same myth—affording me examples of lives carried out above the cover of reactionary violence. Reverend Ed Rodman, David Dance, Bob Heard, Obalaji Rust, and eventually ex-commissioner John O. Boone all offered models of Black manhood that I could strive to emulate, which I had not had up to that point. Max Stern and Jonathan Shapiro gave me different prototypes for manhood, too. I grew to understand the meaning of the phrase "there is a rose in the fisted glove, and the eagle flies with the dove," from the lyrics of a popular song in the 1970s.

My participation in the NPRA afforded me the ability to perceive, empathize with, and accept another individual's point of view, sometimes contrary to my own, often incorrect, one. I had grown up fast in prison. In 1969, I was a fearful child confronting the prospect of growing old and possibly dying in prison. Four years later, I had learned how to embrace a world far greater than my own, and found myself in the process of life-altering change. My conscious decision to undertake an insurmountable task, for the collective good, came at a price that I was then willing to pay. I continue to pay it to this day, willing still.

I believe that my decades of commitment to the struggle for prison reform have aided me in my attempt to pay the extremely high debt that I have been judged to owe to society. Although the justice system I had sworn to protect and die for when I enlisted in the army in 1967 came to betray me, my consciousness and commitment to the community outside these prison walls have never wavered.

Ralph Hamm
Walpole, Massachusetts
December 2007

A FOREWORD

by edward rodman

WORKING ON THIS BOOK WITH JAMIE, RALPH, AND BOBBY HAS brought back many memories, both good and bad, painful and funny. My last visit to Walpole State Prison (now MCI Cedar Junction) was a year and a half after the events depicted in this book. Some prisoners who had taken guards hostage requested that State Senator Bill Owens and I try to resolve the situation. Attorney Margaret Burnham accompanied us, so that whatever settlement we might negotiate would be respected. The primary objective of the four Black prisoners and one white prisoner who were involved was the release of Ralph Hamm from solitary confinement, where he had been for nearly a year. The guards were released; our efforts to take the target off Ralph's back did not work as well. He has continued, these many years, to bear the brunt of the backlash of the events about which you are about to read. The "success" of our negotiations left one last bitter taste in my mouth as I realized that the repression that we had struggled with the prisoners to end was mutating into a different and more permanent form. The lasting impression was to indelibly impress upon my conscience the futility of the prison system and to steel my resolve to advocate whenever possible for its abolition.

Many questions will arise in your minds as you read this amazing story of a brief moment in the struggle for justice that was enacted at Walpole State Prison from 1971 to 1973. I will offer three points of context to guide you: first, a description of the racial climate that provided the context for the prisoners' struggle in a post-Attica environment; second, some insight into how I became involved in this saga; and third, an explanation of why nonviolence worked in that moment and how Black consciousness became a transformative tool for the prisoners of color.

To fully appreciate all the dynamics that were in play, it is important to first understand the ethos of eastern Massachusetts during this period, culminating in the infamous Boston school desegregation crisis. The great Celtic player/coach Bill Russell, of the perennial world-champion basketball team during that period, was

3

quoted as saying that Boston was the most racist city in America. The howls of protest that greeted this harsh assessment of the "Hub" (as Boston is affectionately known) were many and mighty. To his credit, Russell did not back down from his judgment; the subsequent events tragically bore him out. You will find critical evidence of the validity of his observation in the chronicle of the rise and fall of the first Black commissioner of corrections—John Boone. His treatment at the hands of some local politicians, too many in the media, and ultimately the very administration that hired him, is a case study of institutional racism at its worst. As the flames licked at Boone's heels during the turmoil at Walpole, the racist opposition to what ultimately became court-ordered desegregation reached unprecedented heights and was a bellwether of the tragedy that was yet to come.

I was not a neophyte to the peculiar form of racism that existed in Boston, which became typified by the distinction between de facto and de jure segregation. Growing up in Portsmouth, Virginia, in the 1950s, I was painfully aware of de jure segregation, which is simply the legalization of what we would call today apartheid. It was in the context of my leadership of the sit-in movement in that city that I came to Boston for the first time in the spring of 1960, as a spokesperson for nonviolent resistance as promoted by the Congress of Racial Equality (CORE). That speaking engagement carried me to Harvard University, liberal white churches throughout New England, and several radio and television appearances. It was an eye-opening experience; at the tender age of 17, I hadn't known there were so many "good white people." Thus, it was with little resistance that upon graduation from Hampton Institute and completion of a significant tour of duty with the Student Nonviolent Coordinating Committee (SNCC), I returned to the Boston area in the fall of 1964 to attend the Episcopal Divinity School in Cambridge, Massachusetts.

Two important experiences during my tenure there deepened my understanding of the true face of institutional racism and the depth of the resistance that had to be overcome if things were to change. The more significant for the purposes of the Walpole story was the three years that I spent in mandatory field-work education at Saint John's Episcopal Church in Roxbury and the Boston University chaplaincy. They afforded me an opportunity to get to know the leaders in the Black community and elsewhere who were truly committed to equality and put me at the heart of their struggle. The second occurred within the student body at the Episcopal Divinity School when one of my white colleagues was murdered in Hainey, Alabama, as he tried to carry out the work of SNCC, following the famous Selma to Montgomery march. While I had attempted to dissuade Jonathan Daniels and the others who accompanied him on what they saw as a noble quest, my principal argument to them was that if they wanted to combat racism in America they need not go all the way to Alabama; it was right here in their own backyard. Sadly, Jonathan's death blinded folks to that reality, and it wasn't until Boston erupted in 1974 that I got the call from many of my classmates sheepishly saying, "Now we know what you mean."

Upon graduation, I was ordained as an Episcopal minister and took a job in New Haven, Connecticut (which is another story), where I met Phyllis Ryan, who was to play a pivotal role in the work of the second Ad Hoc Committee on Prison Reform. The first Ad Hoc Committee, in New Haven, started to address the many amazing and bizarre things that were happening in the run-up to the Bobby Seale Panther trial and the May Day demonstration that followed. In each instance, our primary objectives were to continuously promote nonviolent protest as the appropriate strategy and to create communication tools that would give voice to the targets of oppression—the beleaguered Black community in New Haven and, in Walpole, the prisoners.

Ironically, when I returned to Boston in May of 1971, my new boss, the Right Reverend John Melville Burgess of the Episcopal Diocese of Massachusetts (the first Black Diocesan bishop in the Episcopal Church), asked me to interview the plaintiff in the Boston school desegregation suit, who had just filed the complaint with the help of the NAACP. This landmark case was the first of its kind in a northern state challenging de facto segregation, which until that time had not been recognized as a legitimate cause for federal court action. Many in the Black community had been fed up with the lack of change and had chosen this route to force the issue. Bishop Burgess's question to me following the interview with the plaintiff was "How big a problem are we facing?" I recall telling him that the case and the furor surrounding it would be huge, because it would blow away the façade of white liberalism and unmask the true nature of racism as a national and not a regional problem.

Phyllis and her husband, Dr. William Ryan, had also relocated to Boston, where they had become affiliated with Packard Manse (an interfaith peace group). Packard Manse was trying to keep faith with the civil rights movement, and it became the initial core group responding to the aftermath of Attica. Given the wonderful working relationship Phyllis and I had developed in New Haven, it was natural that we found ourselves thrust into a new struggle to champion the prisoners' cause and avoid a second Attica in the state prisons in Massachusetts. The story that follows chronicles these efforts, with the prisoners at the helm, and is admirably described by Jamie Bissonette and the voices of Bobby Dellelo and Ralph Hamm.

It is important to note that as we struggled with the governor and his minions, we actually achieved two essential breakthroughs before we engaged in the struggle between the prisoners and the guards at Walpole. The first was the principle of establishing citizen participation, which was evidenced in our work with the governor's staff and ultimately the legislature in the fashioning and passage of the Omnibus Correctional Reform Act, and subsequently in our work in the Observer Program.

Because of our efforts, early in the process many of us were able to gain admission to Walpole State Prison, initially as part of the Elam Committee and then as friends and supporters of the Black prisoners' organization known as BANTU. In these early days I was to meet Ralph Hamm for the first time and engage in conversations with many of the politically aware white prisoners as they were beginning to formulate their strategy. During these conversations I began to plant the seeds of the importance and utility of nonviolent resistance, and a proper understanding of Black consciousness. What happened was neither magic nor incomprehensible but rather one of the remarkable things that can happen when oppressed people come to truly understand the reality of their situation and the authentic power that they possess to bring about change in themselves and then in their context. Let us take each of these in turn so that you will have a grasp of the dynamics that lie at the heart of this story.

As far as nonviolence was concerned, the gist of my argument was very simple: violence had gotten the prisoners into the situation in which they found themselves. Violence was being used to suppress them through the age-old tactic of divide and conquer, which in their case was black versus white. Various attempts at violent resistance, whether at Attica or the recent riots in the inner cities, had accomplished nothing. What was needed was a different approach, one that had worked for periods of time in other situations as a counterpoint to the ever-present threat of violence. Another important point that I made is that at its best, nonviolence is more than an alternative form of dispute resolution; it should be a way of life rooted in a deep spirituality that respects all people. However, I told the prisoners, I did not expect them to adopt nonviolence at such a deep level, but more critically, to understand it as a strategy for bringing about change.

The key to the strategic approach was discipline. When I explained that there was a role for everyone to play in a nonviolent movement and how even the most violent could be an important part of the struggle, the men began to listen. Simply put, the essence of nonviolence is non-cooperation; this they understood. The objective was not passive resistance, but active nonviolent confrontation that exposed the cruelty of their oppression. Finally, when I pointed out that there is always a need for some people to enforce the discipline, if necessary, so that the objectives could be obtained, everybody got it. This latter point is a controversial part of my understanding of how a nonviolent movement must function. I firmly believe that if everyone is not involved in the struggle, in a role in which they are comfortable, it will not work. At Walpole, the strategy of active nonviolent non-cooperation did work, for the entire time that the Observer Program was in the prison, and almost carried the day. The observers were present throughout the prison in the spirit of nonviolence and solidarity and trusted that the prisoners would reciprocate in kind.

While these general conversations were being held with the full prisoner leadership, BANTU members were engaged in their own struggle to understand what it meant to be Black men in the most oppressive environment that exists in the United States—maximum security prison. Through many long nights, the people whose story follows deconstructed American history, analyzed negative and positive behaviors of oppressed people, and provided the prisoners with the tools for critical self-reflection and political analysis. Without giving away any secrets, it is fair to say that at the end of our dialogue, they came to understand that when Malcolm X said, "by any means necessary," he did not necessarily mean for them to pick up a gun. Even more importantly, they came to understand that manhood and courage are measured not by how you die, but by how you live, not by how many people you intimidate, but by how many people you empower.

Having achieved this understanding of both strategic nonviolence and enlightened Black consciousness, they were able, with confidence, to forge an alliance with each other and the white prisoners that was, for the duration of their control of the prison, remarkably solid. As you read this story, understand that this could not have happened had it not been for the courage and foresight of Ralph Hamm and Bobby Dellelo and the unlikely friendship and trust that developed between these two remarkable men, requiring each of them to put aside the cultural norms and historical behaviors that had taught them to fear each other and to believe that the only recourse was violence. Once they made that personal change they were able to provide creative and disciplined leadership to a united group of prisoners who for the first time in their lives accepted a disciplined nonviolent approach to their natural resistance to the outrageous conditions to which they were subjected. Jamie could only begin to capture in this book the degree of their sacrifice and the pain and suffering they endured in order to provide the critical leadership necessary to avoid a second Attica and write the first chapter in the struggle to abolish prisons as they have existed and continue today.

The telling of this story is an important reassertion of a history that must never be lost for those who still believe that there is a way to achieve justice and peace. This is a story of hope that even fallible and finite creatures can claim a common vision and struggle together to attain it. I am proud to have played my small part in this struggle, to have the opportunity to use my experiences and learning to its benefit.

Edward W. Rodman
Cambridge, Massachusetts
January 2008

INTRODUCTION

FROM THE BEGINNING, THE CRIMINAL JUSTICE SYSTEM IN the United States has been focused on reform. From the Quaker initiative to turn the criminal poor into the working poor that resulted in the construction of penitentiaries in the 19th century to the impulse to make gentlemen out of convicted criminals that resulted in the parole system in the early 20th century, each reform was designed to protect property, increase the stability of civil society, and manifest the ostensible responsibility of every sovereign nation: to keep those who were recognized as citizens safe from harm. Each major reform has compounded the problem of crime, reinforced a race-based class system, and deepened the nation's reliance on punishment.

Parallel to this history of penal reform, there is another history. It is a history that is largely unrecorded, a history of people—prisoners, advocates, policymakers, judges—who really wanted to "solve the problem" that crime presents. These people initiated programs that actually reduced crime and recidivism and decreased the numbers of men and women who sit idle, as do more than 90 percent of the women and men in the jails and prisons of this country. Largely, these impulses caused great social upheaval during their implementation. The chaos caused by this social change is reported, but the successes—the valuable lessons gleaned from the attempt to actually reform or abolish the system—are buried. This book is the story of such an attempt at prison reform, an attempt that reduced the prison population in the state of Massachusetts by 15 percent and the recidivism rate from over 60 percent to 23 percent during the course of the 18 short months that are critical to this story, from January of 1972 to July of 1973.

THIS IS ANOTHER BOOK ABOUT PRISONS, CRIME, PUNISHMENT, AND SOLUTIONS.

I could begin by telling you about the more than 2 million people who are held captive in US prisons. And that more than 1 million of these people are young Black men. And that at least two-thirds of the 2 million have been in prison before or will be in prison again. I could also tell you that a scandalous percentage of prisoners are prescribed psychotropic medication, not necessarily because they are mentally ill but because it makes them easier to control. I could explain that half a million of these individuals return to their communities each year with the intent of starting their lives over—homeless, jobless, and impoverished. And that more than 24,000 men and women will be imprisoned for their entire lives.

But this is not that kind of book. This book is a story told in many voices. It is a story about people—prisoners, their families, their allies, prison administrators, legislators, and advocates—who surveyed the political landscape in the fall of 1971 and, witnessing both society's angry rejection of penal welfare policies and the horror of the prison yard in the aftermath of Attica, decided that radical reform was the only way out. Rather than increase the size of the prison system, they decided to depopulate the large prisons, develop a community corrections model, and create a way for prisoners to participate in the public debate on crime and its solutions. And, to a certain extent, that's exactly what they did. They were right to have done so then. And they would be right to do so today.

This book is the result of a 30-year conversation among people who dare to believe that 2 million people need not be imprisoned to make the rest of us safe. In fact, they would point out, because there are 2 million people in prison, the rest of us are much less safe. The people of this story are manufacturers, educators, students, lawyers, clergy, and workers. A few are prison guards and prison administrators. Some are politicians. Many are prisoners. All are pragmatists. They challenge our ideas about security and dare us to examine and confront the problems that prisons create for society. They also tell us how we may construct solutions to these problems.

Prisoners, their families, and those from the communities where crime most often occurs know that one deep root of crime is the prison itself. If we are to cut out this root, prisons must ultimately be closed. Indeed, prisoners have shown us that they know what all the roots of crime are. Those who are in prison, the guilty and the innocent, know why they are there, and they know what needs to change to make their communities safe and allow them to build balanced lives.

All along, many of the men and women most directly affected by the prison system have, through their actions and through their very existence, challenged the racial and class structure of a society that was founded on the punishment and captivity of the poor and powerless. With scant support and fewer resources, from behind prison walls and within their communities, prisoners and ex-prisoners have created programs to reduce crime. They have mentored youth who appear to be walking a path directly to the prisons, sponsored furlough programs allowing prisoners to maintain their connections to society, developed job-training programs that are linked to employment after release, and set up halfway houses where formerly incarcerated people can teach those who are coming out the skills they need to rejoin their families and communities. Many of these programs work. They contribute to creating healthy and safe communities. While corrections departments largely continue to warehouse prisoners in institutions devoid of opportunities for growth and change, they prove that current penal practices are dangerous and offer few solutions for the men and women in their custody.

THIS IS A STORY OF PRISON ABOLITION.

First and foremost, this is a story about a group of men who led an entire maximum-security prison. These men, these leaders, refused to see themselves as prisoners. Instead, they became primary actors determining the shape of their lives. These men and their allies knew they could present a vital solution to the problem of crime and punishment. This is also a story about a Republican governor, Francis Sargent, who believed that the prisons under his jurisdiction were a moral embarrassment; about public officials who took upon themselves the mandate to close these prisons and replace them with a statewide network of community-based corrections; about legislators who passed laws to create the framework for these changes; and about a commissioner of corrections, John O. Boone, who was committed to closing prisons. It is also about guards who saw prison reform as a threat to their livelihood and their culture.

In 1955, after a brutal standoff in the state's maximum-security prison in Charlestown, public discussions about prison reform took place. A commission was convened, the commission issued a groundbreaking report, and a new law was proposed. And, over the following 16 years, prisoners were once again forgotten. Resources were never assigned to support the proposed prison reform and regulations were never adopted to facilitate the implementation of the law.

Then, in early 1971, the public struggle for human dignity for prisoners in the Commonwealth of Massachusetts began in earnest. Through a concerted effort on the part of prisoners, their families, clergy, liberals, and labor, the untenable conditions in the Departmental Segregation Unit at Bridgewater State Hospital were exposed. Prisoners there were held in filthy isolation cells and denied clothing and sanitary food. Ultimately, prisoners and advocates forced the state to close this unit and put in place a far-reaching correctional-reform program. This is our story.

The prisoners confined at Massachusetts Correctional Institution at Walpole (MCI Walpole) formed a chapter of the National Prisoners Reform Association, or NPRA, which had begun at the Adult Correctional Institution in Cranston, Rhode Island. The NPRA defined prisoners as workers. Using a labor-organizing model, the NPRA intended to form chapters in prisons throughout the country. The goal of the association was to organize prisoners into labor unions or collective-bargaining units. Prisoners' unions could then act as a counterbalance to the notoriously powerful guards' unions in negotiations with prison authorities about how the prisons were run. Prisoners throughout the country began to look at prisoners' unions as a catalyst for prison reform. But only at MCI Walpole did the NPRA become a recognized bargaining unit, democratically elected by the prisoners—the workers—to lead their struggle for reform within the prison.

The NPRA at Walpole remained the recognized representative of the prisoners for two years, and sought State Labor Relations Commission certification along the way. Even after its petition for recognition as a labor union was denied, the NPRA continued to exercise its power as the prisoners' elected representative for an additional two years. During its tenure, prisoners not only conducted arbitration with Department of Correction administrators, but also actually ran the prison for a period of almost three months while the guards staged a work stoppage—moving freely throughout the prison, establishing programs, and democratically determining policy and the structure of their day-to-day lives. They engaged the media and the public in a conversation about crime and how to stop it, what conditions were like within the prison, what needed to be done to keep released prisoners from returning, and ultimately, what needed to be done to close prisons.

The NPRA argued that prisoners were entitled to every constitutional right exercised by the outside population except the liberty to leave the confines of the institution. Prisoners, as human beings, had the same needs as people who were not in prison, and these needs are fundamental requirements not to be denied. Since prisons are governmental institutions, the NPRA held that the public has the right of access to them and to information about them. Maintaining that prisoners do not suffer "civil death" upon incarceration was radical then. It remains so. The Massachusetts prisoners took this argument further and challenged both their chattel status and the loss of their freedom—they demanded fair wages and the right to vote in all elections, run for public office, exercise freedom of speech, and participate in the development of public policy.

The voice of the prisoners was pragmatic, strong, and unrepentant. Their vision was positive, creative, and hopeful. More than 1,300 hundred men and women responded to this voice and came to volunteer day and night inside the maximum-security prison, acting as civilian observers at a time when that prison had the highest murder rate in the country. Together, prisoners and civilian observers dropped the murder rate to zero. Together, they learned that when a prison becomes a tool for self-development, it becomes a smaller prison—and that perhaps it could become so small that it would no longer be a prison. It is these voices, the voices of the prisoners who believed that they could change the prison and seized the moment, that form the conversation that underpins this book.

THIS IS A STORY ABOUT PEOPLE WHO CHOSE TO ACT.

Ralph Hamm was barely 20 years old when our story began. He graduated from the US Army Leadership Preparation Course in Fort Sill, Oklahoma, in 1968, and had been scheduled to be shipped to Vietnam two days after "his" crime occurred. He had been in prison since he was 17. After being convicted—at a jury-less trial— for a brutal assault on a white couple, this young Black man was sentenced to two concurrent life sentences with an additional 40 years after the completion of the life sentences. While maintaining his innocence, he used his agile intellect and honed his anger to fend off attacks from guards and prisoners alike.

Robert Dellelo was a larger-than-life character. The unacknowledged son of a mafia figure, Bobby had grown up in the state's notorious Department of Youth Services. He knew how to survive and he knew how to escape. More than any other convict in our story, he understood the relationship between power and leadership. He was a shrewd politician who was able to negotiate the complex alliances within Walpole. And when this failed, he was tough. He would fight and he would win.

The Reverend Edward Rodman organized a sit-in at his high school in 1968, at the age of 16. Two years later, Rodman was an unpaid field secretary for the Congress of Racial Equality in Virginia. Later, in college, he was one of the founders of the Student Nonviolent Coordinating Committee. He became an Episcopal priest and a professor at Yale University. While in New Haven, he coordinated community support for Bobby Seale throughout his trial. He came to Boston a committed prison abolitionist dedicated to eradicating slavery in all its forms. He taught prisoners and allies crucial skills for engaging in this struggle.

Phyllis Ryan was in her 50s, a veteran of the labor and civil rights movements. Ryan came to the movement with a fully developed organizing strategy, which she taught while she implemented it. She and her husband, William Ryan (author of the seminal book *Blaming the Victim*), were the bedrock of the outside support for the prisoners. Undaunted by the progression of her multiple sclerosis, Ryan used her razor-sharp intellect to motivate the press and hold politicians accountable.

Governor Francis Sargent was serving his first term in office. He was a career civil servant. Scandalized by both juvenile and adult penal confinement, he committed himself to reforming the penal system in Massachusetts. He used public outcry about the conditions at the Bridgewater State Prison and the slaughter at Attica to garner support for implementing a plan that he had already conceived.

John O. Boone was appointed by Sargent as commissioner of corrections in Massachusetts. He was a career prison administrator. He broke the color barrier in the federal Bureau of Prisons as the first Black caseworker, director of parole, and superintendent of a federal penitentiary. He was the first Black man to head the Department of Correction in Massachusetts.

Peter Goldmark was 30 years old when Sargent named him the executive secretary of Health and Human Services. He had worked as a city planner under Mayor John Lindsay in New York. Goldmark made successful de-institutionalization of human services the focal point of his office.

James Isenberg was 26 years old and a recent graduate of the University of California at Berkeley's School of Criminal Justice when Goldmark tapped him to oversee corrections for the Office of Health and Human Services. Isenberg had studied in Europe and had witnessed the success of the "community corrections" model. He came to Massachusetts to implement that model.

The *Boston Herald American* became a character integral to this drama. The newspaper openly became the mouthpiece for the guards' union, even publishing an editorial declaring the paper itself the victor when John Boone ultimately was fired. The *Herald American*'s openly racist rhetoric was a clear reflection of the blatant racism that would erupt in South Boston as school desegregation was enforced.

WHO GETS TO TELL THEIR STORY?

Many years after the drama that unfolds within these pages was largely erased from public memory, both Robert Dellelo, the first president of the NPRA at Walpole, and Ralph Hamm, his vice president, confessed that if they had their lives to live over there was little they would have done differently. While both wish that the events that put them in prison had never happened, and both express deep remorse and responsibility for their crimes, both also believe strongly that their struggle for dignity within the maximum-security prisons in Massachusetts has made them into the men that they are today.

Hamm and Dellelo were joined by the Reverend Edward Rodman, who not only became their staunchest ally, but unwaveringly took their direction and supported their agenda, even if there were differences of opinion. Both of these leaders have said that this brilliant, radical, young priest who dedicated his life to ending modern slavery was the unsung hero of our story. These three men are my cowriters in this project, for even if they are not responsible for the words that finally made it on the page, this is their story. They not only lived this history, but preserved it, in document and memory. And then they entrusted me with it. They read, responded to, and eventually approved every word in this book. Through six years of conversations and letters, offering cartons filled with observer reports, newspaper clippings, and prisoner letters, they generously shared their own understanding of their struggle and worked with me until I understood, too.

Another strong influence was Phyllis Ryan. She kept notes on every aspect of this project. She saved every press release and every piece of paper given to her. Her commitment to preserve the passion, beauty, and promise of the moment made this book possible. Her rigorous thinking is reflected throughout this book. Their authorship—then and now—is vital; it is through them that we get a glimpse, firsthand, at what many say is not possible, not practical—that prisons can and should be abolished. Here, in this story, is the beginning.

A LASTING COMMITMENT

The actions of these committed individuals would successfully shift the paradigm by defining true prison reform as abolition. Eventually all the actors in this story entered into the conversation about prison abolition. By the end of his tenure as commissioner of corrections, John Boone admitted that he came to Massachusetts as a reformer and left as an abolitionist, the Catholic Priests' Senate had issued a statement supporting the abolition of prisons, and the Ad Hoc Committee on Prison Reform became the Committee to Abolish Prison. This commitment did not end in the mid-'70s. It has continued even during the massive construction boom of the prison industrial complex, and the development of super-maximum prisons. It has continued despite the paralyzing rhetoric of the War on Drugs. All of the participants in the conversation have aged, some into their 80s, but the debate is still lively, the arguments are still strong, and the challenge is still ours to meet.

And it has made a difference. Massachusetts had one of the most successful furlough programs in the country. Despite the infamous Willie Horton scandal that ended Michael Dukakis's bid for the presidency, the state has never removed the furlough statute from its General Law. The legislature still works from the premise that a prison system's responsibility is to provide programming and educational opportunities to prisoners. In recent years, amid all the demands that government be tough on crime and tougher on criminals, members of the ranking legislative leadership have publicly and vocally resigned from special commissions when they have understood that the governor did not plan to act upon their recommendations. The state's prison population began dropping in 1999. There is an active and vocal prisoners' rights movement that has always connected those most affected by crime to allies from middle-class communities. This movement has grown in strength at times, and weakened at others, but it has never disappeared. The prisoners and members of the churches, nonprofits, and communities have remained vocal—clearly asserting that we not only *can* solve the problems of crime and punishment, but we *will*.

1

PREAMBLE

constructing punishment in massachusetts

THE FIRST HALF OF THE 19TH CENTURY HERALDED MASSIVE prison expansion throughout the United States. Massachusetts was no exception. The state's first maximum-security prison, the Charlestown State Prison, was completed in 1805. The Framingham State Prison followed in 1827. Framingham was designed exclusively for women and could house up to 400 prisoners. Twenty-four years later, the Charlestown State Prison was expanded and renovated as a classic penitentiary after the Auburn model, which combined utter solitary confinement with congregate forced labor. These two prisons marked the beginning of penal reform in Massachusetts. A short 20 years later, the Charlestown State Prison would be condemned but not closed. In 1878, the state attempted to ease overcrowding at the facility by constructing the Concord Reformatory. It quickly filled to overcapacity and fell into disrepair.

In 1919, with the passage of the first law governing punishment in the state, the Department of Correction (DOC) was formally created. The department was mandated to achieve two objectives: "Protection for the public and rehabilitation of the individual."[1] These replaced the twin goals of the penitentiary: containment and repentance. Twenty-two years later, during a period in which corrections aimed to make "gentlemen" out of criminals, the DOC built the Norfolk State Prison. Norfolk was designed to replicate a small town with industry, school, and government (administration). It was to be a place where prisoners could practice the responsibilities they would shoulder after their release. It was to be a place where men could better themselves by attending classes, learning a trade, and participating in the running of the institution through an active inmate council. Norfolk Prison Colony was considered the first "community prison" for males in the United States.[2]

By 1955, the Department of Correction was in crisis, as each of its underfunded prisons was filled far beyond capacity. On January 18, four long-term prisoners tried to escape from Charlestown State Prison. When their escape failed, the prisoners took guards and other prisoners hostage. The causes of the ensuing rebellion were described by *Time Magazine*:

> The Massachusetts State Prison, a cramped compound of blackened granite and dilapidated brick buildings in the Charlestown section of Boston, is the oldest, most disreputable prison in the US. It was built in 1805, has been damned for 80 years as a verminous pesthole, unfit for human habitation.
>
> In the past two years the prison has been the scene of 16 disorders, including riots and attempted escapes. Last week, in the seventeenth and most spectacular try, four armed convicts held five guards and six fellow prisoners hostage.[3]

In the aftermath of the rebellion, Governor Christian Herter appointed a special commission to study the Massachusetts Penal System, naming the president of Tufts University, Nils Wessel, as chair. Interestingly, the commission's charge was not to investigate the actual rebellion at Charlestown; the uprising was seen as symptomatic of the problems plaguing the DOC. Instead, the commission was asked to study the penal system itself. As a result, the Wessel Commission, as it was known, authored the first omnibus penal-reform bill introduced in Massachusetts. One year later, the new state prison at Walpole opened. This reform bill and the opening of Walpole State Prison is the beginning of our story.

THE WESSEL COMMISSION

> *Punishment for punishment's sake*
> *alone is a discredited theory.*[4]

Governor Herter simultaneously released the Wessel Commission's report and the proposed Corrections Reform Bill bundled in one publication. He stated that the contents of the report were "a recital which should be pondered by every citizen of the State, for it concerns the moral obligation of every citizen to interest himself in a problem which is basic in the structure of our society."[5] The governor's opening remarks reminded the legislature of its obligation to reform the prisons but cautioned that "the ultimate responsibility for action or inaction lies with the people of the State." Here, Herter was articulating his belief that prison reform depended completely on public demand for it. This framing ensured there would be no substantial change, for it provided no mechanism to hold "the people" accountable; indeed history demonstrated that "the people" only focused their attention on prisons when there was an uprising or a rebellion. The commission had been convened as little more than an exercise to clear the Herter administration of any responsibility for the recent prison rebellion and, more important, for the failure of any future correctional policy.

Still, the commissioners had taken their job seriously. The Wessel Commission's groundbreaking report was a scathing indictment of the appalling conditions inside all the state's jails and prisons. It condemned the run-down and dirty plants, the poorly paid and trained staff and administrators, the forced idleness of the prisoners, the lack of educational and vocational programming, the court's reticence in using probation as an alternative for first-time offenders, and a parole department that was so understaffed it only served to apprehend violators and furthermore, operated independently from and without the cooperation of the DOC. The commission's report laid the foundation for the thinking of some of the prison reformers involved in our story.

The Wessel Commission found that each prison was an isolated fiefdom over which the warden and his deputies had complete control. Since there were no DOC-wide rules, the marooned prisoners were completely at the mercy of their captors. No one was monitoring these rat-infested holes, where prisoners were fed bread and water or starved, and there was no semblance of a correctional philosophy.[6]

To address this lack of organization and accountability, the commission proposed the obvious: a coordinated program involving probation, institutional care, and parole should be developed; competent administrators and staff who were trained educators should be hired; all prison guards should be trained; and "well-prepared, understandable and written rules" should be drafted and promulgated.[7] The commissioners considered the community-prison connection fundamental to rehabilitation, and the report urged "every effort to mobilize community resources as an aid to the correctional program."[8] The commissioners envisioned adult-education programs that could enrich the educational opportunities inside the prison, trade groups that could be involved in vocational training, and civic and local groups that could volunteer in the prison, forming natural connections to "specialized community agencies."[9] They encouraged the administrators of the prison to be open to visits from clergy, civic groups, religious volunteers, and the press.[10]

All of the commission's recommendations followed this pattern. They were well founded and pragmatic but required a level of competence and training that neither the administration nor the guards in the prisons had. They required extensive resources and a radical realignment of the DOC. Furthermore, in most cases the report offered recommendations without any suggestions as to how to implement them, thus compromising any potential for systemic change.

Commission members had visited the solitary-confinement cells inside the Charlestown prison and Concord Reformatory and were shocked by their filth and the dirty, hungry, desperate men that inhabited them. They did not go so far as to condemn solitary confinement, but they did recommend the "elimination of solitary confinement in dark cells for recalcitrant prisoners."[11] The Wessel Commission was the first official organ in Massachusetts to go on record questioning the use of solitary confinement as punishment.

However, the Wessel Commission also opposed the creation of inmate councils that would act as a conduit for prisoner complaints, while elsewhere in the country penologists were advocating for such councils. Ironically, the commissioners believed "well-trained staff" would be adequate to ensure that the prisoners' voices would be heard, that prison industry would be created, and that a sound educational program would be implemented.[12] Furthermore, since the commissioners assumed that specialized personnel would be hired, they did not stress the vital necessity of this. Guard training did not even make it into their proposed legislation. Given the criminal ineptitude of the existing prison staff, this failure to mandate an adequately trained staff would undercut the success of any reform efforts.

The commission also recommended the creation of a voluntary advisory committee on corrections. This board would review complaints, make recommendations, and evaluate programs. The penal-reform bill that passed in 1955 mandated both that the board be created and that it should report semiannually to the governor. Nonetheless, it was never assembled.[13]

Commission members saw parole as an integral part of corrections.[14] They recommended that all prisoners—except those condemned to death—become eligible for parole after seven years, and that consideration for parole be a continual process that ideally would start with classification when a person entered prison.[15] The commission even recommended that the parole board see prisoners proactively within the first year of their incarceration to "assess progress, evaluate potential, and correlate impressions with the individual's social history."[16] This would allow the parole board to determine when a prisoner was most ready to leave state custody. The commission condemned the withholding of parole hearings for disciplinary reasons as contrary to accepted parole practices, which require continual evaluation regardless of behavior.

Two appendices accompanied the Wessel Commission report. Appendix A addressed the reasons for the rebellion at the Charlestown State Prison with draft legislation for prison industries—a thinly veiled forced-labor program. Commissioners identified four reasons for the rebellion: personnel shortcomings, idleness among the prisoners, the influence of hard core "recalcitrants," and failure to provide compensation for good work and good conduct.[17] Of these, the primary concern was the idleness of the prisoners. They recommended a full industry program mandating employment for all prisoners—forced labor. For the men, the industries would be located on state premises. Some of the women would be offered as domestics, as chattel.[18] At the time of the report, prisoners were paid nothing for their labor, with the DOC claiming that the state realized so little income from the labor of prisoners that it could not afford to pay daily wages. Commission members proposed that a "small daily wage [would] encourage morale and workmanship."[19] They offered no discussion of the ethical problems involved in unpaid or poorly paid labor—a daily wage was conceived only as a route to more satisfied prisoners, and hence, a better-functioning institution. This section is the longest and most detailed of the report.

Unlike the other recommendations, the prison-industry program was implemented. Not surprisingly, it resulted in the utter exploitation of prisoner/workers. It also became the focal point for the National Prisoners Reform Association (NPRA). The prisoners' union would demand full wages and entrepreneurial rights for prisoners. Wielding the ultimate power of "the strike," the NPRA exposed prison labor as slave labor. It also demonstrated that prisons functioned because prisoners worked—and that working was cooperation in their confinement. Prisoners could control their environment if they controlled their level of cooperation with it.

Appendix B was the draft of the omnibus penal legislation, "An Act Reorganizing the Correctional System of the Commonwealth of Massachusetts." This bill mandated, for the first time, that the commissioner and deputy commissioners of the DOC possess professional experience in the field of corrections; this provision was mainly intended to ensure qualified leadership, although it also was a challenge to the rampant nepotism within the department. At this time, when a prisoner was sent to prison in Massachusetts, it was simply to the "state prison." There was nothing to balance the arbitrariness of administrative decisions, including whether an inmate would be held in minimum or maximum, in general population or in a segregation unit. The proposed legislation would change this directive, sentencing the individual to the "care and custody of the Commissioner."[20] This change was intended to give the commissioner more flexibility in determining a prisoner's placement and moving him within the system to ensure him better access to necessary programming.[21] The proposed law also gave the commissioner the authority and discretion to publish and promulgate regulations without legislative or public hearings beforehand.[22]

The Wessel Commission report and appended legislative proposals were bundled into one penal-reform bill and received broad support from the public and the legislature. The bill was passed despite the fact that the statutory demands were complex and it was clear from the outset that neither DOC administrators nor prison staff were capable of implementing the recommended framework, nor prepared to do so. Since prison hiring processes were rooted in nepotism, with jobs granted to cronies or family members, there was scant impetus to replace the existing staff with specialized personnel who could create educational or work programs.

Instead of being the object of the wide-sweeping reforms Wessel recommended, the prisons were again ignored.

WALPOLE

When the new Massachusetts Correctional Institution (MCI) at Walpole opened in 1956, it was quickly filled with young men who had spent their adolescence in the state's juvenile detention centers. With Walpole's opening, the notorious Charlestown State Prison, condemned more than 80 years earlier, was finally closed.

The DOC opened Walpole a year after the release of the Wessel Commission's report with little pretense that it would solve any penal problems. The new state prison was hidden behind 20-foot walls topped with 8 guard towers, and had 10 cellblocks with 40 cells each. Every cellblock had an observation deck and was separated from the rest of the prison by an elaborate grilled section. Two blocks, known as 9 Block and 10 Block, were designed as segregation units. Within them there were four isolation cells aptly called "blue rooms"; they had floors covered with cold blue tile and were lit by a single bulb, with no windows to the outdoors and only a hole in the floor for a toilet. These blue rooms would figure largely in torture of prisoners—and their resistance against it. The death row was located in 9 Block—as was the electric chair.

The prison operated two industrial programs: one, a metal shop that manufactured the license plates for all Massachusetts motor vehicles and the other, a print shop that handled the production of stationery and publications for the commonwealth. Largely, however, the population was idle. Even though there was a school building and teaching staff, there were few educational programs. The prison was geographically remote from the population centers and phone calls were not allowed. Walpole quickly gained a reputation for brutality.

2

CONFRONTING THE MORAL DILEMMA OF MASSACHUSETTS PRISONS

francis sargent and his administration

DURING THE 1960S THE UNITED STATES HAD BEGUN TO CREATE the legal framework for equal protection and equal opportunity for people of African descent. The world had witnessed the consistent dignity of Black men and women as they laid claim to the protections offered by the Fifteenth Amendment. The "simple" act of voter registration had brought cataclysmic change to the accepted and legally protected apartheid of the South. The self-determined actions of Black men and women unleashed a wave of non-cooperation throughout the country. Native Americans formed All Tribes and began to act upon treaty rights, declaring their "homelands" to be sovereign nations. Young white people refused to participate in the undeclared, hegemonic war in Vietnam. Highly conscious dissidents of all races began to fill up the prisons and jails of the country. Prisoners increasingly exchanged ideas and shared skills. Prisoners already understood that since they were locked up, they were defined as slaves—the captives, this time, of the State. By 1969, prisoners began to resist the domination of captivity and refused to cooperate with the US penal incapacitation project.[23]

That year, President Richard Nixon nominated the governor of Massachusetts, John Volpe, to his cabinet as the secretary of transportation. Volpe's lieutenant governor, Francis Sargent, became acting governor of the commonwealth. In 1969,

Massachusetts's capital remained a highly segregated city. While many New England liberals participated in the civil rights movement, the privileges of white supremacy and the political and economic deprivation of poor people were firmly ensconced within the state's institutions and legal framework. Sargent was keenly aware of the changes that were sweeping the country. He saw himself as a practical reformer—a Brahmin liberal of the old school. He believed that social change was inescapable and he committed his administration to fundamental reform in Massachusetts.

Sargent was ambitious; he had aspirations for the presidency and he planned to establish a record as a competent reformer at a time when the whole country appeared to be clamoring for a new social compact. But Sargent was also motivated by a deeply rooted Protestant sense of goodness and decency.[24] He wanted to do the right thing.

An architect by training, Sargent had worked for state and federal agencies in the field of natural resources until 1963, when he returned to Massachusetts to accept a position in the Department of Public Works. Sargent believed that the actual structure of governmental institutions greatly influenced the way that government met the needs of citizens. His first action as governor was to initiate broad institutional reform. Sargent introduced the "secretariat" structure of cabinet-level superagencies each headed by a secretary. He placed the Department of Correction under the largest of these agencies, the Office of Health and Human Services. He had seen the problems within the state's prisons and believed the primary reforms needed to come by way of services provided to a dangerously deprived population.

> By God, when I was lieutenant governor, I went to a number of the institutions. (And you know, lieutenant governors don't have a damn thing to do except cut ribbons and go to banquets, but I did go.) I went to a lot of institutions, and I was horrified to see them, and I thought, "Jesus, I don't know exactly what I'll do about it, but these things ought to be changed somehow or other."[25]

Immediately after his appointment as acting governor, Sargent began campaigning to be elected in his own right. In 1970, he won his first term. On taking office, Sargent began planning how to get people out of big institutions and into neighborhood centers, to the extent that it was possible and practical. To accomplish this, he appointed Peter Goldmark, who at age 30 had distinguished himself as New York's city planner under Mayor John Lindsay. Goldmark then hired Jerome Miller as director of the Department of Youth Services (DYS). Within a year, Miller would successfully deinstitutionalize juvenile corrections.[26] Goldmark also hired James Isenberg as his aide in the area of corrections. Isenberg was 26 years old and a recent graduate of the School of Criminal Justice at the University of California at Berkeley, where he had focused on the emerging field of community corrections. While at Berkeley, he had studied with European criminologists who had been implementing community corrections since the early 1950s.

Isenberg clarified the central idea of community corrections for the Sargent administration. He worked from the premise that there were many people in large institutions who did not need to be incapacitated and that most necessary supervision could be easily and more efficiently provided at the community level. While Isenberg envisioned a penal system that actually posed a solution to the problem of crime by keeping prisoners, whenever possible, rooted in their own communities and active agents in their own lives, Goldmark maintained a much more conservative vision:

> I defined [community correction] as a series of structured, differential (depending on the levels that different guys could stand) settings, in which a guy begins to acquire the disciplines for work or managing himself or semi-independent living, and then independent living.[27]

Both supported "community corrections" but they had radically different visions of what the system would look like. For Goldmark, the institutions were to remain a point of entry to the system, while for Isenberg, ideally, the offender would do his time under supervision close to or within his community.

BUILDING ALLIANCES AGAINST REPRESSION

As Sargent was discussing prison reform in Massachusetts, prisoners and their allies at ACI Cranston in Rhode Island were forming the first chapter of the National Prisoners Reform Association. The NPRA defined prisoners as workers entitled to the rights and protections offered by the US labor code. By looking at prison through the lens of labor, they sought to address some of the serious challenges under confinement: job training and preparation, education, health, and safety. Through a labor union, prisoners could shift discussion of these issues out of the disputed framework of prisoners' rights and into the accepted and legally protected framework of workers' rights. Chapters of the NPRA and other prisoners' unions were eventually formed in other states—most notably, at MCI Walpole in Massachusetts. Later, representatives of prisoners' union chapters in Rhode Island and in California were to travel to Walpole prison to support the Walpole NPRA. In late 1971, the NPRA national office in Providence, Rhode Island, made contact with prison reformers in Massachusetts, and its representatives unsuccessfully tried to make direct contact with prisoners. Ultimately, it was John Boone, Sargent's appointee, who would open the doors of Walpole to the NPRA. Later he would reflect, "A prisoner union just seemed to make sense."[28]

The path to prison reform is dangerously uneven. The Sargent administration's first move toward penal reform was an abysmal failure, which, nonetheless, ultimately laid the foundation for public support of prison reform.

When Sargent took office the Bridgewater State Hospital confined men who had been committed through civil court because they were diagnosed with mental illness and men who had been convicted of crimes. Surrounded by the ever-expanding Bridgewater Correctional Complex, the state hospital was operated by the

Department of Mental Health, with security provided by the DOC. Two sections of the hospital were under the direct control of the DOC: one contained "defective delinquents"—mentally ill people who had been convicted of crime—and one contained those imprisoned for public drunkenness, a crime in Massachusetts until 1974.

In 1967, Frederick Wiseman released a documentary, *Titicut Follies*, exposing the horror of life at Bridgewater State Hospital. Immediately, the commonwealth lodged an injunction prohibiting him from showing the film. Bridgewater State Hospital became a target for reform. Two years later, the DOC responded to public pressure by closing the "defective delinquent" section, and the facility for the treatment and rehabilitation of alcoholics became a freestanding unit within the Bridgewater prison complex. This action resulted in a serious labor problem later inherited by Peter Goldmark. The various guards' unions[29] had negotiated contractual rights to bargain on "all appointments, assignments, vacations and shift selections."[30] The DOC was unable to fire or lay off any of the guards who had worked in these units without permission from their union, despite there being nothing for these guards to do. Ultimately, the problem was resolved by opening a DOC-wide segregation unit to collect the "worst of the worst" across the system. This Departmental Segregation Unit (DSU) at Bridgewater added to the existing punitive segregation units at Concord Reformatory, Walpole's 9 and 10 Blocks, and MCI Norfolk's Receiving Building. Almost immediately, the Bridgewater DSU became the holding facility for prisoners who were involved in political organizing.

In the fall of 1970, ten Walpole prisoners were taken from 10 Block and moved to the Bridgewater DSU. They were placed in one of the two corridors. Among these ten were Robert Dellelo and Ralph Hamm—soon to become key organizers and presidents of the National Prisoners Reform Association.

At 30, Dellelo had been in prison since he was 14 years of age—more than half his life. His adolescence was spent in the Massachusetts "Training School" system.[31] Released at 18, he soon picked up a three-to-five-year bid. Then, three months after he wrapped up this term, he was arrested on a robbery and murder charge, even though prosecutors did not even claim he was on the scene when the murder was committed. After his conviction, he was sent back to Walpole, this time to serve a natural life sentence. Deciding that it was time to do something constructive about the prison environment, Dellelo began organizing the prisoners. After he had led several work stoppages at Walpole, he was soon shipped to the DSU.

Ralph Hamm, an 18-year-old Black man, had arrived in prison after being convicted of assaulting a white couple. At 6 feet 5 inches and 175 pounds Hamm towered over most men. White prisoners and guards took it upon themselves to avenge the victims. Hamm fought for survival throughout his first year, spent at Walpole: he was spit upon and assaulted, and his cell was set on fire. Ultimately, the guards and some prisoners attempted to kill him. They beat him badly and cracked his skull. He survived, only to be charged with assault and sent to the DSU in Bridgewater.

Hamm would walk the Bridgewater yard alone, fighting an internal battle defined by complex emotions and anger over both his conviction and what seemed to be an undeniable reality: he would live out his life as a targeted man. He caught the eye of Bobby Dellelo.

The conditions in the DSU were appalling. Prisoners were placed in cells where they could neither see nor hear each other, often without clothing or personal belongings, and time in the yard was severely limited. Highly medicated residents of the state mental hospital delivered unpalatable food to their cells by passing it through a slot in the door. A pot served as a toilet. Each room had a window and a mattress. Sometimes there were blankets and sheets, sometimes not. The prisoners were kept in these conditions for weeks or months. Often, they were sedated—sometimes forcibly. As Bobby Dellelo recalls:

> All kinds of drugs were given out. Shots were given that made prisoners into babbling idiots, then we would be shipped to Bridgewater State Hospital. As bad as the DSU was, you did not want to be in the state hospital. They tried to do this to us when we were on our hunger strike.
>
> They were giving people three thousand units of Thorazine. They were experimenting on prisoners. When we went on our hunger strike, people were dying one a week.[32]

The mentally ill men who had been the wing's residents in its previous incarnation as the defective-delinquent unit had often smeared feces and urine on the walls of the rooms. When the unit was prepared as a punitive segregation unit, the walls were not sanitized. They were simply washed and painted. Many of the people who lived in the wards above the DSU were so highly medicated they were incontinent. The building was in such disrepair that when it rained, feces and urine would run down the walls. Many of the DSU prisoners contracted hepatitis. Often gravely ill, and always knowing that they were in a dangerous situation, the Walpole prisoners began to develop unity among themselves.

This unity was hard to achieve, given the utter racial polarization of the prison population. The commitment to racial equity that allowed the development of unity began as a personal commitment between Ralph Hamm and Bobby Dellelo. Dellelo had grown up in prison; he knew what Hamm was up against. He liked him and feared he would not survive. As Hamm remembers it, "Between Bobby and me, it was never about race. It was about coming together as two equal men."[33] While in the DSU, Dellelo taught Hamm the skills he thought the younger man would need to survive as a Black target of white prisoners and guards alike. Through Hamm, Dellelo made a fundamental connection between oppression and race. He realized that white prisoners' struggle for dignity and power was impossible without racial equity. To be successful, not only would prison organizing need to cross racial lines, but also white prisoners would have to understand that being in prison made them "Black." Hamm says, "Bobby got this. In a sense, he became Black. He was not going to go forward without us."[34] This understanding that reform is impossible without racial equity informed all subsequent organizing initiatives undertaken by these Walpole prisoners. If Black prisoners were left behind, soon all prisoners would be right back with them. As Dellelo put it, "If we continued with racism, we would have been dead, dead in the water."[35]

As their friendship deepened, Hamm and Dellelo began laying the groundwork for cross-racial organizing. The ten Walpole prisoners in the Bridgewater DSU agreed that they would end the practice of harassing Black prisoners, known as "niggering." The trust engendered by this commitment provided the foundation for the organizing project the prisoners were to undertake at Walpole a year later, after the Bridgewater DSU was finally shut down. In hindsight, Dellelo mused, "It is amazing that this kind of unity could have emerged in these circumstances; you just had to be there to fully appreciate it."[36] In the midst of deprivation, the prisoners in the DSU agreed to treat each other as equals, across racial lines and across organized-crime affiliations. Once they created solidarity among themselves, the prisoners began to look for allies, ultimately reaching out to volunteers in the chaplain's office. Some of these volunteers were from an ecumenical group known as Packard Manse.

SOLIDARITY AND RESISTANCE

On September 9, 1971, the prisoners at the New York state prison in Attica staged a work stoppage. Prisoners had long complained about the meager pay of 25 cents a day; oppressive working conditions, with temperatures that rose to over 100 degrees in the metal shop, known as "the black hole of Calcutta"; and the blatant racism—the guards even called their clubs "nigger sticks." On this day, the guards—armed only with their clubs—tried to force the population to go to work. The prisoners resisted. With the guards outnumbered and overpowered, the prisoners gained control of one cellblock and the yard it faced. They also captured 38 hostages. They held the yard for three days, asking the prison administration to negotiate a set of grievances. The grievances paled against the proclamation that the prisoners made: "We are men. If we cannot live as people, we will at least try to die like men."[37] On September 13, pepper gas was dropped from helicopters and more than 500 heavily armed officers took sniper positions and stormed their way into the yard, shooting indiscriminately. An hour later, 26 prisoners and 9 of the 38 hostages were dead. Many other prisoners were injured; 83 required surgery.[38]

Over the course of these five days, people across the United States and around the world were confronted with images of blindfolded guards in prison clothing, and the men of Cellblock D, who had organized their society in the yard, replete with law enforcement, leadership, and democratic procedures. The word "prisoner" now evoked images of strong, articulate Black men who fearlessly faced the cameras, weld-ed the gates of the yard shut, and prepared themselves to die—unrepentantly. After the bullets flew and the media published photos of men in the yard—naked, hands on their heads, waiting to be returned to their cells—public attention was turned to the prisons and jails across the country. Attica was not unique. Attica was Walpole.

Prisoners in Massachusetts decided to show solidarity with the prisoners in New York State and, simultaneously, draw attention to the strikingly similar problems that they confronted. The Inmate Advisory Councils at Norfolk and Walpole organized peaceful demonstrations. Some prisoners walked around the yard carrying signs while others gave passionate speeches decrying the appalling conditions within the prisons. Walpole prisoners issued a list of 120 demands for changes.

The administration's response was tepid: it encouraged the Inmate Advisory Councils to form grievance committees. In response, Walpole prisoners capped the demonstrations with a work stoppage.

Governor Sargent believed that the DOC, established in 1955 to improve conditions in the prisons, had failed in its goals. There was an inescapable and immediate need for prison reform. The conditions at the Bridgewater DSU, the rebellion at Attica, and the unabated resistance within the Massachusetts prisons had brought this need to public attention. Sargent knew that there was little to be gained politically from embarking on a campaign for prison reform, but he felt both morally compelled and pushed by circumstances to address the problem. Peter Goldmark, in turn, felt that it was as good a time as any to try reform.

> No matter what you do ... it was going to be awful, it was going to be trouble; because the system was so rotten, and everybody's expectations were so conflicting and so hot. So when whatever you do was going to be trouble, that's when you try and do something serious in government.[39]

With organized prisoner resistance developing on the inside and a fear of prisoner rebellion developing on the outside, the time was ripe to initiate substantial change in the system.

Goldmark and Isenberg seized the moment.

SARGENT'S RESPONSE: THE CITIZENS' COMMITTEE AND THE COLO COMMISSION

On September 28, Sargent, capitalizing on the pressure generated by the prisoners at Walpole, formed a Citizens' Committee on Corrections and charged it to identify the grievances of the inmates, the officers, and other staff of the penal institutions; to assess channels of communication; and to identify the highest priorities for improvement of the correctional system.[40] Sargent named Harry Elam, a Black Municipal Court judge in Boston, chair of the committee. Elam was highly respected and intimately connected to Black leadership in Boston.[41] Three of the members were highly visible leaders of Boston's Black community, three were white, and one was Latino. Throughout this prison-reform initiative, there was a consciousness about Black representation and leadership within the prison, among the allies, and in the Sargent administration. At Elam's request, the Citizens' Committee also included former prisoners and current prison employees. This inclusion would prove crucial.

To complement the Citizens' Committee, the governor also created a Legislative Commission on Corrections. It was to be known as the Colo Commission, after its chair, state representative Tom Colo, of Athol. Appointed were three state senators, seven state representatives, and five DOC staff. The commission had a far-reaching mandate.

> This commission shall in the course of its investigation study, consider the public and official attitudes and conditions of probation, the laws of the commonwealth related to crimes and sentencing, procedures and attitudes of due process, the facilities for confinement, attendant and administrative personnel, the needs and progress of vocational training, education, physical and mental development and rehabilitation of inmates, psychiatric treatment, and the procedures and attitudes employed in the release and parole of inmates, the causes of recidivism and suggestions and needs for reduction, the forces and attitudes that may exist or be found lacking in society, prior to arrest and conviction, confinement and after release of any person, and the fostering of programs to prevent juvenile delinquency.[42]

To fulfill this tall order, the commission was given subpoena power over citizens and officials of the state and federal governments. But given the commission's heavy DOC representation, it was slow to respond to prisoner complaints. Furthermore Colo had no experience in corrections and had great difficulty leading the commission. Although it existed for two years, the commission never published a formal report.

On September 29, the day after the Citizens' Committee was empanelled, its members traveled to Walpole prison for an all-day meeting initiated by the Inmate Advisory Council. Prison administrators and the press accompanied the committee. Dellelo, who had just returned from Bridgewater, reports:

> When the Elam Committee got to Walpole, the administration had chosen a group of prisoners to speak to them. Red Kelley, a former prisoner and member of the committee, said, "These are the wrong men. You need to talk to Robert Dellelo, Ralph Hamm, and the other prisoners they recommend." Then the committee sent for us. We told them what was happening inside the prison. They were pretty upset. Before the committee left Walpole, they called the governor on the phone. When Commissioner Fitzpatrick heard that we had been called out, he collapsed with fatigue.[43]

At the meeting, prisoners not only aired their grievances, they also presented a strategy for change. This meeting provided a rare glimpse at the men who inhabited the maximum-security prison—and the meeting was televised and covered extensively in the print media. Once the door was cracked, prisoners and advocates refused to allow it to close. Eventually, the door was shaken off its hinges, exposing the waste of prison and the hopes of the men imprisoned behind the high, white walls of Walpole.

RESISTANCE CONTINUES

Sargent responded to the prisoners' demands with a promise to introduce a prison-reform bill. But promises were not actual changes. By October 5, the prisoners had resumed their strike. Robert Moore, the superintendent (or warden) of Walpole, claimed that the prisoners who had emerged as spokespersons had instigated the strike. He described these men as "a small hardcore group of agitators."[44] He locked down the prison, confining all prisoners to their cells 24 hours a day. This behavior was predictable. As Dellelo later reported, "Robert Moore was known as More Gas Moore. He earned the name in Charlestown during the rebellion there. He kept insisting that more gas be poured upon the prisoners in the segregation unit. One guy lost his lung."[45] Rather than breaking the back of the prisoners' organizing initiative, this lockdown only increased their solidarity.

Despite this increasing unity, the October 5 strike and lockdown highlighted the power struggle between the white prisoners who had control of the prison and the new leadership, represented by Dellelo, that was emerging. The white hard core, led by Vincent "the Bear" Flemmi, was able to intimidate the line guards by convincing them that it was in their best interest to let the hard core control the population. This worked well because the guards responsible for each block were able to shirk many of their duties as long as their blocks stayed calm.

Dellelo had to demonstrate that he was the strongest of the hard core. Hamm explained that Dellelo achieved this by challenging Vincent "the Bear" Flemmi, who ran all enterprises in the prison, and whom no one had dared challenge up to then.[46] Dellelo recalls:

> Right after the Elam Committee came into Walpole, we had a lot of strikes. We were just beginning to challenge the old structure that the Bear and others had negotiated to feather their own nest. The Bear tried to make a power play against me in the yard in front of everyone. He came up to me when I was standing and drinking a can of soda and he sucker-punched me. My head went right and I just rolled with it. I had a soda can in my hand. As I brought my right arm back to hit him I was trying to drop it. I actually hit with open hand; that is what saved him. I hooked him, and he immediately curled up. I went up under the front—bam, bam, bam—and when he protected his face, I got the sides of his head. We went back and forth like this. I was a tough kid who was not afraid to fight. I came up fighting and I had survived the Training School. I beat the Bear up in the yard. People were suing for peace. They were afraid of what might have happened.

From that point on Dellelo would refuse to cooperate with the Bear's agenda.

> Because of one of the strikes, we were locked down—but the Bear was let loose. Some guards came and got me at my cell and brought me down to the grate and the Bear was there. He sees me and lets me know that they are going to snatch 55 guys and ship them out. The Bear suggests that we choose five guys from each block. He asks me to pick out the people. I say, "Fuck you—let me get this straight. You want me to choose who is going to be shipped out tonight. No way. And what are you doing running around loose? Isn't the whole prison locked down?" He looks at me and screws. I go back upstairs.
>
> That night, the screws bring me to 9 Block. I was taking Nalidar for a sleep medication. If you take more than one, they make you sick. The screws came by early. They gave Nembutal, which is much stronger. I thought, "What a score!" And I popped it. I was feeling kind of nice, then it dawned on me. SOB—they are taking me out.[47]

They "took him out" as far as the federal penitentiary USP Marion, in Illinois, where he stayed until the following spring.

By November 1971, the population of MCI Walpole was in open rebellion. In the beginning of the month, prisoners set a fire at the foundry resulting in $30,000 in damages. Shortly after the fire, in a display of unity, the entire prison population staged a work stoppage. The administration responded by locking the prisoners in their cells and shaking the prison down for weapons. At a subsequent press conference, the guards displayed shanks, pipes, and a pipe bomb they claim to have found. Hamm and Dellelo explained that the guards had a ready display of "prison-made" weapons. Every time there was a shakedown, they would bring out this display. The prisoners were amazed that the press never picked up on the fact that the same weapons were always attached to the same pieces of wood in exactly the same manner. It's not that there *weren't* weapons in the prison. Given the level of violence in the prison, the prisoners were indeed armed and remained so, even after they adopted nonviolence as an organizing strategy.

The prisoners remained relentless in their resistance. Each day they engaged in concrete action to challenge the DOC. In the midst of this tension, William Fitzpatrick, the commissioner of corrections, resigned. Again, Governor Sargent capitalized on the moment, playing on the fear of Attica, the unabated prison unrest, and the public push for change to bring in a reform-minded commissioner.

THE AD HOC COMMITTEE ON PRISON REFORM

A key part of that public push for change was the Ad Hoc Committee on Prison Reform, which had formed largely due to the work of Packard Manse, an interfaith community of people committed to nonviolent social change brought together by a group of white leftists who had been sidelined from civil rights work with the rise of Black Power. The members of Packard Manse saw prison reform as an issue that would allow them to continue their social activism. During the summer of 1971, members had become aware of the onerous conditions in the Bridgewater DSU. They informed their churches and synagogues about the horrors the prisoners were enduring. This educational campaign was initiated against a backdrop of increasing prison unrest that eventually came to a head at Attica State Prison in western New York state.

Packard Manse used the creation of the Citizens' Committee and the increasing prison unrest as a call to action, quickly becoming the outside voice of the prisoners. Phyllis and Bill Ryan provided the organizational leadership for this project. Phyllis was a seasoned organizer who had worked as an organizer in the civil rights movement, building support in New York City and New Haven. Her friends described her as hard-driving, passionate, and unable to accept the word "no." Through the increasingly debilitating effects of multiple sclerosis, she would attend rallies and pickets in support of the prisoners. Often Bill, her husband and a professor at Boston University, would walk behind her with her wheelchair, in case she tired.[48] He did this burgeoning movement a great service; Phyllis Ryan was the glue that held it together. She never missed an opportunity to exploit an opening; whatever her physical limitations, with her pen and her phone she was relentless. Ryan kept copious notes on all of her conversations. She wrote on anything that was at hand—napkins, backs of message pads, scraps of paper—chain-smoking all the while.[49]

As a result of her work handling press relations for the Southern Christian Leadership Conference in New York City, Phyllis Ryan had an enviable list of contacts— her "little black book" was actually an annotated photocopy of a media directory. She had noted issues that each reporter focused on, their preferred names, and sometimes their home phone numbers. Because of her extensive work in the civil rights movement, Ryan also had connections to organizers throughout the country, many of whom were already involved in prison reform, having been exposed to prison life as a result of their participation in civil disobedience over the years. Ryan had also determined her role as a white activist within a movement to end racist oppression. She was committed to mobilizing and organizing supporters for the prisoners and ex-prisoners, who were the primary decision makers and voices of the reform project. This commitment would cement her relationship with the Reverend Edward Rodman.

During October and November of 1971, Packard Manse initiated a conversation about prison conditions with the membership of the Massachusetts Council of Churches.[50] Although the uprising of the men at Attica Prison prompted these discussions, their focus was closer to home: the resistance of and the issues raised by the men at Bridgewater, MCI Walpole, and Norfolk throughout the fall. Packard Manse also paid close attention to the Elam Committee's preliminary reports.

At Phyllis Ryan's insistence, Packard Manse made the strategic decision to be led by and to stand in common cause with the prisoners and ex-prisoners whose lives would be directly affected by any prison reform. This group of advocates quickly expanded to include an active and vocal group of recently released ex-prisoners. The ex-prisoners were clear. They wanted: to speak for themselves, a face-to-face meeting with Governor Sargent, new leadership for the DOC, and a concrete commitment to implement real prison reform. Getting this meeting with the governor became the first concrete initiative undertaken by Packard Manse.

On November 22, Packard Manse sent a telegram to Governor Sargent requesting that he meet with a delegation from the Manse to discuss "the deteriorating and volatile conditions at our prisons, particularly Norfolk and Walpole."[51] It challenged the governor to address the general public, the prisoners, and the guards, declaring that public interest was not well served by teaching "criminals to be more criminal, hopeless and dehumanized."[52] It also encouraged the governor to assure the prisoners that he was concerned about them and wished them to refrain from self-destructive action. The signatories of the telegram asked Sargent, as a sign of good faith, to issue an executive order immediately closing the departmental segregation units at Bridgewater, which they described as "medieval chambers of horrors, which are used as ever-present threats and intimidations."[53] Lastly, they urged the governor to assure the guards that he was "sensitive" to their fears and the role they were "required" to play, and to remind them that their own self-interest and safety was intrinsically tied to prison reform. The executive board of Packard Manse and 108 "religious, labor, legal, academic, and community leaders," including Judge Harry Elam, signed the telegram. More than 600 postcards reiterating the request followed from citizens across the state.[54] While Packard Manse was mounting its postcard campaign, the administration was engaged in its search for a new commissioner of corrections.

Immediately after Packard Manse sent its telegraph, Norfolk County district attorney George G. Burke initiated a search of Walpole prison. During the search, Walpole prisoners released a letter stating that the prison administration had broken its contract with the Inmate Grievance Committee. The grievance committee was formed after Attica, and constituted the first committee ever organized by the prisoners, without administration sanction, unlike the Inmate Advisory Council.[55] The committee had presented a list of 160 demands at a meeting in the presence of outside observers on November 5. After making their statement, the prisoners voluntarily walked back into their cells. They had been in lockdown ever since. Even though the warden, Robert Moore, acknowledged that many of the prisoners' complaints were legitimate, he made it clear that he preferred working with the Inmate Advisory Council, composed of prisoners elected by the general population, and "mature" and "concerned" outsiders as opposed to grappling with the clear, vocal criticism leveled at the prison's administration by the former prisoners who were working with Packard Manse and would soon provide leadership to the Ad Hoc Committee on Prison Reform.[56]

On Wednesday, December 1, 1971, Phyllis Ryan and Jim McClain of Packard Manse double-teamed the governor's staff. Steven Teichner, the governor's aide assigned to interface with the DOC, responded. He refused Ryan's request for an immediate meeting with the governor. Further, he explained that the governor was not obliged to close the Bridgewater DSU because the federal courts had ruled that DSUs did not constitute cruel and unusual punishment.[57] On the other hand, he argued that closing the DSU was an obvious prison reform that the administration might use to feather the cap of a newly appointed commissioner. He argued that Sargent couldn't make a public speech because he did not want to scare off candidates for commissioner. According to Ryan's notes, Teichner called Packard Manse "inflammatory" and the prisoners "humbugs," and tried to play McClain and Ryan off against each other. This interaction made it clear to the members of Packard Manse that even though the administration was interested in reforming the prisons, it did not welcome public involvement.

Teichner offered to set up a meeting with the sitting commissioner, William Fitzpatrick, and Peter Goldmark. Even though Goldmark was known to be committed to prison reform, Ryan refused. Teichner offered a future meeting with the new commissioner—once that selection had been made. Ryan refused. When Teichner conceded to a meeting with the governor but was indefinite about when—maybe the following week, maybe the week after, maybe after the new commissioner was hired—Ryan seized on the promise. Capitulating, Teichner offered a meeting between the governor and one representative of the group. Ryan asserted that the signatories of the letter were "the best game in town," and that their meeting with the governor was necessary to move along reform. She explained that a meeting with "one representative" was not what she had asked for. He agreed to give her an answer on Monday.[58]

Ryan prevailed. Not waiting for Teichner's response, on Friday, December 3, Packard Manse sent out a press release stating that Governor Sargent would meet with a number of groups who were active on the issue of prison reform on Monday, December 6 at 11:00 AM.[59] These groups were later to join in a coalition known as the Ad Hoc Committee on Prison Reform. A young, Episcopal priest by the name of Edward Rodman was asked to chair the nascent coalition.

Rodman was the Cannon Missioner of the Boston Episcopal Diocese. The NAACP had recruited Rodman in 1958, when he was 16, as a potential candidate to integrate the public high school in Portsmouth, Virginia. Later, he was trained by members of a nonviolent direct-action group, the Congress of Racial Equality (CORE), and received national attention when he salvaged a lunch-counter sit-in staged by Portsmouth high-school students in February of 1960. For the next six months, Ed Rodman was the first national spokesperson for the organization that emerged from the sit-ins: the Student Movement for Racial Equality, which ultimately became the Student Nonviolent Coordinating Committee, or SNCC. In 1960, at the age of 18, he attended the founding meeting of SNCC, called by Ella Baker, in Raleigh, North Carolina. He participated in SNCC's first national gathering in the spring of 1962. He would serve on SNCC's steering committee until September 1963. Rodman collaborated with Stokely Carmichael (Kwame Ture) and others in drafting a call to Black Power. In this version of the speech, the call to Black Power was explicit. Ultimately John Lewis capitulated to political pressure demanding a rejection of Black Power as antithetical to the doctrines of civil rights and nonviolence, and did not give the speech as drafted by Carmichael, Rodman, and the others. Rodman then resigned from SNCC. Carmichael finally delivered the original address in 1965, after Malcolm X was assassinated. So when Rodman arrived in Boston in May of 1971, he was 28 years old, a recognized intellectual rooted in the Black Power Movement, and a radical. He was also committed to the abolishment of prisons, "among other things."[60]

THE ELAM COMMITTEE REPORT

On December 5, 1971, the night before the governor's scheduled meeting with Packard Manse, his Citizens' Committee on Corrections, known to the public as the Elam Committee, released its final report on the conditions inside Massachusetts's prisons. The report began with the following assertion: "That punishment remains as the state's primary response to a convicted criminal is a critical flaw in the correctional system."[61] Among its many recommendations, the Elam Committee called for the immediate closure of the DSU at Bridgewater.

The first page of the report the Elam Committee issued, entitled *Corrections 71, A Citizens' Report,* admonished the governor and the citizens of the commonwealth that while in 1955 the Wessel Commission had clearly stated that "punishment for punishment's sake alone is a discredited theory,"[62] the Elam Committee found in 1971 "that this discredited theory is not a discarded reality."[63] The report went on to describe obsolete vocational training, lack of job preparation, inadequate educational programs, disrespectful staff attitudes, and a DOC-wide focus on control rather than correction. The Elam report described "an urgent need for policies, programs, and attitudes within the Department of Correction to adapt to the clear fact that today inmates are people not just under custody but with needs to which the system must respond."[64] The report was an open challenge to the governor and the legislature to act upon the recommendations of the committee. This group of citizens left no room for equivocation. They knew from their own professional and personal experience that the penal system was built on a flawed foundation; for the good of all, it had to change.

The committee drew clear connections between the struggle for equity and self-determination being waged by people throughout the United States and the struggle of the prisoners. They rejected the characterization of the prisoners as hardened militants, noting that "the demands for change that have infused society are also present in the prison, a justified call for change must be met."

POLICIES

The Elam Committee was composed of individuals who were pragmatic realists. Their extensive recommendations began with a list of reforms and practices that could be implemented without changing the law or augmenting the budget. The primary goals underpinning these recommendations were the creation of an effective administration and meaningful roles for staff, and the empowerment and involvement of prisoners in the corrections process. The committee believed that "the inmate should participate in his own correction and that correction should occur in a manner that respects the inherent dignity of every individual."[65]

The report asserted that many important systematic issues were not addressed because the lines of authority within the corrections system were not clear. Instead, these problems would be referred to the legislature and the courts for resolution, even though these bodies were not willing to solve them. Consequently, few issues were resolved, and each prison operated as an unconnected fiefdom. Later, John Boone recalled,

> The thing is in this system, every prison is an island unto itself. And every superintendent is sort of like a dictator of that island. And in some institutions he doesn't run it. The deputy superintendent runs it, you see, and he knows everybody. He runs it out of the top of his head. I couldn't find a piece of paper, a rule or a regulation, a guideline in *any* of these prisons. All of it is in the top of somebody's head.[66]

This situation was recognized as a primary cause of instability within the DOC.

Both Bobby Dellelo and Ralph Hamm concurred with this assessment. The deputy superintendent did run Walpole, largely because the deputies stayed in place while the superintendents were regularly replaced. The deputy's allegiance was to his staff, and he exercised a lot of power to change rules and procedures for their benefit. Under this system, there was nothing to balance the arbitrariness of administrative decisions. Paramount among Elam's recommendations, therefore, was the establishment of an operating structure within the department.[67] And again, the creation of a committee to advise the commissioner was encouraged.[68] Furthermore, the report urged that Black and Spanish-speaking guards be hired in response to the shifting demographics of the prison population.

PROGRAMS

The report reiterated that the basic needs of prisoners must be met and went on to define them. Prisoners required a decent environment, with clean living accommodations, wholesome and properly prepared food, proper toilet facilities, and decent clean clothing.[69] They needed to receive necessary and timely medical care and services, to have access to educational facilities and programs both inside and outside correctional institutions, to receive job training and work experience that conformed with their capabilities and desires—and with available employment opportunities. The committee recommended that prisoners be given access to adequate legal information, including law books, individual legal advice, and any necessary legal counsel. Furthermore, recognizing the fundamental importance of family ties, the committee advocated prisoners be provided timely counseling in matters that concerned their families. The report stipulated that these resources should be made available for prisoners of all financial means.

In more than a nod to the importance of personal sovereignty, the committee spoke to prisoners' participation in the planning and selection of correctional programs. A key element in recommended program development was fiscal responsibility. The committee scrutinized the department's budgetary procedures, commenting, "The committee sees no justification for spending money from the educational allocation to an institution for tear gas."[70] Publications available to prisoners were overly censored, family visiting spaces inadequate, and libraries in need of educational material. Finally, the Sargent administration was admonished to assign someone the task of "seeking funds from all available sources to implement a variety of correctional programs."[71]

After meeting with many prisoners over its three-month tenure, the committee was convinced that the incapacitation of many of the prisoners was wasteful. It recommended educational release—modeled after work-release programs—allowing a prisoner to attend school or training programs in the community. Additionally, the report recommended the expansion of work release and the creation of a furlough program.[72] The committee also advised that certain prisoners be allowed to "leave the institution for speaking engagements and other educational contacts with the public," because "this communication would be productive, [and] what the inmate and public may learn might be influential in reducing crime."[73]

THE SIGNIFICANCE OF *CORRECTIONS 71*

Important themes permeated *Corrections 71*. The members of the committee believed the prisoners and were grateful for their clarity, expressed in their understanding of the problems they faced, and the comprehensive solutions they suggested. The report frequently refers to the prisoners as a resource and cautions against overlooking them. The prisoners and staff were both recognized as laborers, entitled to advocacy and representation, who needed a well-organized environment to do their jobs. The committee viewed prisoners' participation in their own "correction" as their most important "job"; communication within the department and between the department and the public as crucial; and transparency and uncensored communication with maximum accessibility as an ideal. The committee knew that these prisoners were returning to live in the same communities most of us live in. The goal of *Corrections 71* was to see that every effort was made to assure that prisoners were afforded as many opportunities for change as possible before release so that when they left prison they could contribute to their communities, provide for their families, and stay out of prison.

The committee ended the report with a reminder that the prisoners were justified in feeling aggrieved when an injustice had been committed or their rights had been infringed upon and that procedures must be available for the redress of these grievances.[74] Such fundamental fairness was a basic responsibility the state could not shirk.

SARGENT AND THE ADVOCATES

On December 6, the day after the Elam Committee released its report advocating close administrative monitoring of Walpole and Norfolk, 20 people attended the meeting Phyllis Ryan had managed to win with the governor. By the end of the meeting, the governor had made two commitments to the group. He promised to visit the prisons himself and he agreed to assemble legislation that would mandate reform of the prison system. He followed through on both promises. In mid-December, Sargent visited all the penal institutions in the state and was "torn apart."[75] His visits, unprecedented and unpublicized, were conducted with Sargent's closest staff. They met with prison personnel, guards, and prisoners to develop a "feel" for the problems. Sargent came away from these meetings with a deepened commitment to prison reform.[76]

On December 20, the governor unveiled his six-point prison-reform program. This plan proposed the institution of a statewide system of halfway houses coupled with work-release programs; the establishment of a nonprofit prison industry corporation to provide on-the-job training; the repeal of the two-thirds law governing parole eligibility;[77] improved training for correctional officers; increased recruitment of Black and Latino personnel for the DOC; and the establishment of staff/inmate councils in all of the prisons.[78] Sargent announced his plan in a speech televised statewide.

It was an eventful week. On December 22, two days later, the state education commissioner announced that the Boston School Committee had violated the Fourteenth Amendment through actions "which could have no other intent than to maintain racial separation."[79] The next day, Sargent cemented his commitment to corrections reform with the appointment of John Boone as commissioner of corrections.

Letters to the editor in publications across the state voiced criticism of the governor's plan. On December 31, the prisoners at Norfolk responded to the complaints with a letter to the *Boston Evening Globe*. At the close of the letter signator Nicholas C. Fryar linked the prisoner to the reader.

> Rehabilitation is something that can work but not without a proper foundation. Give us a chance. The governor's plan is not only good for us; it would be extremely beneficial for you. We want to be able to become useful to society—please help us to do so.

Fryar's formulation that what is good for the prisoner is ultimately good for society, and prison reform will increase public safety, became the bedrock of the prison-reform initiative mounted by those who were imprisoned within Massachusetts prisons.

Two months later, John Boone was sworn in as commissioner of corrections. Boone had had a long career in the federal Bureau of Prisons. He was known as a radical reformer who believed that, given the opportunity, individuals would choose to better themselves. Through the implementation of a variety of programs, Boone gave prisoners this option.

John Boone was also a Black man suddenly handed the responsibility of leading an entirely white staff. Boone's appointment placed institutional power into the hands of a Black man, a rarity in Massachusetts at the time. Black leadership, from the community level, with the Black Panther Party, to the state level, with elected legislators, would form a network around the new commissioner. They not only supported him, they would consciously and strategically use his access to power to reveal the racism of the criminal justice system.

3

THE NEW COMMISSIONER

from corrections to abolition

They found Boone and they really wanted him. They were excited. He was a symbol. He was the only Black in the Department of Corrections. You don't understand what that meant. And for those officers, when they looked at John Boone, that was the first powerful Black man they had ever seen who wasn't behind bars. (They were used to dealing with powerful Black men who were behind bars!) Now here's a guy who was really a different thinker. That was a major symbol.[80]

—Assistant to Goldmark

BUT JOHN O. BOONE WAS NOT JUST A SYMBOL. BOONE HAD grown up in Cedartown, Georgia, in the years following World War I. His understanding of the world was shaped by parents who were devoted to their church, the education of their children, and the struggle for dignity and equity for Black people.

As a boy about the age of 10, John went with his father to bring food for an uncle sentenced to hard labor on one of Georgia's notorious chain gangs. His crime: possession of a handgun. Yet, possession of a weapon seemed a necessity. Boone told me a story about the danger his family faced when his mother returned a pair of shoes that did not fit properly. Six armed men had to protect her from a mob of angry whites who tried to storm her home.[81] The chain gang worked directly outside of

Cedartown, so John and his father could walk right up to the men at lunchtime. The men were fed on a meager diet of what Boone described as "gruel." Many of them perished from malnutrition, exposure, dehydration, overwork, and untreated illness. Their odds for survival increased if their families were able to care for them. Boone's father was faithful to his brother, visiting every day. Boone remembers the loneliness of the laborers, the way they were chained together, the songs they sang. Seventy-four years later, thinking of them, he shook his head and closed his eyes. When he finally lifted his head, he said, "It was a terrible place, a terrible place."

Boone recalls one Sunday, when he and his father visited his uncle after church. The Sunday atmosphere was different. The men were not chained to each other but were surrounded by armed guards. All the local families with relatives on the chain gang would come to the clearing outside of town where the prison camp was set up, bringing baskets of food and money. They ate together as families. The "bosses" brought in prostitutes. There, in the open, the families paid for their services. Boone remembered, "There was a God-fearing mother dressed in her Sunday best after church. Her son was sitting next to her and she averted her eyes while a woman did an unspeakable act." His impression of this mother's dignity and composure never left him.

Two years later, two of Boone's cousins decided to go berry picking. They invited John and his brother Joe.[82] The brothers rushed home to ask their mother for permission to go. She refused because these cousins were known to swear and cause trouble. She locked John and Joe in their room for the afternoon. Boone claims he owes his life to his mother's strict discipline and her intolerance of cussing.

That day, his cousins encountered some white landowners who informed the boys they were not permitted to pick berries at the abandoned quarry. According to a woman who had hidden in the bushes, the boys responded, "No one owns this land. These berries are free to pick." The men lynched them, pushing both boys into the quarry, where they drowned. The witness told the family how the boys struggled for their lives in the cold water, searching the sides for a way out, and how the men pushed them away from the steep walls. William, who was the older of the two, fought for a long time. There was no investigation. The family, afraid to protest for fear of the violent consequences, quietly buried their sons.

Cedartown was well known for lynching. Another of Boone's cousins recalled a day when 16 men were hanged from a single tree outside of a courthouse where the trials of Black men always ended with a guilty verdict. He said the men would be taken to the attic, where a rope would be tied around their necks. They would stand above a trapdoor, the door would be opened, and each man would drop through the ceiling and "hang 'til his death" in the middle of the courtroom. For these men there was no due process, no appeal, no prison, not even a chain gang—only judgment and immediate death. It was in this environment that Boone, at the age of 12, vowed that he was going to change the criminal justice system.

Boone would go on to serve in World War II. Shipped home with appendicitis, he nearly died because the standard of treatment for Black soldiers was so poor. But Boone survived both his illness and the military hospital. He took advantage of the GI Bill to enroll in Morehouse College, where he met Benjamin Elijah Mays, later to become the mentor of Dr. Martin Luther King Jr. Mays is recognized as the architect of Morehouse's international reputation for excellence in scholarship, leadership, and service, and his influence on Boone's professional demeanor cannot be overstated. Boone credits Mays with his determination to present himself as a gentleman, keep his voice calm, and resolve conflict with dignity. His comportment—professional, capable, soft-spoken, and polite—later caused profound confusion in opaquely racist Massachusetts, where his demeanor was perceived as confrontational.

After earning a degree in social work at Morehouse, Boone went on to pursue his master's in social work at Clark College. When he graduated, he went to work at the United States Penitentiary (USP) in Atlanta, Georgia, as a guard. Well over 90 percent of the prisoners at USP Atlanta were Black, but Boone was one of only two Black guards. Eventually, he was asked to facilitate group therapy—with no change in pay. He took on this role, and later became a program director as well, but because of the racism at the federal Bureau of Prisons, he would not be promoted any further in Atlanta. Finally, he accepted a position as director of parole at USP Terre Haute, in Indiana. Each place he went, he brought his unique perspective as a social worker, not a criminologist, and each place had to adjust to his vision as well as to his race. Boone was always the first Black man to occupy these positions of leadership in the corrections field.

THE DEVELOPMENT OF A BLACK CRIMINOLOGY

> *Even under ideal circumstances, nothing much good happens in prison.*[83]
>
> —John O. Boone

Although Boone was a social worker, he did not use a traditional social-work philosophy. He believed that each prisoner knew the limits of agency and amount of freedom that he or she could handle. If prisoners were able to think through and articulate a plan of rehabilitation that would not put the individuals, their families, or their communities at risk, Boone was willing to give them permission to execute their plans.

Boone had a deep faith in human beings. He believed that if the prison functioned only to deprive prisoners of their liberty—not to punish them—and if the prisoners exercised their power of self-determination successfully, they would eventually be able to manage their liberty. He believed that the public was more interested in knowing that prisoners could become productive members of their communities and exercise power in a lawful manner than in whether or not prisoners were punished. He was right. He was also wrong.

The idea that prisoners might know what they needed and be able to execute a better rehabilitation plan than a social worker was not only radical, it subverted those who thought that *they* were radical. Some radical criminologists believed that prisoners should work with educators to develop higher education and social programming within the prison. Boone took this philosophy in an entirely different direction. If a prisoner determined that he or she would benefit from a particular program or educational experience that was not available in the prison, and if the prisoner demonstrated the ability to manage his or her personal freedom, Boone believed the prisoner should be awarded the opportunity to test him- or herself within the community. This philosophy was extended to education, to jobs, and to church attendance.

For Boone, justice was fairness. Over his career in corrections, he had seen little that was fair. This led him to oppose parole procedures that favored those prisoners who were able to influence the parole board. It also made him skeptical of "reformed" prisoners who simply followed the rules or played the game. He wished to turn the game into a transparent structure, so that prisoners could concentrate less on getting over, and more on demonstrating their constructive control over their lives.

Boone opposed indeterminate sentencing, but he cautioned that determinate sentencing might lead to the court's being the arbiter of the kind of opportunities that would be possible in prisons. He saw that the focus could easily become the short, determined sentence, rather than the creation of an environment where prisoners could take control of their lives and change them for the better. This, he said, could become a new source of indeterminacy. This is exactly what happened in the 1990s when mandatory minimums were instituted. The sentence itself determined what kinds of resources the prisoner could access by prohibiting the individual from ever going to minimum security or work release.

From his experiences in the South, Boone knew that society did not want Black people to exercise power and self-determination—even when they were living their lives as lawful citizens. The Georgia chain gangs, the lynching of children, and the mass incarceration and enslavement of convicted felons had amply demonstrated to him that the criminal justice system had, as its goal, the oppression and deprivation of Black people. It was founded on the racism Boone defined as an "immediate deadly form of violence."[84] In the South, prisons inevitably created tension that exploded in racialized violence, simply because the entire staff was white and the vast majority of prisoners were not.

RESEARCHING THE PRISONS

In the late 1960s, Boone traveled through the South to document the racial and class composition of prisons under the auspices of the Southern Regional Council, a social-justice organization that emerged out of the Commission on Interracial Cooperation. He found that poor people, and particularly poor Black people, were disproportionately represented in prison. Even though poor Black men and women would labor all of their lives, they rarely approached "working class," while the people staffing the prisons were almost always white and usually working class. Neither the prison administration nor the guards came from the same communities as the people who were sentenced to confinement. Boone concluded, "Rules, regulations and treatment methods reflect the ways and manners of the community immediately surrounding the prison rather than the communities from which the prisoners come."[85] He was one of the first administrators to argue the importance of cultural competency in the penal environment.[86] Because of what his research revealed, Boone was committed to changing the class and racial composition of the custodial and administrative staff so that it more closely resembled that of the prisoners, at the same time that he challenged the fundamental premise of incarceration.

Boone never lost sight of the thin line that separated him from the Black men who were confined in prison; he identified himself as part of the community that prisoners come from. In analyzing the effects of racism within the criminal justice system, Boone used the first person. "We must acknowledge the deplorable conditions in the community on one hand and that we are also caught in its trap. We must outline a strategy of survival."[87]

COMMUNITY ORIENTATION

Boone's strategy for survival involved "self-help endeavors." As a student of Mays, he was taught that survival required demonstrating ability and integrity. Rebellion against prison authority undermined any such demonstration. And yet, he understood, rebellion was inherently created by the existing total repression of the prison. The answer was the development of community programs—both for prisoners returning to their communities and for those who already lived in these communities. It was not enough for programs to be located in the physical community (community based); they also had to be integrated into the community—following its direction and receiving its support (community oriented). Despite the pragmatism of this approach, however, the "corrections power block" demonstrated that it had no interest in the community, whether for location or orientation.

Boone was realistic about what it would take for prisoners to succeed outside the walls, and sincerely wanted all prisoners to have these necessary resources. Rehabilitation would require skill training, education, and integration into the workforce. He condemned the prevalent concepts of rehabilitation because they focused only on the individual, as if there were no institutional barriers to re-integrating prisoners. He warned, "Crime will continue to destroy individuals, neighborhoods, and communities if programs and opportunities do not go hand in hand."[88] Accordingly, the only way to ensure success was to create tangible links to the community. Every program that he created had a community component. And they largely worked. During his tenure in Massachusetts, recidivism fell from over 60 percent to an unprecedented 23 percent.

As a prison administrator, Boone considered his primary role to be a problem solver, not a punisher of criminals. He knew that the people who populated prisons throughout the country had already suffered enough and that their crimes sprang from the punishing circumstances of oppression and deprivation. If, as he hypothesized, oppression and deprivation were the root cause of crime, they could not be the solution.

At the center of Boone's philosophy were the following tenets: prisons must be fair; prisons must not be harsh; staff must not abuse power and must model nonviolence; problems must be resolved through conflict resolution; and most important, the prisoners know their own paths to liberty.

SUPERINTENDENT: USP LORTON

I went to Lorton, and I was completely blown away.
The prison was humming. Everyone was involved
in programs. I knew we had found our man.

—Jim Isenberg

After a short tenure as the director of parole at USP Florence, Boone arrived, during the winter of 1970, at USP Lorton, 18 months after a bloody "rebellion" at the prison—a rebellion that an independent commission called a "guards' riot."[89] USP Lorton was the District of Columbia's prison, located just outside the nation's capital in Virginia, beside the Potomac River. Prisoners were brought down the river on a barge in cuffs and manacles in a way that reminded Boone of the Georgia chain gang. He ended the practice, an act that made him his first enemy there. The wife of the deputy superintendent had been receiving a salary as the "Barge Master," even though she never oversaw the barge.

Many of the prisoners inside Lorton had either participated in or had relatives who had experienced the 1968 and 1969 urban rebellions that shook Washington, DC, and many of the country's urban centers. The Nation of Islam (NOI) was strong inside the prison. When the white guards at Lorton refused to follow the orders of the new Black superintendent, the NOI came forward and took responsibility for security within the prison. They also administered some programs.

Boone initiated a college program through which Lorton prisoners with high-school equivalencies could complete their freshman and sophomore years inside the institution with the assistance of peer tutors. Then they would attend classes at the City College in Washington, DC. Each day buses would carry students from the prison to the college. If the men demonstrated they could handle this freedom well, they would be assigned to a halfway house to complete their course of studies. As an immediate consequence, the number of high-school students inside the prison doubled. Boone has reported, "The new opportunity turned on the whole prison population."[90]

In Lorton—and later in Walpole—Boone's approach demonstrated that prisons run better without custodial staff. To implement his rehabilitation philosophy, Boone needed staff capable of job training and educational counseling; unable to fire existing staff, he hired teachers, psychologists, and social workers. The guards became idle and the prisoners demonstrated that they could maintain order in their blocks, cook their food, and repair the facilities. This further undermined the traditional staff role in the institution.

One night Boone received a phone call at home. He was told that strong rain and thunder had knocked the power out at the prison and that the population was rioting. He was told to meet his staff in the front of the institution and that they would take him in to see the damage the prisoners had caused. Boone went immediately to the prison but decided to enter it through the back. He walked through dark corridors, past cell after empty cell. When he got to the prison yard, he found all the prisoners standing in lines under the rain. There were no guards present. The prisoners told him that when the electricity had gone out, the guards had run through the blocks, opening the cells, and then fled to the front of the prison. Then they must have called Boone to notify him of a riot. The guards had probably hoped that either the prisoners would react to the situation by fighting each other, or Boone would believe there was a riot and give the guards permission to enter the prison with police backup. Then they could use force to show the prisoners that they, not the prisoners, were in charge—and blame the prisoners for any damage.[91] Boone asked the prisoners to remain disciplined, standing in the yard until the electricity was restored. All but one did. (That one took a guard's uniform and escaped; he turned himself in a few days later.)

Boone then surprised his staff by walking out through the front door of the prison. He informed the staff, the police, and the media assembled there that there was no riot, and that the prisoners were peacefully gathered in the yard waiting for the electricity to be restored.

"Guard riots" were a frequent phenomenon at Walpole during Boone's tenure in Massachusetts. But Boone had already learned at Lorton that if he respected the men and supported their desire to better themselves, they would struggle to control their own and each other's behavior.

Lorton marked a change in Boone's self-definition. For the first time, Boone was truly in charge. In each of his previous positions, he was constantly required to convince both his superiors and his staff of his competence. At Lorton, he caught his staff off guard. They had to recognize that he was competent and that he had developed a philosophy of criminology, he was not window-dressing. He was a sharp, energetic young man with a vision and a "few good ideas"[92] about how to enact it.

COMMISSIONER OF CORRECTIONS: MASSACHUSETTS

> *Governor Sargent says, "You come from out of state,*
> *you are a reformer, your skin is black—they are going*
> *to hate your guts the day you walk in." Says, "If you are*
> *prepared to handle this, I am willing to give you the job."*
>
> *When I said I was prepared and asked how*
> *long Sargent will give me to turn the system*
> *around, Sargent replies, "Two years."*[93]
>
> —John O. Boone

Boone had built his career on his reputation for being fair. Until Lorton, he had believed that a prison could be operated in a just and fair manner. But his experience at Lorton led him to believe that, instead of being fairly operated indefinitely, prisons needed to be phased out. He described his philosophy as "shortening the line," or depopulation. At Lorton, he had developed a model based on self-determination and the population did shrink. When he arrived in Massachusetts, he was well along the road to becoming a prison abolitionist.

Once in Massachusetts, Boone was awarded grant money to develop a prison industry inside Concord Reformatory. Instead, he closed an ancient wing of the prison and proposed that the DOC build the factory in the surrounding community—not behind the prison wall—so that prisoners and laborers who were not imprisoned could work side by side. Through this kind of project, the prisoners would naturally create the connections that would support them upon their return to the community. He reacted similarly when money was donated to build a new chapel: he wanted the prisoners to be able to go to church in the community instead. Boone had tested these ideas at Lorton. There, prisoners were working and going to school during the day and returning to prison at night, and the prison ran smoothly.

In Walpole, where there were only a few psychologists or social workers, Boone saw an opportunity to implement his particular criminology while he developed his own team of professionals. Adamant and vociferous objections came from guards who saw the prisoners as their own captives in an institution where they created the law, mostly on a day-to-day basis. Boone thought that correctional officials should meet the highest standard of lawful behavior. The Walpole staff's conduct fell far short of the mark. It became apparent to Boone that the guards at Walpole saw their positions in the DOC less as jobs than as entitlements that they could pass on. The changes that Boone planned to implement destabilized the guards' social compact.

Boone's goal of reforming and depopulating the prisons was to collide with Peter Goldmark's goal of implementing community corrections. Boone believed that the prison institution, as long as it existed, had to meet a standard of operation that maximized prisoner agency and modeled the benefits of a lawful society. Goldmark asserted that the institutions were fundamentally flawed and unworthy of reform, that instead they should be simply stabilized while new institutions were constructed along the model of community corrections. Goldmark's vision of community corrections only meant substituting smaller, staff-led institutions for the larger, staff-led prisons, in a cycle that eventually would send prisoners back to the street. Boone resisted this. The existing staff was responsible for the chaos at Walpole and throughout the system. He knew he had to permanently change the culture that staff had created, or the new project did not stand a chance.

In Atlanta, John Boone had worked alongside his brother, the Reverend Joseph Boone, a prominent civil rights leader. Boone knew that the prison system was being used as a wedge between the growing national consensus that segregation was morally and constitutionally wrong and the ultimate conclusion that government had to legislate equity.[94] He also saw that some prisoners across the country had embraced the tool of nonviolent resistance in order to bring about social change inside prison. When Boone arrived in Massachusetts, prisoners had already adopted nonviolence as one strategy for change. Boone recognized the struggle of the prisoners as a civil and human rights struggle.

In the largely white Massachusetts prisons that remained mostly untouched by the civil rights movement waged outside, staff, guards, and administrators alike dismissed Boone's embrace of nonviolent conflict resolution as a means of social change as a "Black thing." In his willingness to speak directly with prisoners and respond to their demands, they recognized a paradigm that would dispossess them of a coveted and illegitimate power. Their power was predicated upon their ability to terrorize the prisoners through humiliation and coercive force. Nonviolent resistance to such force was a powerful threat.

Boone came to Massachusetts after playing a significant role in the crafting and implementation of the Law Enforcement Assistance Act of 1965. This law stated that rehabilitation must take place in the community. After his arrival in Massachusetts, Boone focused on the construction of Governor Sargent's promised correctional-reform bill. Boone knew from experience that writing a reform bill without supporting its determined and earnest implementation would change nothing on the ground. Boone was determined to construct and implement this law to reform prisons, enact community corrections, and reduce the prison population.

Boone's philosophy was difficult to implement. In dealing with the Walpole prisoners, he would come very close to abandoning it all together. Even though he was the prisoners' greatest ally, he also posed a substantial threat to their success.

After his tenure in the Massachusetts prison system (1972–1973), Boone continued to push against the tide. By the mid-'70s, liberal criminologists were saying that rehabilitation was no longer an acceptable purpose of imprisonment; rehabilitation and programming should be voluntary and parole should be abolished. Boone agreed that corrupt and perennially indeterminate sentencing policies like parole had to be abolished. By 1973, he had already come to the conclusion that prisons themselves must be abolished.

Because he was a Black man who was an administrator of prisons, a Black man who had survived the Jim Crow South, only to experience the no-less-virulent racism in the North, a middle-class Black man who had seen how class status determined who became prisoners and who became guards, he refused to avert his eyes from the racial and class drama being played out within the criminal justice system. He spoke loudly and clearly. After his one and a half years as commissioner of corrections in Massachusetts, he never held another position within the prison system. In 1976, he formed the National Coalition to Abolish Prisons.

In 1977, when he was invited to present a paper to an audience of California policymakers, Boone told them he saw a criminal justice system that was headed in the wrong direction.

> Fear and anger now permeate the criminal justice system to an extent which seems unprecedented in our lifetimes and which has yielded a vindictiveness, or sternness if one prefers, being translated into ever increasing average sentences that is widely accompanied by a not-so-tacit assumption that the social programs of the '60s failed and through no fault of our generosity. So that while we cut back one of those programs after another it is believed that justice and social wisdom now require that we take more and more young men, who mostly happen to be Black, into custody.[95]

Boone's assessment was already accurate in the mid-'70s—a time widely recognized as one of penal innovation. Reading it almost 30 years later, it is eerily understated.

In 2002, Boone presented a workshop to the anti-prison activists who had gathered in New Orleans at the third national Critical Resistance conference. The young people in the workshop asked him how they could talk to prison administrators in order to encourage reform. He replied,

> I think you all have a lot of energy and a lot of good ideas but I don't think you should be talking about reform. You can't reform this corrupt system. It is rotten to the core. Abolishment is the only course of action. And don't say it can't be done. I have seen a lot of abolishment in my lifetime. I only wish I was as young as all of you.[96]

4

THE BEGINNING

constructing corrections
in massachusetts

> *[Penal reform is] one of those intractable areas where*
> *we have no theory—we go from crisis to crisis, from*
> *Attica to Rahway, and we don't know what we are do-*
> *ing. Prisons may have outlived their usefulness.*[97]
> —Congressman and Catholic priest Robert Drinan
> after visiting prisons across the country

WHEN JOHN O. BOONE WAS SWORN IN AS COMMISSIONER OF corrections in January 1972, the prison population in Massachusetts numbered 1,800. Of these prisoners, 450 were lifers. Half of the lifers were at Walpole. The DOC employed 1,150 penal personnel in all. And the DSU at Bridgewater remained open.

The state of Massachusetts would pursue two strands of funding: one to promote prison reform and the other to prepare the state police to contain civil unrest. State officials had reason to believe such unrest was on the horizon; the US Supreme Court's decision that the segregation of the Boston schools was unconstitutional, rendered the day before Boone was appointed, would pit the two poorest communities in the city against each other.[98]

In the North, segregation was and is de facto. Racism and oppression that are manifested in practice are as real and as damaging as the historic de jure segregation of the South that was manifested through force of law. The fact that the outward representations of segregation and its legal framework were not visible allowed Northern liberals to pretend that it did not exist. Whereas racism in the South resembled the thin glass that covers the electric filament of a light bulb, racism in Boston more resembled the thick one-way glass that divides rooms and hides the occupants of cars. Those who were inside looking out were all too aware of what surrounded them, while those on the outside could go about their lives and escape the potent questions posed by deliberate racial segregation.

The Sargent administration knew that desegregating the Boston schools—the only response to the High Court's decision—would be met with violent resistance that would in turn expose the ugliness of the liberal apartheid structures to the world. Training the police was an attempt to contain the inevitable fire. By the spring of 1973, a year after Boone's arrival, the state police would have a fully trained SWAT team. The first community it entered would be Walpole prison. There they would hone their newly acquired riot-control techniques.

In late August of 1971, Dellelo had been transferred back to Walpole, where he began organizing in the aftermath of Attica. After he had secured power from the "hard core," he was shipped to USP Marion in November of that year. Hamm remained at Bridgewater until October of 1971, when he was returned to Walpole and placed in the 10 Block segregation unit. He was not in general population but did exercise his leadership through his membership in the Nation of Islam.

Soon after Boone's arrival, the pace of events and the atmosphere grew ever more intense. Governor Sargent's reform bill was introduced; advocates criticized its gaps. Advocates stepped up pressure to close the Bridgewater DSU; Boone complied. Conditions at Walpole and Norfolk deteriorated. Boone's work was obvious— and daunting.

CREATING A CORRECTIONS DEPARTMENT

When Boone arrived in Massachusetts, he was met by an active, vocal, and highly organized prisoners' rights movement. Responding to its pressure over the targeting of prison organizers for removal to the Bridgewater DSU and placement in isolation there, Governor Francis Sargent had appointed a prominent leader in the Black community, Judge William Davis, to investigate all the transfers. Over the next few months, many of the affected Walpole prison leaders argued their cases before this special magistrate. Eventually, Davis would rule in favor of each prisoner who brought a case before him. After these cases were disposed of, the Walpole Inmate Advisory Council pressed for Dellelo's return from Marion at the request of the Inmate Grievance Committee.

The ground was partially cleared. Boone had a mandate from the governor and a call for community involvement from the vocal prisoners' rights movement. His first task was to identify resources to advance his reform effort.

ACQUIRING THE FUNDING

For financial resources, Boone looked to the Law Enforcement Assistance Act of 1965, which he had helped to craft and implement during his tenure in the federal prison system. The act created the central framework for a nationwide police network, and was a precursor to the Omnibus Crime Control and Safe Streets Act of 1968 that mandated the formation of the Law Enforcement Assistance Administration (LEAA).[99] Although both laws were intended to expand law-enforcement powers, they also included substantial provisions for corrections reforms. Boone had exploited these provisions already, using the block grants available for corrections initiatives to introduce radical corrections reforms in the federal Bureau of Prisons at both Terre Haute and Lorton.[100] In Massachusetts, he would again turn to the LEAA to fund various initiatives, including pulling together the staff he needed, and he would use his experience to advance Sargent's corrections-reform bill.

ASSEMBLING THE TEAM

The reforms required more than just funding. The Massachusetts DOC had never been professionally administered. Boone had to put together a team that could implement the far-reaching community corrections strategy envisioned by the Sargent administration. Sargent's office secured almost half a million dollars in LEAA funds for Boone to develop core management staff, and Goldmark assigned Gary Robinson and James Isenberg as special assistants to the commissioner.

Boone divided the responsibilities of his staff into six divisions. Robert Moore, a former superintendent of MCI Walpole, headed Security and Management.[101] Boone brought in an associate from USP Lorton, Lawrence Solomon, to head Classification and Parole, and tapped Walter Williams, the former director of Boston's Manpower Program, to head Community Corrections.[102] Boone developed the Office of Planning and Research and created the Office of Volunteer Services and Office of Public Information, the last of which was headed by Mel Bernstein.[103] William Farmer, a former prisoner and colleague who had worked with Boone at the Southern Center in Atlanta, would eventually become Boone's administrative assistant.[104] According to Arnold Jaffe, an attorney for the DOC, the appointment was apt.

> Bill Farmer was one of the smartest people who walked on the planet....And Bill was devoid of ego. He was the quintessential "behind-the-scenes guy." He listened, he really heard everything that everyone said and he remembered it.... He was invaluable because of his brains and heart, economical and efficient in the way he did things.[105]

All of these men had considerable experience in their fields and together they would create, for the first time, an institutional framework for the Department of Correction in Massachusetts. In early February, Boone also named Robert Donnelly, the former superintendent of Soledad State Prison in California, as the new superintendent of MCI Walpole.[106]

THE AD HOC COMMITTEE

Claiming Voice

The Sargent administration's quick response to the need for prison reform created unprecedented space for public dialogue. By the time the Ad Hoc Committee was established in December 1971, the advocates for prison reform were so well positioned to move into this vacuum and lay vocal claim to the public discourse that it would take an additional seven months and a cataclysmic event for those who opposed prison reform to enter the dialogue. Ryan, whose files were replete with photographs, newspaper clippings from across the country, and dense public-policy analysis on prison reform and abolition, made sure the advocates had done their prep work. From September to December, when the AHC was formally named, the members of Packard Manse had learned everything they could about the Massachusetts prison system.

So when Packard Manse joined with former prisoners and their family members, as well as other organizers, to form the Ad Hoc Committee on Prison Reform, the AHC was ready for Boone and ready to claim its place as the community component of correctional reform in Massachusetts. The organizers of the coalition were eventually able to bring a broad group of organizations together to support prison reform. (To this day, many of these organizations are still active in prison reform and abolition.) Among these organizations were the Massachusetts Committee for Crime and Correction, the Civil Liberties Union of Massachusetts, the American Friends Service Committee, the National Association of Social Workers, the Ex-Con Self-Help Organization, Citizens and Relatives Concerned About Prisons (CARCAP), the Roxbury Defenders, and religious groups, in addition to individual lawyers and ex-prisoners. And the membership of the Ad Hoc Committee would continue to grow over the course of its first years. Yet, throughout its tenure, the AHC remained exactly true to its name: ad hoc. It did not waste its time creating an institutional structure for itself or raising funds for its work.

At its inception, the AHC's primary focus was on educating the public about prison reform.[107] The committee would work to promote discussion about administrative, legislative, and citizen action, and it would define prison reform as a self-determination project. Direct access to prisoners, especially those confined at the embattled Walpole prison, was central to its strategy. The AHC knew that accountability for prison reform could only be achieved through the participation of those who were currently incarcerated. Without direct contact with prisoners, the AHC's work would lack authenticity. The coalition was committed to creating the opportunity for prisoners to lay claim to a position of legitimate authority. The group nurtured a link between ex-prisoners and current prisoners, and agreed to develop strategy through consensus, which would help assure that less powerful voices would be adequately considered.[108] (The process also made for long and passionate meetings.)

Besides pressing for the closing of the Bridgewater DSU, the AHC's particular concern rested with the Walpole prisoners who had been using work stoppages to draw attention to their situation. Conversations had already begun between ex-prisoners and national representatives of the National Prisoners Reform Association, the NPRA. Now, some of the ex-prisoners introduced the AHC to the NPRA.

The AHC had also accompanied Judge Harry Elam to Walpole when he met with the prisoners in September 1971. One of its members had also been appointed to the Elam Committee. Fully aware of the Walpole prisoners' commitment to resist their oppression, the Ad Hoc Committee understood that what happened at Walpole would determine the success of the reform endeavor to which John Boone was committed.

Thus, on the heels of Boone's appointing Donnelly superintendent of Walpole, the Ad Hoc Committee sent Donnelly an open letter, offering to be the link between the prison population and the public. Members used their widely respected work exposing conditions in the DSU at Bridgewater to leverage the group's position. The letter argued that no reform can succeed unless prisoners have a mechanism to address their grievances, and that, furthermore, successful reform required community involvement. It ended:

> We do not foresee that real change can take place without citizens involving themselves, informing themselves, and most importantly listening. We propose to begin this process as quickly as we can work out arrangements to meet with the prison population.[109]

The Ad Hoc Committee also sent a long telegram to the commissioner, outlining the AHC's expectations for the new commissioner and requesting a meeting with him.[110] With the leadership of the Inmate Grievance Committee at Walpole still locked down in early 1972, it was urgent that Boone affirm the right of prisoners to negotiate through their own elected committees. Throughout the previous fall, the DOC's response to the prisoners' organizing initiatives had been arbitrary and capricious. The committee wanted Boone to protect the prisoners from reprisals by establishing due-process safeguards for disciplinary actions and transfers. Committed to increasing the transparency of penal institutions, the AHC asked Boone to support free communication between the prisoners and the public. It also offered to take responsibility for both the arbitration of the prisoners' grievances and the evaluation of the rehabilitative results of prison programs. Not wanting to ally himself with a group who had been a thorn in the side of the governor, Boone did not respond to the telegram.

On February 9, 1972, the reform bill Boone worked on for Governor Sargent was introduced in the legislature.[111] The AHC sent a copy of the bill to prisoners throughout the system. While the committee waited for responses from behind the wall, it began its own study of the legislation.

Shortly after the bill was released, the AHC tried to arrange for representatives of the NPRA and the Walpole Inmate Advisory Council to meet, but Donnelly refused to allow it. Donnelly was adamant, confirming that the "counter-NPRA policy [would] continue."[112] Resolutely ignoring this negative response, the Ad Hoc Committee continued conversations with the warden, pushing for access to the prison.[113]

While waiting for a response from Donnelly, the AHC finally secured its initial meeting with Commissioner Boone. It was scheduled for February 16, and the agenda included prisoners' rights, advocacy, citizens' access, and DOC accountability.[114] The meeting was polite. The AHC pushed for the closure of the DSU at Bridgewater. Later that day, Boone went to the DSU himself. When I discussed this tour with John Boone, he reported that he had visited the DSU well after the mandated hearings for each prisoner had been concluded, although other sources point to the Davis hearings continuing into April. During his DSU tour, prisoners remained. Boone only saw one of them. The staff, with no one to guard, was playing squirt-gun war through the cavernous halls and empty cells. The conditions were still squalid. Boone was disgusted.[115]

The next day, Boone held a press conference and closed the unit "because it lacked the facilities to meet the standards of basic health and human dignity." Boone stated that the closure reflected "a new policy that dictates treatment rather than punishment for those inmates who have adjustment problems."[116] Prison records indicate that seven prisoners were still at Bridgewater when Boone closed the DSU. All were returned to Walpole.

At the press conference announcing the closure, Boone also detailed the immediate reforms he planned to implement. Demonstrating that community corrections would be the centerpiece of his plan, he announced that four halfway houses would be opened later in the spring: two in Boston and one each in Worcester and Springfield. Boone also reported that interdepartmental regulations governing disciplinary infractions, grievances, transfers, censorship, medical care, and other crucial areas of concern would be ready for public commentary in March. Sargent, also present ,declared the penal system "a monumental failure" and urged the adoption of the new prison regulations Boone was to release, promising that both officers and inmates would "have a voice in setting correctional policy."[117] By appearing with Boone as he unrolled his plan for penal reform, Sargent demonstrated that he intended for Boone to be the person who would make real the promise embedded in his reform bill.

Setting Boundaries

Yet, the AHC found the bill itself to be faulty. With substantial input from prisoners and ex-prisoners, the Ad Hoc Committee launched a public attack on the proposed act. By March 2, it had determined its strategy.[118] In his testimony before the House judiciary committee Ed Rodman outlined the problems inherent in the proposed legislation.

> Unless it is changed substantially—by additions and deletions— blindly supporting it simply because it carries the label of reform would be a violation of our reason for being. The bill contains features that deserve our support and yours: community based programs, minimum wages for prisoners who work, and giving the new Commissioner the authority and responsibility he needs and should have. But it authorizes many of the punishments which have caused despair, desperation, and, most important, the failure of our prisons. *You cannot rehabilitate a man at the same time you are dehumanizing and humiliating him.* Not only does this bill affirm isolation, segregation, and transfers all over the United States—but it provides no due-process safeguards to prevent their malicious use. It does not even *fully* guarantee religious freedom. Its best provisions deal only with a small percentage of the prison's population. In short, prisoners' human rights—the issues that *caused* Attica—are unprotected by this bill as it now stands. We cannot sit on two chairs at once—claiming reform and using revenge. We are tired of supporting so-called reforms that do not, for the most part, alter inhuman conditions that destroy men and women. We could support this bill only when it is transformed into a real reform bill.[119]

The real sticking point for the AHC was the fact that the bill contained no entitlements or guarantee of human rights for prisoners. Without entitlements, they reasoned, every improvement the prisoners obtained would be considered the granting of a privilege, which could just as easily be taken away. The committee suggested to Sargent's administration that certain rights be enumerated in the law and that the commissioner be given a mandate to enforce and protect them. The coalition focused on "censorship, religious freedom, visitation, medical rights, right to counsel, and inmate-guard relationships." But Sargent's team had constructed the law to allow significant structural change to penal institutions; it was about vision, large strokes, not individuals or the particular human rights of those who had to endure imprisonment. Because the Sargent administration would not budge on this point, the AHC never did actually support the Omnibus Correctional Reform Act, known simply as Chapter 777. In the end they agreed not to oppose it, but they fought for a number of changes.

Legal Representation

Armed with the Elam report and the voices of the prisoners, the AHC advocated for access to legal counsel for prisoners. They lobbied for an amendment to the legislation ensuring that any prisoner's request for legal counsel would be relayed to an attorney within one working day. They lost on this matter. However, Boone eventually enlisted DOC attorneys to work with the NPRA's Legal Committee, and one of their joint projects was a collection of prisoner rights and responsibilities.[120] Attorneys from the Roxbury Defenders, led by Patrick Ireland, who would one day sit on the Massachusetts Supreme Judicial Court, worked with civil rights attorneys to establish the Prisoner Rights Project, which would eventually be court mandated to provide civil legal services for prisoners.

Transparent Regulations

The first draft of the Omnibus Correctional Reform Act had not explicitly required the publication of departmental rules and regulations. This change was made to the legislation only after outside pressure by the AHC. The AHC also wanted records of grievance proceedings opened to the public. Ultimately, they would prevail on this, although not through legislation; their recommendation would be written into DOC regulations.

Parole

Chapter 777 recommended that parole management be moved under the control of the DOC. The Ad Hoc Committee opposed this. They counseled, "The combination of parole and correction with expanded possibilities for custody in community based correctional programs is seen as a means of extending the control of the DOC over the inmate/parolee." The AHC reasoned—wisely, as it turned out—that since the DOC constituted a punitive correction system, there was no reason to assume that a parole department under its control would be able to play a supportive role. Instead, the AHC recommended that more resources be procured for the parole department or that parole be eliminated entirely. They asserted that a separate parole-reform bill was needed. Boone also saw parole as problematic, and had worked to abolish it elsewhere, but since it was firmly established in the Massachusetts system, he had decided that it was his best mechanism to depopulate the prisons there. He advocated for placing parole under his purview. This way he could begin to move prisoners who were ready for release out of the prison in a more efficient manner. Ultimately, he won. Although this structural change served Boone's short-term strategic interests, the poor thinking behind it was to become evident 20 years later, when the DOC was moved from the Executive Office of Health and Human Services to the Executive Office of Public Safety. Today, every member of the Massachusetts Parole Board has a law-enforcement background.

Medical Treatment

Prisoners had revealed that they had been subjected involuntarily to medical experiments. One of the proposed experiments involved brain surgery on recalcitrant prisoners.[121] Additionally, the Medical Advisory Committee to the DOC had identified substantial problems in the provision of medical care in the state prisons, combined with an alarming use of psychotropic drugs to control the prisoners. The AHC therefore advocated for a line in the bill that would prohibit "medical or scientific experiments conducted in any state correctional facility." The committee was to lose on this recommendation, but raising the issue allowed it to publicize the scandalous medical treatment prisoners received.

Religious Freedom

With its members deeply committed to religious freedom, the AHC also recommended the following amendment:

> A committed offender shall have the right of free exercise of his religious beliefs, the right to change or adopt such beliefs, and the right to receive visitations from a clergyman or the representative of his faith. No committed offender shall be ordered or compelled to participate in any religious activities.

This unheeded recommendation preceded the landmark federal Religious Freedom and Restoration Act, which guaranteed religious freedom in the United States, by six years, and the Reorganized Land Use and Institutionalized Persons Act (RLUIPA), which guaranteed religious freedom for prisoners, by thirty years.

Public Access

Because prisoners' ability to establish direct contact with the outside world was crucial in defining the reform project, the AHC attempted to secure broad media and civilian access to the prison. However, since the AHC had positioned itself as a key player in the conversation about prison reform, the Sargent administration saw the committee as a problem. Being a prison administrator who had often been criticized publicly for his far-reaching reforms, Boone was not enthusiastic about media access to the prison. He did not want the guards to gain control of the media. Initially, Boone also identified Ed Rodman as a problem—he saw him as radical, stubborn, and meddlesome. Ultimately, Boone prevailed here as well; neither media nor civilian access was guaranteed in the legislation. Yet strategically, this was a mistake. As Dellelo puts it, "The administration had the media on their side. But then they started, through Ryan, identifying with us, because while we brought them in, the administration pushed them away."[122]

Disciplinary Procedures

The AHC was particularly concerned that unregulated disciplinary procedures had led to profound prisoner abuse. It argued that prisoners should be awarded due process[123] in all disciplinary procedures, especially those that led to solitary confinement, or isolation. Due-process protections were not included in the law and it would take more than ten years to win them in the courts. The 1955 penal law had imposed a maximum 15-day period for isolation and declared that solitary confinement could not be used as punishment. The AHC argued that a 15-day maximum time limit be imposed for administrative segregation too. This revision would, in effect, eliminate segregation as a disciplinary tool by removing any distinction between isolation and segregation. But the committee lost on this recommendation, and the standing distinction between segregation and isolation has made it impossible to shut down any super-maximum units in Massachusetts. To this day, the DOC has been able to argue that solitary-confinement units are actually segregation units and, through semantics, legitimize the torture of prisoners through forced solitude. Nor was the AHC successful in requiring that "segregated" prisoners be guaranteed three meals a day.

Transfer Procedures

The AHC took the position that involuntary out-of-state transfers should be completely prohibited and in-state transfers should be allowed only with the inmate's consent or after procedures that would guarantee due process.[124] It argued that prisoners should have the opportunity to appeal a transfer decision, a hearing on the potential transfer, and timely notice of a transfer to relatives and attorneys. The DOC countered that the complete prohibition of interstate transfers would conflict with existing provisions and contracts under the New England compact, which allowed the states to address long-term protective-custody issues on a case-by-case basis. Some institutional protocol for in-state transfers would ultimately be built into the prisoner-classification procedure, but it would fall far short of "due process."

Staff Job Requirements

Acknowledging that there were distinct benefits to having a social worker as commissioner of corrections, the AHC urged that the bill mandate job requirements for the commissioner's position, including background in other allied professions, as well as correctional administration. Again, this was never written into the bill.

THE OMNIBUS CORRECTIONAL REFORM ACT OF 1972—CHAPTER 777[125]

The Correctional Reform Act of 1972 was remarkable. In the end, it did not include entitlements for prisoners, nor did it end the torture of solitary confinement, but it did provide a unique framework for community corrections and for prisoners' agency in their own rehabilitation.

The act was not popular among the members of the state legislature. Because a civil war was being waged behind the walls of the state's maximum-security prison, many lawmakers did not want to go on record as supporting the legislation. They did not want to be associated with the prisoners who appeared to be committed to tearing down the prison from the inside out. But they knew something had to be done. The governor wanted Boone to have a reliable tool to force the radical change he had outlined though his six points of correctional reform (see p. 39). In the end, the leadership of both the House and Senate decided that the only way to pass the legislation was to put it to a voice vote, so there would be no public voting record. The act, which became known as Chapter 777, was signed into law on July 16, 1972, at a special signing ceremony held in Norfolk prison.

Chapter 777 focused on the mandated, unequivocal responsibilities of the Department of Correction. The prisoners in Walpole had turned the DOC on its side, allowing all to look directly into the institution and witness the utter depravity of the living conditions. Chapter 777 gave the DOC its work plan. The verbs throughout the legislation were predicated with "shall"; the usual legislative qualifiers "to the extent possible" and "consistent with security needs" were, for the most part, absent. Chapter 777 made it clear that prisons would be reformed.

The act also stipulated that the DOC was immediately responsible for designing and implementing that reform. Those who benefited from the corrupt corrections system were expected to clean it up.

The guards' unions had another concrete reason to declare war on John O. Boone. This soft-spoken, intelligent Black man had just been given the responsibility and the mandate to "break the box." He had been given the tools and the authority to take away the entitlements of white supremacy, entitlements that were predicated on prisoners' chattel status. The act gave the commissioner the power to establish, maintain, and administer the state correctional facilities "as he deemed necessary." Conversely, he could petition the legislature to close any prison.[126] During Boone's short tenure he would act on this provision to permanently close an entire wing at the Concord prison; he had already closed the segregation unit at Bridgewater. Later, Boone reported that as both the recidivism rate and the prison population dropped, the guards became angrier and angrier, saying, "Look at Boone, he's taking *our* prisoners away."

RESTRUCTURING THE INSTITUTIONS OF PUNISHMENT

Other provisions of the law were not left to the commissioner's discretion. Like the 1955 reforms, Chapter 777 required the commissioner to establish standards for all prisons and jails. It required programming in education, training, and employment. These programs were to be designed so that each convict would be prepared "to assume the responsibilities and to exercise their rights of citizenship." However, the legislation did not follow the Elam Committee's recommendation to involve prisoners in the development of programming and in the creation of their own individual rehabilitation plans. In that respect, the law fell far short of the goals of the reformers. Yet, by the time the act was passed, Boone had already begun to implement the first set of uniform regulations for the DOC. And he did expect prisoners to design their own furlough plans.

ACCOUNTABILITY

Chapter 777 required that all institutions be inspected by the public health inspector twice a year and that a report be issued following those inspections.[127] The reports were filed with the secretary of human services, the commissioner of corrections, the superintendent of each institution, and the state legislature. Accountability was built in at all levels of governance. Because the Ad Hoc Committee had demanded that the

DOC operate with complete transparency, the reports were a matter of public record. They are kept on file at the State House Library, and any citizen can review them.

In response to the pressure to identify entitlements for prisoners, the drafters of the legislation decreed that the commissioner establish minimum standards for the care and custody of all persons committed to a penal institution. However, these standards were not completed during Boone's tenure and, to this day, no minimum standards exist. Unfortunately, this lapse allows the DOC to continually lower the decency bar.

Chapter 777 also called for the establishment and maintenance of research programs within the DOC, requiring regular reporting of statistics and departmental planning. The research and planning department was expected to conduct studies on correctional programs and evaluate the DOC's execution of all its mandated responsibilities.[128]

CLASSIFICATION

Chapter 777 ordered the department to establish a prisoner-classification system that would help in developing a rehabilitation program for each person. The legislation changed the purpose of classification from maintenance of security to provision of necessary services to prisoners. Ideally, the classification process would determine the program requirements for each prisoner and assign or transfer the prisoner to appropriate facilities, where the needed programs were offered. The DOC was ordered to "utilize, as far as practicable, the services and resources of specialized community agencies and other local community groups in the rehabilitation of offenders, development of programs, recruitment of volunteers and dissemination of information regarding the work of the department." In other words, the department was to develop substantial ties to community-based organizations. When a program existed on the street, the DOC was to invite the program to develop a "behind the wall" component.

PUBLIC ENGAGEMENT

The legislation called for the DOC to develop civic interest in the work of the department, educate the public, and advise the legislature on the needs and goals of the corrections process. Sargent was particularly concerned that the public be engaged in his correctional-reform project. Like Governor Herter, he knew that the project's success or failure depended on the development of a convinced citizenry.[129] He wanted the DOC to take on the task of creating buy-in for his ideas. To this end, Boone traveled around the state and spoke with civic groups and churches about the department's commitment to prison reform. He also created the first public-relations department within the DOC.

Boone, Goldmark, and Isenberg understood that the work they were doing in Massachusetts was groundbreaking. They knew that it would not be enough to shift from carceral to community corrections. Ultimately, they had to prove that community corrections and correctional reform reduced recidivism and crime. Isenberg was well aware that some radical criminologists were publishing results of studies that demonstrated the failure of correctionalism. He wanted to make sure community corrections were seen as being outside this rubric.

PRISON LABOR

The Sargent administration's efforts at correctional reform were first and foremost practical. They knew that prisoners would return to the community. If they were to succeed at the community level, the DOC would need to be able to work with the prisoners during their incarceration to make them employable after release. In 1971, the national unemployment level was at a record high. The numbers in Massachusetts were particularly high.

Chapter 777 required the commissioner to establish and maintain education, training, and employment programs for all prisoners. This included academic and vocational education, vocational training, and "other related pre-vocational programs and employment." To structure rehabilitative programming, the commissioner was to evaluate the training value of the program, and assess the current job market and employment conditions in the community so that prisoners would be prepared to assume jobs upon their release. Where the employment programs articulated in the 1955 act were constructed to end idleness in prison, the drafters of Chapter 777 had much higher expectations. They were serious about job training and saw employment preparation as one of the most important issues to be addressed while an individual was confined.

To get the prison employment programs off the ground, the administration had to negotiate with radical elements of organized labor who insisted prison work programs conform to labor law. Mainstream organized labor was particularly concerned that prisoner work programs, given the potential incentives for employer participation, not compete with organized labor. Labor was well aware that Sargent planned to develop manufacturing programs within the prison. This aspect of prison programming became the central aspect of NPRA organizing. Chapter 777 also required that the skills-training programs developed within a correctional facility conform to the types of goods and services required by the commonwealth and its subdivisions. In other words, the print shop could print state documents and stationery, the furniture shop could build furniture for government offices, the sewing program at Framingham could make flags for state buildings, and so on. Prisoners could be prepared while inside the prison to join the ranks of tradesmen upon release, and they would not be able to compete for private contracts with labor outside the wall.

As much as radical, organized labor unionists were supportive of prison reform, they were deeply concerned that the DOC itself not profit from the labor of prisoners. To safeguard against exploitation of prisoner laborers, all profit from the sale of products, by-products, or services of committed offenders was paid into the Correctional Employment Fund. This fund was to be used to defray operating expenses of employment programs; cost of materials, supplies, and equipment; maintenance of industrial facilities; and compensation to convicts who were employed in the programs. If there was any unexpended balance, it would go into the state's general fund.

DOC EMPLOYMENT STANDARDS

The Elam Committee's report had made it abundantly clear that there were two labor issues within the Department of Correction. The prisoners were largely working-class men who would need to be prepared as workers, and the prison staff were also workers who had jobs to do. As Boone would later recall, the committee had passionately argued that these jobs had to be meaningful and the current staff needed to be prepared to do the work that correctional reform would demand.

The crafters of the legislation outlined two aspects of job preparation. The first related to security. The behavior of guards throughout the fall of 1971 and spring of 1972 made it abundantly clear that they had not been trained in law enforcement. The law established a training program for guards in cooperation with the municipal police-training council. This was the first attempt to create a "professional" staff. The law also made provisions for current correctional staff to prepare themselves to take on the new roles that would be required of them. The DOC was mandated to develop employee-training programs. Because these programs were not defined in the law, there was space left to design them according to the reformers' priorities. Some of the first trainings implemented were intended to develop the line staff's nonviolent conflict-resolution capacity.

Corrections 71 built a strong case for the commissioner—not the unions—to take the lead in establishing work conditions for the DOC staff. The legislation required the commissioner to promulgate rules and regulations that would include provisions for hours, conditions of employment, wage rates for employment-program participants, and deductions from such wages. The law also gave new power to the commissioner. For the first time, the commissioner had the right to hire trainees outside of the union's purview. Boone would use this right to bring in cadet trainees who were young men of color, setting off a racialized struggle within the staff.

This section of the bill, more than any other, created immediate antipathy between the line staff and the commissioner. Over the years, the unions had successfully negotiated all conditions of employment. Through nepotism, they controlled all hires, and through control of the final review process, they were able to block any fires. Chapter 777 threatened to change the very foundation of their world; the guards' unions were no longer able to unequivocally determine what would happen when they went to work. The multiple guards' unions (see p. 26) joined to protect their interests and began a highly personalized and racialized war against one man: John O. Boone.

TEAR DOWN THE WALLS

The heart of Chapter 777 was completely radical. It actually created the framework for shutting down the large penal institutions in the state. Although the commissioner could not shut down a prison without approval from the legislature, the commissioner was given the authority to "designate, establish, maintain and administer such state correctional facilities as he deems necessary."[130] Isenberg was to explain, "This allowed us to declare any place a correctional institution. If you wanted to open your home to create a halfway house and we approved of your proposal, we could do it." One small sentence would allow for infinite flexibility in the construction of a new correctional system.[131] The Boone administration envisioned closing the prisons through staff attrition.[132] Prisoners would be moved to smaller community settings where their needs would be better met, thus driving down the recidivism rate and emptying the larger institutions.[133]

The law formalized the prisoners' ability to participate in programs outside the correctional facility. Prisoners within 18 months of parole eligibility would be eligible to participate in work, training, or educational programs within the community. These programs could be under the direct purview of the DOC, or administered by public or private employers. Successful participation would be credited toward the serving of their sentences in the manner of added good time. Through concrete, structured experience, prisoners were to become accustomed to life in the community well in advance of their release. The only caveat to participation: the prisoner would be subject to the rules and regulations of the institution, such as curfews and mandatory reporting, and to the supervision of prison staff. All prisoners were eligible for these programs, but lifers could only participate at the recommendation of the superintendent and with the approval of the commissioner.

The centerpiece of Boone's correctional philosophy was the furlough program. Unlike educational or employment programming, the furlough fostered the intimate connection of the individual prisoner to his own community. Any prisoner, regardless of his or her sentence, could apply for a furlough. The language of the furlough program again pushed the conventional boundaries of penal incarceration:

> The commissioner may extend the limits of the place of confinement of a committed offender at any state correctional facility by authorizing such committed offender under prescribed conditions to be away from such correctional facility but within the commonwealth for a specified period of time, not to exceed fourteen days during any twelve month period nor more than seven days at any one time.[134]

Prisoners were encouraged to go home for an afternoon or weekend, to visit their families, to watch their children graduate from school, or simply to become a part of the communities from which they were exiled. The furlough program challenged the fundamental premise of incarceration—that these individuals could not be trusted to behave responsibly in society.

Under Boone's tenure, 97 percent of prisoners receiving furlough conformed to these rules. The men and women in Massachusetts's prisons demonstrated that, if given the opportunity, they not only could but would make substantial contributions to their families and to their communities. If allowed, they would help solve community problems.

The stage was set. The script was written, but all of the actors wanted revisions. And all were committed to continued struggle. Soon, the guards would demonstrate that they would have their needs met by any means necessary. But first, the prisoners were to make themselves heard.

5

RESISTANCE, REBELLION, AND DECLARATION

creating a culture of resistance

*A culture is an environment where creativity is honored as
a great value; it happens around and through the people.*
—Ralph Hamm

BY THE FIRST OF MARCH, THE PRISONERS WERE FINISHED WAITING
for action from the advocates, the commissioner, or the legislature. Despite its radical premises, Chapter 777 fell far short of their expectations and they had become frustrated with the indirect process of influence through the Ad Hoc Committee. They decided they might speed up the process if they took action themselves. The Inmate Advisory Council threatened another work stoppage unless representatives from the public and the press were allowed in.

Superintendent Robert Donnelly capitulated, and 50 observers, legislators, and advocates organized by the AHC were invited into MCI Walpole to talk with the prisoners. At this meeting, the prisoners aired their grievances, the cameras rolled, and the reporters took notes. The prisoners had achieved one of the AHC's primary goals. The Walpole prisoners finally had direct access to the press so that they could tell the public exactly what was going on there.

With this accomplishment, the prisoners reconfirmed the power that with-holding labor could afford them. They made a tactical decision to be the primary actors in their lives, and self-determined action had proven to be the best route to immediate and tangible results. No longer would the prisoners allow policy to happen to them. To drive home the point that they would exercise their power, im-mediately after the meeting ended they declared the work stoppage anyway, despite Donnelly's concession.

This marked a critical turning point in the prisoners' strategy. The men under-stood that there were two separate, although related, initiatives: the prison-reform movement and their own struggle for dignity and self-determination. While the AHC and other supporters were willing to take the time to work through the system without directly challenging it, the prisoners were the quintessential outlaws—they did not work through or "respect" the system; nor did they trust any outsiders to re-ally have their interests at heart. Prison reform was an "issue"; but they were men. As human beings, they had dreams and aspirations that could not be addressed under the banner of "prison reform." For the prisoners, the reform movement was a vehicle through which to assert their humanity. The tension created by this unapparent but critical dichotomy was to frame their entire struggle for self-determination.[135]

With the hubris common to many committed activists, some AHC members believed their advocacy was the catalyst for the effort to reform the prisons. The pris-oners viewed the AHC and its work as one prong of a broad, strategic effort whose goal was liberty. They were well aware, however, that many of the advocates would settle for reform.

Because of her experience in the labor and civil rights movements, Phyllis Ryan knew that advocates' attempts to "control" the prisoners would compromise the struggle to end their oppression. Always a foil to liberal self-involvement, she made sure that the AHC never tried to direct the prisoners. The prisoners continued as they'd started: setting their own agenda and respecting their supporters' strategies, but adopting only the aspects that bolstered their own plans.

Ralph Hamm was finally released to general population at MCI Walpole on March 10, 1972, after being held in various segregation units for over 14 months. Because he had worked to build unity across racial lines in the Bridgewater DSU and because he had demonstrated his ability to fight the guards and prevail, he had won respect among the prisoners, both intellectually and physically. He knew that whether he was perceived as innocent or guilty, he would always have to be the stron-ger, more capable individual in any conflict with prisoners or staff. His life depended on his ability to convince people they should listen to him, to make good on his leadership, and to prevail when challenged. It was not surprising, then, that despite his age, he had become a leader in the blocks where the majority of Black prisoners were housed. Shortly after his return to general population, he was elected to the Inmate Advisory Council.

RAISING BLACK CONSCIOUSNESS

While Hamm had been in segregation, the Nation of Islam had seized one of the cellblocks and, as Dellelo reports it, declared,

> This is ours. They put their stuff up on the wall, and the white prisoners said, okay, it's yours. Just like the Italians had claimed 6 Block, the Irish had claimed 4 Block, they were taking this block for the Black prisoners.[136]

In the first week after Hamm's release from segregation, David Dance, a Harvard undergraduate active in Black Panther support work in Boston, received the administration's permission to start a Black history course inside Walpole. Aware that prisoners needed to understand the historical context of their imprisonment, John O. Boone strongly supported the study of African American history in prison settings. Twelve students were to participate in the class, with Ralph Hamm among them. Dance co-taught the program with Robert Heard, a high-ranking Panther Party member who had recently arrived in Boston. Together, they would introduce the students to the canon of Black Consciousness literature through the guise of a general Black history class.

While Hamm had already begun to re-define himself within the context of the Nation of Islam, the Black history classes opened all the windows and doors and let a clean breeze that smelled like possibility into Walpole, where previously even the simplest things could appear impossible. These classes were to shake the philosophical, psychological, and spiritual foundations of the men who participated, and give them an intellectual framework for their personal experiences. Ralph explained:

> This was the first time that I heard my history. Reading Ralph Ellison turned my world upside down. I knew nothing about slavery, nothing about the South. David Dance's class opened my mind to the world of Black Consciousness and Big Bob [Heard] exemplified what a Black revolutionary actually was. I went overnight from the former military man to a participant in the Black Consciousness movement. I couldn't read enough. Learning our history started the ball rolling. Our world was turned upside down and then right side up.[137]

The obstacles these prisoners had to confront came from all sides. As Ralph describes it,

> In many regards, living in Walpole during the 1970s was like living in the Wild West during the 1800s. I knew many prisoners who would wear magazines tied around their torsos as armor against a knife attack. Some even took the metal mirrors off cell walls and fashioned them into back and chest plate armor that hung from their neck. It was a rough environment that needed an extreme façade of bravado to control it. We used to liken it to Pandora's box, where whenever the prison administration refused to concede to

an issue pertaining to prison reform we would open the box's lid so they could take a peek at all of the demons imprisoned within its confines.

The least armed of all the prisoners were the Black prisoners, because we were the minority and we had no control of anything. Those of us who could secure weapons formed a small unit that would have to run from one racially charged crisis in the prison to another in order to protect the lives of Black prisoners—this meant even protection from the guards, who were in league with their white prisoner counterparts when it came to racially motivated attacks against the minorities. If organized crime or the guards (often one and the same) wanted a Black prisoner killed ... [they] would set up the black "militants" in the cellblock and have them either locked up or transferred to segregation whereby the murder could be carried out without any opposition; after which, the whole prison would be locked down and we would have to negotiate its reopening under the promise of no further violence.[138]

Yet, because he had come to understand the importance of solidarity within the prison population, Hamm understood that equity for Black prisoners in the prison at large would be determined by their ability to build internal unity. He began to work within the small Black population to end any internal fighting. Almost immediately, he had an opportunity to put his ideology in practice.

THE ST. PATRICK'S DAY REBELLION

On March 17, prisoners at Walpole rebelled against guard manipulation. Hamm tells the story:

It began with a knife fight that ensued between [a Black prisoner] and [a white prisoner] in max end Cellblock #2. I had recently been released from Segregation Block 10, [where I'd been locked down] as a result of the firebombing and beating by the guards in 1971. I was a member of the Nation of Islam (NOI) then. The entire NOI prisoner congregation had been removed from population to Segregation Block 10 prior to my release, and I was attempting to keep the program alive in their absence. After a service on the night of March 17, I stepped out of the door of the mosque into the main corridor when I heard [corrections officer] John Dumbrowski and other guards yelling that there was a race riot, while they ran toward inner control. They had all abandoned their posts in the max end corridor and cellblocks, leaving most of the barred gates open in the predominately Black cellblocks so that [other] prisoners had easy access to Cellblock #2. When I reached the housing corridor, Black prisoners came running down the corridor from Blocks #3 and #4, and were massing up to head for Block #2. I followed, but once inside of Block #2, I found that the Black prisoners had eased their way behind me so that I was now the one up front.... They pointed out [the white prisoner] and told me to get him. I had spent months in Segregation Block 10 with [him], and although I knew him to be a bigot and prideful of his Irish heritage—belonging to an Irish-American prison gang ... I didn't interpret him to be one who would start a full-scale race riot.

I stepped away from the crowd, took [the white prisoner] to the side, and asked him what happened. He informed me that he and [the Black prisoner] had been going at each other for some time, and eventually that it erupted into a one-on-one knife fight. I believed him, turned and told everyone who did not live in the Block to get out. After which, we went from Block to Block in the max end to inform everyone that there was no race riot, and that the guards (with their prisoner allies) were attempting to encourage us to fight one another. The situation eventually evolved into a major property damage riot, where prisoners turned their frustration and anger on the prison itself. Some of us prisoners attempted to quell the disturbance, as did Superintendent Fred Butterworth, but it was too late.... The violence had spread to the minimum section of the prison thanks to the guards.[139]

To stop the property destruction, Donnelly brought in state police armed with shotguns and tear gas. Five prisoners were injured in either the rebellion or the state police takeover. After all the damage was tallied, it was estimated that repairs would cost $1.6 million. But Boone recognized the uprising for what it was: a guards' riot.[140] His first response was to meet with the prisoners. Afterwards, Boone held a press conference with 30 of the prisoners, among them Hamm and all the participants of Dance's Black history class. The prisoners explained that, despite the guards' claims, the conflict was not a race riot, but rather a protest against the conditions in the prison.[141] The AHC released a statement to the press predicting that the St. Patrick's Day disturbance would be the beginning of an ongoing crisis at Walpole unless the problems there were addressed.[142] Together, they planned to use the rebellion, and the threat of more to come, to leverage a long-term policy of public access to state prisons.[143]

REBELLION BRINGS REFORM

For three days, from March 18 to 20, the Walpole prisoners met with Boone and the AHC within the prison.[144] On March 20, Boone held another press conference, declaring that the response to the St. Patrick's Day riot "should be prison reform" and asserting that reform meant more than seeing to the extensive repairs necessary within the prison and that actual reform had to be funded adequately.[145]

Boone's decision to discuss the rebellion with the prisoners and then stand with them in demanding reform was seen as an outright betrayal by the Walpole Guards Union. Up until this point, the relationship between the commissioner and his staff was one framed by cautious suspicion. The guards did not share his corrections philosophy and had never invited Boone to join the guards' "old boys' club." By siding with the prisoners, Boone tipped his hand; he didn't even aspire to be a member.

Not closing ranks with his staff demonstrated that Boone was dead serious about prison reform.

BECOMING BANTU—BLACK CONSCIOUSNESS AT WALPOLE

The next few months were critical for Black prisoners. The class participants' study of Black history and Black Consciousness deepened. Their commitment was to abolition, not reform, and their dedication was rooted in their newfound consciousness, pride, and understanding of the unique way the penal system had been built not only to oppress them, but to re-enslave them. The history-class students formed their own cultural organization—the first cultural organization for Black men within the Massachusetts prison system: Black African Nations Toward Unity. BANTU was to become the vehicle the Black prisoners used to ensure racial parity within the prisoners' union. Hamm explains the group's impact on him and the other prisoners, and the context within which it had been created.

> I arrived at Walpole Prison in June of 1969. Years of watching Dr. King's marches for civil rights, reading of the lynchings and murders of Black people "down South," the FBI and COINTELPRO attacks and murders of Black Panther members, the riots in Watts and Grove Hall [in Boston], to name a few events of the times, had conditioned my attitude toward white authority figures. The above mentioned came in light of my own personal experiences with similar authority types during my years in the community, Essex County Training School, and the military. I despised them all.
>
> Upon entering Walpole Prison, my first observation was the small number of Black prisoners confined there, in comparison to the number of white prisoners. In a population of approximately 465 prisoners, 48 were Black, 2 were Hispanic, and 1 was Asian.
>
> Christian Action, the Italian-American Heritage Group, and the Irish-American Heritage Group were the three major programs of the time; with the Christian Action program the only one with Black prisoner participation (2 or 3). African-American books, specific newspapers and magazines, and Black History periodicals were all deemed contraband by the prison administration.
>
> During the years 1969 to 1973, a number of significant events occurred in the community that radicalized the mindset of most of the 48 Black prisoners in Walpole—especially myself. These events were the Attica Prison revolt, the American Indian Movement take-over at Wounded Knee, the political rise of the Republic of New Africa, the formation of the Weather Underground, and the slaughter of students at Kent State University by the National Guard. These events gave me the ideology and blueprint to structure an organization of resistance that could benefit prisoners in their quest for meaningful rehabilitative programs designed around the outside community, with the assistance of community activists.
>
> The idea and belief [that I'd been] betrayed by the judicial system via my conviction—an institution of just-us that I had been

brainwashed by the educational system and the military to defend—as well as my compelling need to find my own spiritual identity as a Black man unfettered by what I had heretofore been forced to believe, by what I perceived then as the missionary-to-slave teachings of Christianity, led me to Islam and the Honorable Elijah Muhammad in 1970. Muhammad's teachings were at the far extreme of what I had heretofore been forced to believe, and fit my need to rebel against the establishment—while at the same time affording me an alternative spiritual foundation. However, my stay in the Nation Of Islam was short lived, as my quest for knowledge and love of books revealed to me Islam's role in the slave trade, and eventually afforded me with the perception that most of its upper echelon adherents were nothing more than poverty pimps (living high off the lower echelon's monetary contributions and ignorance).

Prior to the March 17, 1972, rebellion in Walpole Prison, David Dance persuaded the prison administration to allow him to teach a Black history course to 12 Black prisoners. The group was afforded space once a week in the prison general library. The prison administration pre-approved the books that we were allowed to read, by such authors as Richard Wright, Langston Hughes, Lerone Bennett Jr., Ralph Ellison, and Herbert Aptheker. It was within the framework of the Black History course that I met Big Bob Heard who not only entered as one of our course instructors, but also as a standing member of the Black Panther Party of Boston. It was through Big Bob that we received the Black Panther Party Paper, Weather Underground written material, and books authored by Franz Fanon, Paolo Freire, Kwame Nkrumah, Amilcar Cabral, Patrice Lumumba, Yusuf ben Jochanin, William Reich, Chancellor Williams III, and J. A. Rodgers, to name a few. This additional reading material rounded out our education of self, and allowed me to circulate the books and newspapers throughout the Black prisoner population via a mobile underground library (it was continuously moved from cell to cell, so that the prison administration would not find it). During this period of time I required that all prisoners who took out books from the library were to write a book report on what they had read; failure to do so would cost the individual a carton of cigarettes (which were donated to newly arrived Black prisoners to Walpole Prison population).

My newly founded education could be attributed to the Black history course.... My greater understanding of the Third World struggle against colonialism, imperialism, white supremacy, and racism ... as well as Black Consciousness awoken within me by Black poets (such as The Last Poets, Nikki Giovanni, Sonia Sanchez, Etheridge Knight, Frederick Douglass, etc.), and the Black musicians of the era (e.g., James Brown, Curtis Mayfield, Gil Scott Heron, Bob Marley, Jimmy Cliff, and Sly and the Family Stone) gave me my marching orders and anthems. All of the above led to the founding of BANTU in 1972, with all the members of the Black history course as its cofounders.

> BANTU was founded because there was a cultural need for representation for Black prisoners that was not afforded by the Inmate Advisory Council then and the other self-help groups that were established within the prison. Also, my newly awakened sense of Black/African history and pride instilled within me an obligation to assist in what I perceived to be the restructuring of the outside Black community. I believed that I could accomplish this feat by providing the prospective communities with educated and highly trained/motivated individuals (ex cons); rather than the uneducated, unskilled social parasites that the prison system was forcing down their collective throat. Community activists such as Obalaji Rust (Boston Black United Front), Amina Greene (college student), David Dance (Harvard University Undergrad), and the Reverend Edward Rodman were some of the people who made up BANTU's external board of directors. These community members were the individuals who continually impressed upon me the need for BANTU to become a voice in the newly recognized NPRA.
>
> This was the most difficult period in my young life, as I had been conditioned up to this stage to react to political/social racial violence with violence. Ironically, it was not until the 1980s that those sessions on nonviolence with Ed finally took root in my conscious mind, so I could fully understand and appreciate the political and social significance of the principles of nonviolent resistance.[146]

Although BANTU came together in early spring, it would be officially formed with an internal and external board in September of 1972, as would the NPRA. Initially, BANTU members were not interested in even joining the NPRA, because the mainstream labor movement had always overtly excluded Black workers. Eventually, however, all of the BANTU leaders were on the board of the NPRA. Even so, BANTU maintained its own identity.

COMBATING THE NOD

By 1972, the prison administration at Walpole was using psychotropic drugs to control the prison population. Prisoners were put on Talwin, an analgesic narcotic usually used to control chronic or intense pain; it is used today in the preparation of Oxycontin, known to be highly addictive. Side effects included severe drowsiness, inability to focus, impaired reactions, and impaired thought processes. Talwin was the ideal drug to control the Walpole population.

Combating "the nod" would be a constant struggle for the NPRA. Dellelo describes a meeting of the general population where whole sections of the auditorium could not keep their heads raised. "The whole front row. It was like watching synchronized swimming. They all crossed their legs, folded their arms, and dropped their heads."[147] The guards would give each prisoner an entire day's worth of meds at one time. These prisoners would take all the pills at once and become "worthless."

By the end of 1972, the administrators of Walpole were intentionally turning the population into narcotics addicts. Once prisoners ceased being behavior problems, they would be transferred to Norfolk prison, where they would go through rapid detoxification. Sunny Robinson, who later became an observer, worked at the Medical Project in Norfolk. She reported what she was seeing to the AHC. When the AHC eventually was able to enter Walpole, they brought in doctors who could assess the extent of drug dependency within the prison. These doctors were scandalized. But undoing narcotics addiction is a very nuanced task.

Talwin also made people heroin addicts. Prisoners would be deliberately addicted to Talwin at Walpole, and then they would be transferred out to Norfolk, where they would begin to detox. The guards at Norfolk would then sell them heroin. All family members whose loved ones were bounced back and forth between the prisons attested to this pattern.[148] Many prisoners were unable to kick their habit even after they were released to the street and struggled for many years, cycling back and forth between prison and home because of addictions they picked up in prison.

The guards at Walpole not only manipulated the availability of Talwin to pacify the population, they also stemmed the supply to destabilize it. In the end, the NPRA had to secure its own supply of Talwin. When the guards would turn off the supply, the NPRA would use its stash to maintain the prisoners' self-control. They never sold it; they just gave it out one pill at a time. Dellelo and Hamm have spoken at length about the challenges presented by the dramatic substance-abuse problems within Walpole. Dellelo explains the problem with Talwin during the NPRA tenure.

> All prisons have drugs, even the super-duper ones. Most drugs come in through guards. They are the only ones who can bring that quantity.... The prison held 580 people; 265 people were on Talwin. When the NPRA had responsibility for running the prison, we came up with the number. What often happened was a deputy would send people to the hospital to put people on Talwin for a few days. It was very addictive. After a few days they were hooked.... Once someone was on Talwin, the supplier owned his ass. So they would make a round-up, put people in segregation and take away the Talwin. After a day or so they would go around and check with the cons and say, "What's wrong? Oh, you need Talwin? What are you going to give me?" They would pull a guy in and trade Talwin for information.[149]

ASSUMING LEADERSHIP

Despite the complexity of race relations and access to power Hamm described, he played a pivotal role in the Walpole prisoners' transition from a dispersed group to a body acting democratically in its own interest. Hamm describes the first step in this process.

We elected Bobby [Dellelo], in absentia, as the chair of the Inmate Advisory Council. Then we put pressure on the administration to return him to Walpole so that he could fill the position. He was returned [in April] and agreed to take the position on one condition: that he could determine if the Council was a sellout—if he determined it to be such, he could dissolve it. He would [come to] exercise this privilege when the NPRA was successfully elected the representative of the prisoner population.[150]

Robert Dellelo remembers how the administration tried to undercut the prisoners' choice.

Right after the rebellion, they elected the new Inmate Advisory Council. Joe Higgins was deputy commissioner—the new Inmate Advisory Council elected me as board chairman.[151] Higgins said, "No, no, he is happy in the Feds." The guys said, "You bring him back have him tell us he is happy and doesn't want to come back, okay. Otherwise, it is no business until our chair is back in Walpole.[152]

Dellelo returned from USP Marion, arriving back at Walpole from Illinois in early April. He agreed to head the Inmate Advisory Council. Dellelo insisted on reserving the right to dissolve the council, as Hamm explained, because many other inmate councils served to cover up for or work on behalf of the administration or the guards—Dellelo was determined that such cooptation would not be allowed at Walpole. The rest of the council agreed to his proposition and Dellelo assumed his post.

Dellelo had a very difficult task in front of him. Despite the prisoners' bold demands for reform, the population was still bitterly divided. Walpole prison had the highest homicide rate in the country. As we heard in Hamm's description of the Walpole "Wild West," many prisoners were highly armed. Some had homemade knives or shanks. A few had guns. At least one had access to explosives. Dellelo was perhaps the only person who could walk among the various rival groups within the white population. Having grown up within the prison system, he knew everyone.[153]

At the Lyman School for Boys, where Dellelo first entered the system, the children, rather than attending classes, spent their weeks on their hands and knees scrubbing floors with brushes. On weekends, the employees entertained themselves by goading the children to fight each other to win a treasured Hershey's candy bar. Upon his arrival at Lyman, weighing barely 80 pounds, Dellelo was forced to fight every older boy until he finally defeated the largest young man in the school. Shortly after his release from prison at the age of 64, Bobby told me what it had been like. Soon he was standing, reliving the moment, air punching an opponent who was just beyond his reach. Each time he speaks of the Lyman School and the depravity of the adults who were responsible for the care of these children, he begins to sweat with anger. His edict: "No kid should have to survive that."

Dellelo knew how to resist punishment. He had learned to endure solitary confinement at the Institution of Juvenile Guidance (IJG) in Bridgewater, where boys were placed in empty single rooms for days. Like all children, the boys who were imprisoned at the IJG developed a game to pass the hours and tire themselves before the lights went out at night. As Dellelo tells it,

> The cell was small enough so your hands could touch one wall and your feet could touch the other. You would lay on the floor with your feet on one wall, your hands on the other. You would walk up the walls with your hands and feet. When you reached the ceiling you would bang the back of your head on the ceiling, making a distinctive sound everyone could hear. Quite often you would fall and people would bust out laughing. Whoever climbed the walls quickest and the most times won.[154]

Dellelo "won" often. He also refused to stay captive, escaping often, a practice he continued into his mid-50s; he escaped from all of the commonwealth's maximum security prisons. Most important, he refused to ever see himself as a victim.

But Dellelo had to do more than fight now. After Dellelo was elected chairman of the Inmate Advisory Council, the first order of business was to construct unity. Hamm had been working with the Black and Latino prisoners. The white prisoners were left to Dellelo. He was known as a fair man who treated friends and enemies with equity.

There were many groupings among the prisoners, which ran unofficial side businesses within the prison. These enterprises provided food, laundry, haircutting, and drugs, or ran the print shop and the foundry. Each prison-administrated job had a private enterprise attached to it. It was within this web of entrepreneurial activity that Dellelo mobilized with intelligent determination.

As Dellelo negotiated a truce among the white prisoners, Hamm was responsible for keeping violence from erupting inside the prison. Six-foot-six, weighing 230 pounds, and sporting a huge afro, Hamm would walk the halls of the prison in a three-quarter-length military jacket, which hid the two-and-a-half-foot machete strapped to his waist. He only needed to show the cutlass to stop foolishness. Then he would talk to the men—"educate them," as Jerry Sousa would say.[155] While it is tempting to relegate Hamm to a limited role as security—a now emblematic role for Black men, despite the paradoxical fear of Black men that leads to public support of their criminalization—Hamm's real role was a peace broker. As we will see later, his considerable skills as a negotiator enabled him to reason with white prisoners as well as Black and brown, lending to an atmosphere that was secure, not just safe.

Where Hamm had used Black Consciousness to build unity within the small Black population, Dellelo used the "street code" of the institution to balance the interests of powerful associations among the white prisoners. According to Hamm, their differing styles helped achieve the unity they needed to move forward. He reasons that Dellelo's

> impact upon the organization was through his overwhelming personality as a pragmatic realist—he thought through everything

and saw situations, things and people as they actually were ... everyone trusted his opinion. On the other hand, I was more of the romantic idealist—with utopian views that the Social Revolution, the People's Revolution, was at hand.... The prisoners trusted me to put myself out front without fear of the cost—that I would never sell them out. I could force the issue but did not know how to compromise. I was too young and somewhat naïve, but Bobby knew the fine art of compromise and negotiation.... He was also more personable. We used these traits to our best advantage.[156]

OPENING THE DOOR TO BLUE UNITY[157]

Late in March, Boone was approached by the national organizers from the NPRA and decided that a prisoners' union sounded good. Prisoners were workers and as workers had certain rights and responsibilities. Their employer had rights and responsibilities, too. The labor model allowed for mutual accountability and self-development. Boone recognized the capacity of this model to assist in the development of meaningful programming and create a demand for a unified set of regulations governing all prisons. He successfully pressured Donnelly into allowing the NPRA organizers to enter Walpole and meet with the prisoners.[158]

The resulting meeting with the NPRA's national organizers proved pivotal. After the NPRA portion of the meeting was over, as chair of the Inmate Advisory Council Dellelo addressed the population assembled in the auditorium under the watchful eyes of the Walpole guards and administrators. He conveys his memory of this historical moment.

This is what happened in the auditorium, after NPRA formed, when we were pulling everything together before the vote. We still had the Inmate Advisory Council at the time. We got everyone in the auditorium. The racial tension in the prison was thick. Black Power was bouncing. What happened is I said, "There is only one color and that is blue." The guards wore khaki, which was brown; the prisoners were wearing blue. It was blue versus brown. "You are either blue or brown. There is no in-between ground. We are all in this together." ... I explained to everyone, "We can't have no more beefs for six months. We have to agree no beefs. Everyone backs off." The question was, "What if someone nails someone during that truce, what happens?" My answer was, "Anyone who violates the truce, we will take him down." And they knew I would and could. We had the hard core on call, so even if I couldn't take someone down myself, I had someone to do it. That made a lot of people feel very, very safe. The guards could not work us like before. If we refused to fight each other, they lost a lot of their power. There was a peace across the prison that never was there before. We ended the body count.[159]

The guards and the Walpole administration were already uneasy with Boone's direct involvement with the prisoners. He was supposed to be an administrator, away in an office somewhere, not here with his ear to the ground. Boone's support of the prisoners in their bid for a union was the last straw. Donnelly threatened to resign, and the guards decided to exercise their muscle.

On the first of April, 105 guards from four prisons called in sick.[160] They were joined by 27 industrial personnel at Walpole (the people who oversaw the print shop and the manufacture of street signs, manhole covers, and license plates) who were frustrated by the administration's inability to ensure that the prisoners would show up to work. The Walpole Guards Union sent letters to the *Boston Herald American* and the *Boston Globe* detailing their grievances against the commissioner. Boone's ability to respond to the undeclared strike was circumscribed by the union's contract. In the end, all he could do was suspend the 34 Walpole guards for five days.[161]

DISMANTLING DEATH

Boston was not only home to a dynamic Black Panther Party headquarters; it also housed a collective of the Weather Underground, who were active supporters of the Panther Party. Twenty-seven-year-old Stanley Bond, a member of the Weather Underground, was doing time in Walpole. By the fall of 1972, most of the men on death row had been moved to general population. As the prisoners moved more freely around the prison, in and out of the death row, they undertook a distinctive task. They began to dismantle Massachusetts's electric chair. Hamm explained that each time they had an opportunity, the men would break a piece off the chair. Many men kept pieces of the chair in their cells. "Eventually," said Hamm, "one day it was gone."[162]

In the beginning of May, Stanley Bond went beyond this quiet but powerful act of resistance. Deciding to escape, he began to build a pipe bomb in the Walpole foundry. Many prisoners were aware of Bond's plan but none revealed the existence of the bomb. On May 25, as Bond moved the bomb into place, it went off. Bond was killed. Another prisoner was severely injured.

The fact that a prisoner had been able to build a bomb inside the state's maximum-security prison did little to build Boone's credibility as an administrator, and gave the guards another reason to whip up opposition in the press. By June, not only were the prisoners at war with the system, but the guards were in an all-out, public conflict with the commissioner.

RALLYING OUTSIDE SUPPORT

Once Chapter 777 was in place, the AHC began to focus on its own capacity to stay engaged in prison reform. It was obvious that Boone was going to need significant support to be effective—and the AHC needed him. So Ed Rodman began to develop a network around Boone among the power players in the Black community. In his role as canon missioner for the Episcopal Diocese of Massachusetts, he attended many social events, where he cast his net wide, bringing in Massachusetts cultural luminaries such as Elma Lewis, Hubie Jones, and Barry Gaither, and political leaders such as Representative Bill Owens and Senator Royal Bolling Sr. The grassroots leadership—which included the Black United Front, the Black Panther Party, and the Roxbury Action Project—already firmly supported the prisoners; however, they questioned both Boone's leadership and the leadership of the AHC. Rodman would use that tension to push the AHC, which was largely composed of white liberals, further than its members ever thought they would go.[163]

The AHC began a public-education campaign on three fronts. First, its members sent a letter to its entire constituency alerting them that, now more than ever, they needed to support Boone and the concept of prison reform. Explaining that the crisis at Walpole was a crucial part of implementing reform, since Walpole provided a microcosm of the prison system for critique, and action, the representative organizations that formed the AHC engaged their constituents in formal and informal conversation to create and increase support for Boone and the prisoners.

On June 29, the Ad Hoc Committee wrote another letter to Donnelly requesting a meeting. Again, it offered its services as a link between the prisoners and the public. Donnelly was unimpressed with the AHC's arguments, and refused to grant them regular access. However, right up to the point when he resigned, he continued to rely on the AHC when he wanted public support.[164]

Finally, the AHC released their condemnation of the guard union's stance to the public.

> The recent actions and statements of prison guards in striking openly against reform in our prisons, suggests that many of them are interested only in control, repression and punishment. Tragically, they have been so trapped by their roles as keepers that they have been blinded to the fact that these methods are a total failure. Their strike was not for better wages, hours or other traditional union goals; their strike was against better and more effective treatment of other human beings. What could condemn a system more than evidence that it causes one group of human beings to have a vested interest in the mistreatment of others?
>
> We, as the taxpayers who pay the guards' salaries and the cost of supporting the prison system, want to make it clear that we fully support progressive change in our correctional system. The guards who wish to support these changes will be part of the solution; the others are clearly a part of the problem.[165]

THE NORFOLK TRAGEDY

Over the course of the winter and spring of 1972, George Bohlinger had been able, in large part, to return Norfolk State Prison to its original mission. He had begun a wide range of programming and started an inmate/guard council that was responsible for developing new program initiatives and addressing issues of governance. The prison was relaxed and the programs seemed to be running smoothly.

In July, the guards at Norfolk had been given a metal-detecting wand to use while screening visitors, because the standing metal detector was broken. On July 31, the wife of prisoner Walter Elliott visited.[166] Elliott was serving a life sentence. It was widely known among the prisoners that he had been framed. According to Bobby Dellelo, Elliott was tired of waiting for the courts and opted to escape. Under her dress, Elliott's wife had two pistols taped to her legs, presumably to facilitate that escape. That morning, there was no matron present to pat down women visitors, and the guards did not screen her with the wand. Elliott's wife entered the visiting room and was able to pass the pistols to her husband. He brandished them in the visiting room, eventually killing a guard, James Souza. Prisoners suspected he meant to use the guns later, but others speculate that Elliott was set off by visiting-room policies, and he made an unplanned and wild attempt to shoot his way out of the prison. He and his wife fled into the prison complex. An instructor, Alfred Baranowski, attempted to follow and talk him into surrendering. Elliott shot him down. As guards and police closed in on him, Elliott killed his wife and then himself.

James Isenberg accompanied Boone to the prison to deal with the crisis. The prison was in lockdown, four people were dead, and at the front door of the prison a group of guards and their families had assembled. For the first time they gave open voice to their hatred of the commissioner by chanting, "Boone the coon." The racially charged atmosphere was hostile. Isenberg remembered:

> After [our] first hour [inside the prison], I looked around. I became aware that everyone around me was armed. I leaned over to John and said, "There are only two people in here without weapons, you and me. Maybe I should walk behind you."[167]

Isenberg explains,

> It was horrible. Everyone was stunned. There were four dead people. It was so sad. I didn't know what we were going to do from there. But I knew I was hated the moment I arrived at the prison. It became very personal. I was young, I knew I had to figure out how to deal with this.[168]

The Elliott murders released a torrent of heretofore unspoken opposition. The guards and their families blamed Boone, Governor Francis Sargent, and corrections reform for the murders. A report on the murders commissioned by the governor exonerated Boone because he had supplied the prison with a handheld wand, and it was the guards on duty who had failed to follow protocol. The Norfolk County district attorney, George Burke, realizing that he could not prosecute Boone for the murders, indicted Boone's assistant, Bill Farmer, on an unrelated matter instead. Farmer had been working with Bohlinger and had not reported his prior felony conviction as he was required to do to work within a prison. In his tenth year of a ten-year parole, a criminal charge could result in a parole violation that would have sent Farmer back to prison. For the next eight months, Farmer would fight the charges. Ultimately, he prevailed.

Not content with prosecuting Farmer, the Norfolk DA continued to look for a way to attack Boone. He initiated his own investigation. Not surprisingly, he found Boone to be entirely accountable for the murders because he had implemented the "wrong policy"[169]—Chapter 777. Sargent and Boone attended the funerals of James Souza and Alfred Baranowski, the two guards Elliott had killed. Some guards called Sargent a murderer as he walked by. At the funeral he was approached by a woman who wanted to, using his words, "beat his brains in."[170] Boone remembers being spat on as he entered the church. It is interesting that the guards did not focus their anger on Bohlinger, the warden of the prison. With Boone as their focus instead, they intensified the racialized tension. Boone said attending that funeral was the hardest thing he has ever done. He knew that every eye in the church was on him and that he was hated.[171]

On August 4, long before any report was released, the *Christian Science Monitor* endorsed Boone in an editorial, which reminded its readers that, "When trouble starts, the world goes after the man who is making the changes." It went on to assert that such blame "is compounded by the fact that John O. Boone is Black." The editors argued that the real target of the uproar was the reform legislation, Chapter 777. "There is no doubt that Commissioner Boone deserves support at this time. None of the reforms he stands for is responsible for the tragedy this week."[172] In its analysis, the *Monitor* did not duck the security lapse. The paper noted that the absence of a working metal detector made it possible for the guns to be brought into Norfolk.[173] But the editorial argued that bringing about reforms had nothing to do with decreasing safety: "Security and humaneness in prison are not mutually exclusive. Prisons will never be secure until [they] are humane. This is the point which Massachusetts and all other states wrestling with prison reform must grasp."

The rest of August turned out to be a nightmare. On August 8, the Norfolk guards filed a lawsuit challenging Boone's qualifications for the job. Between August and November the lawsuit worked its way up to the state's supreme court. Eventually, the supreme court ruled in Boone's favor. However, this crisis left a deep scar on Boone. He was a career corrections employee. He began as a guard. He was deeply committed to his staff and grief-stricken over the loss of Souza and Baranowski. When I met with him, 30 years later, he gave me both reports and all the records pertaining to the Elliott murders. He urged me to read everything and come to my own conclusion. The fact that his staff considered him culpable in the death of these officers left him doubly pained. When he came to Massachusetts, he knew the guards would not like him, and would not approve of his philosophy, but he expected to be respected. He did not expect to be branded a murderer.

The guards' strategy did not end with the lawsuit. The wives of the corrections officers forced an emotional meeting with the governor, claiming they feared for their husbands' lives. They demanded Boone's removal. A group of legislators with strong connections to the guards' unions formed an ad hoc legislative committee and held public hearings on what was happening inside the prison system and whether Boone was experienced enough in corrections to remain in his post. Throughout the summer and fall, the guards used every opportunity to draw negative attention to the Department of Correction. The *Herald* was their willing ally.

The irony of the Elliott murders and subsequent investigation was that the most promising initiatives implemented by Boone had begun to take hold at Norfolk and Concord. Furthermore, even though this incident took place at Norfolk, it was not the guards at Norfolk who initiated the most vicious attacks on Boone. It was the Walpole Guards Union.

CLOSING RANKS AROUND BOONE

By the middle of August, Boston's Black leadership and community organizations had closed ranks around Boone. They collaborated to organize a large rally at the Elma Lewis School in Boston.[174] Boone, Rodman, and Elma Lewis herself spoke passionately about prison reform. As it closed, Heyward Henry, a member of the Black Prison Community Committee, presented a petition with 800 signatures supporting Boone.[175]

From October to December 29, 1972, the Ad Hoc Committee worked with continued frustration trying to encourage reform and secure access to Walpole.[176] They solidified their connections to Walpole prisoners through continued work with BANTU, the NPRA, and the Walpole Lifers' Group. Because of the constant pressure from the AHC, and the new requirements of the Correctional Reform Act, the DOC issued guidelines for volunteers. Refusing to accept the narrow guidelines, the AHC engaged anyone who would listen in conversation about the important roles that volunteers could play in the prisons.

6

DYNAMIC AND DETERMINED

the national prisoners reform association—walpole chapter

*We do not foresee that real change can take place with-
out citizens informing themselves, involving themselves
and most important listening. We propose to begin this
process as quickly as we can work out arrangements to
meet with the prison population and offer to serve as a
link between them and the citizenry of Massachusetts.*[177]
                                    —the Reverend Edward Rodman

THROUGHOUT THE SUMMER OF 1972, ROBERT DELLELO WAS
developing the NPRA. At Ed Rodman's urging, Ralph Hamm became involved.
Rodman knew that the NPRA had the potential to be the most viable vehicle for
prisoner self-determination.

> I wanted to see Walpole closed. As long as Walpole was open, it
> could be used in any way the administration wanted to use it, to
> manipulate it. The prison was a human tragedy, an economic trag-
> edy. For the prisoners, it was their world; they fought for control
> of that dynamic community. The prisoner alliance community had
> the responsibility to help them keep it in perspective. The pris-
> oners have no other view to the rest of the community. Eventu-
> ally, the community and the prisoners began to see the NPRA as a

vehicle to abolish prisons. It was kind of a proleptic eschatology.[178] This vision involved complex labor relations. The crumbling buildings of the prison were like a metaphor for what was needed: the resources to repair the damage, true reparations.[179]

Rodman wanted to make sure that Black and Latino prisoners had real ownership of this project. His primary commitment remained with the organization that had sprung from David Dance's Black history class, BANTU, but Rodman spent many long nights convincing Hamm that as a leader of BANTU, he had to give more than nominal support to the NPRA that was taking hold among the white prisoners. If the NPRA was going to be a power within the prison, BANTU had to make sure that Black and Latino prisoners had more than a voice. As an organization of Black men who'd studied their situation and possible solutions, BANTU needed real decision-making power within the NPRA. Rodman urged BANTU to participate in the construction of the NPRA so that parity was given to their voices.

Long before the Walpole chapter of the NPRA was officially formed in September of 1972, before the prisoners could even discuss organizing inmate representation or union elections, the ultimate distribution of power among the prisoner groups had to be negotiated. Dellelo decided he would not disband the Inmate Advisory Council until after the NPRA was the elected representative of the prisoners and the NPRA board of directors was officially nominated, reasoning, "I wanted to make sure there was a smooth transition and there was no breakage of inmate power."[180] Meanwhile, the Inmate Advisory Council would serve as a working group to construct the new organization.

Before the prisoner population could support the NPRA, they needed to know how they would be represented on the governing board. John McGrath, an ex-convict who was involved in administering a halfway house in Cambridge, played a pivotal role in the construction of the NPRA board. He reports of this transition period:

> Conversation started just before I was released. I was sent to Cranston, Rhode Island, where I got to know the NPRA. And then before I made parole, I was sent back to Walpole. I told the prisoners about the union. At first, the discussion revolved around representation of Black prisoners on the board. I advocated for a twenty-seven-member board—nine Black, nine white, and nine Spanish. I kept getting overruled because the white prisoners were afraid that the Blacks and Spanish would unite and overrule them. Eventually, the Spanish guys said they only wanted three representatives because of the small number of Spanish guys in the prison.[181] So the board had twenty-one members—nine Black, nine white, and three Spanish. The guys agreed they would vote from their hearts as men not because of their skin color. And it worked, too. But I really think if I hadn't been so stubborn, it might have fallen apart because the NPRA had to be about equality not about *equal opportunity*. That didn't work on the street and it sure wasn't going to work inside.[182]

By the end of August, the prisoners had established the NPRA board's ultimate structure. They maintained the idea of racial equity in selecting the executive board of the NPRA, which had two Black, two white, and one Puerto Rican leader.

Boone, who supported the idea of prisoners' unions, agreed to allow an election to determine whether the NPRA or the Inmate Advisory Council would represent the prisoners in negotiations with the prison administration. It was crucial that the election be transparent and fair so that it could withstand any challenge to its validity. Dellelo reports on the election:

> We wanted to make sure that no one would think that the election was rigged. This is what happened: They put a list out of all the organizations in the prison plus "other" and that was our ballot. The NPRA was listed along with the Inmate Self Help groups, BANTU, and the Inmate Advisory Council. The election was to decide what organization the prisoners wanted to represent them.
>
> The election took place in the dining room. There were three teams of observers. Each team was comprised of four people: a prison guard, a prison administration staff member, an Ad Hoc Committee member [allowed in for this purpose], and a prisoner. One team was at the door checking the prisoners' identification, one team was at the table where the vote was taking place, and one team was watching all sealed boxes.
>
> Each block came in one at a time. All the prisoners were identified at the door. All the representatives had to agree that the prisoner was who he said he was and that he lived in the block that was voting....
>
> Before each block entered the dining room, one box was opened, shown to all the observers to be empty, and then sealed in front of everyone, leaving a slot open in the top. A guard, staff, inmate, and outside observer were at the table watching that box. When the prisoner came in he was given a piece of paper—the pencil was at the box. Then, with the piece of paper, he would write who he wanted to represent him. When everyone in the block had voted, a piece of tape was put across the slot on top of the box in front of everyone, then it was taken to the table where the finished votes were, and another team just stood there guarding the sealed boxes.
>
> There was not any way tampering took place. We went into 10 and 9 Blocks with the same team approach. The same four representatives came into the block, showed the empty box, taped it up, went up to each cell, stood in front of the cell, gave the guy a piece of paper, and the guy wrote what he wanted. Then the box was sealed in front of everyone in the block and brought back to the chow hall.
>
> After the vote was taken, the people in charge of boxes would bring one box to the counting table. All the staff, guards, inmates, and outside observers watched the count. On each piece of paper, the prisoners had written who they wanted to represent them.

Each paper was read out loud, shown to everybody, and tallied with all four reps present. The vote was marked and after all the boxes were counted the math was done. Making the vote such a long, drawn-out thing was important so there would be no way this election could be rigged. No way could anyone force anyone to vote a certain way. No one can see what each person writes down. It was not possible to have a fairer election. But three or four months later the new superintendent, [Raymond] Porelle, calls the NPRA election bogus. He says prisoners were forced to vote for the NPRA. That is why it is important that people know that election was not rigged. Ninety-six percent voted for the NPRA.[183]

After the prisoners selected the NPRA as their representatives, a second vote was held to determine the NPRA board. Hamm wrote:

The Black population wanted someone on the board and in a leadership position that they knew would not sell them out for personal gratuities, and who had their best interest at heart. I realized then that by putting myself in a position of an identifiable inmate "leader" (something that I had tried to avoid up until this point) that I was in fact putting a bull's-eye on my back; but someone had to do it, and I was young and idealistic. I knew I would never benefit from the reforms that we were fighting for, due to the vindictiveness inherent within the system, and I never have to this date....

I do not remember all of the 21 board members' names from 32 years ago; I do know that the "strong-arm" men were there, and that they were there primarily to enforce the truces between the majority white prisoners and to ensure that the dictates of the NPRA were not compromised.... I do know this—that the Black members on the board of directors were there by the legitimate wishes of their constituency, and could and were removed at any time (and replaced). All issues voted upon by the NPRA had to be first cleared by a vote from my constituency group, whom I had to report to regularly. On the same token, we had to stand united against any and all threats ... because we were the minority.

As race was definitely the underlying reason behind the animosity of the guards' union and the *Boston Herald* toward Commissioner Boone ... such racism was 100 times magnified against those of us held captive in the prisons of Mississippi; as whatever support system one might think we had in the outside community, its voice was never acknowledged by the white majority who controlled and maintained the system. So, we were forced out of necessity to fend for ourselves; and I did everything in my limited capacity to ensure that any reform benefits that were forthcoming were meted out with equity.[184]

This first board, composed of people from the various prison constituencies and, as such, unused to working together, would create 15 subcommittees involving more than 300 men in activity throughout the prison. They immediately went to work creating the internal culture of the prison under their negotiated truce. For them, it was crucial to succeed at everything. The prisoner population expected results from the NPRA. The leadership knew that the negotiated truce among the prisoners could easily unravel if the NPRA failed to deliver. The goal of the prisoners' union project was two-fold: to exercise self-determination within the prison, and to demonstrate that the prison itself was unnecessary. The two projects demanded equal concentration. This balance would be difficult to maintain given the amount of energy and focus required to build a safe and productive environment within the prison. Maintaining their ability to be actors in their own destiny would make them come perilously close to losing sight of their ultimate goal—abolition—and defining the NPRA's control of Walpole as their goal instead.

After the election, 80 percent of the prisoners signed unionization cards, signifying that they not only wanted the NPRA to be the inmate group that represented them, but also that they wanted it to be recognized as a union.[185] The NPRA met with its attorneys, including lead counsel Max Stern, to discuss the process of certification. By December 20, the Walpole chapter of the NPRA had filed the Petition for Consent Recognition with the director of personnel and standardization at the State Labor Relations Commission. In its petition, the NPRA requested recognition as a collective-bargaining unit representing "all persons who are incarcerated in the Massachusetts Correctional Institution Walpole and who are engaged by the Massachusetts Department of Corrections in the production of goods and services."[186] After the election, the DOC recognized the NPRA as the representative of the inmate body, but chose to assume a neutral position on the NPRA's petition for certification as a union. Eventually the guards' union would constitute the only opposition to the prisoners' petition.

CORRECTIONAL REFORM: THE PATH FROM ILLUSION TO REALITY

On November 16, 1972, Chief Justice Warren E. Burger gave a speech on prisons, entitled "Our Options Are Limited."[187] Burger spoke at the Bellevue-Stratford Hotel in Philadelphia. The headline of the *Philadelphia Evening Bulletin* that day was, "16 Riot at Graterford, 3 Guards Injured."[188]

Burger used interesting language in his talk; instead of "recidivism" he used the term "recall rate" of prisoners, which recognized prisons as an industry whose "product" was sometimes flawed. He began, "The 'recall' rate for the American penal system varies over the years, but for the present purpose, it is safe to use the figure of two-thirds."[189] He went on to explain that it was in the self-interest of all in society to address the problem of penal corrections. "Our failure represents more than a failure to be practical—it is a retreat from the instincts that have characterized Americans and set them apart as a people always ready to lend a helping hand."

The chief justice outlined two responses to the problems presented by the US carceral system.[190] The first was the obvious: improve the institutions, facilities, and programs. The second was more surprising: develop a better way "to identify those convicted persons who should not be sent to prison, but should be released under close supervision."[191]

Burger was only one person, however powerful, looking at prison reform. In early November, the Massachusetts Correctional Association, an organization composed of corrections personnel and citizens concerned about prisons, released a small pamphlet, *Correctional Reform: Illusion and Reality*.[192] It provides some insight into the mindset of the professionals who were engaged in critical study of penal reform in Massachusetts at that time. It began with a discussion of the word "reform." The authors state that reform demands are usually accompanied by a sense of urgency. The proposed solutions were usually changes that not only would reform the prison system but would alter its very foundation. Noting that these kinds of calls for reform tend to be brought on by "emotionally disturbing situations," the MCA cautioned that reforms that worked in one place might not work in another.[193]

Attacking the Correctional Reform Act, the MCA predicted its failure unless adequate resources accompanied it. Boone had also cautioned that legislation without monies for "tooling up" would not be worth the paper it was written on. Interestingly, the MCA recognized the importance of organizations led by prisoners—and ex-prisoners—like the NPRA and the Fortune Society, founded by former Attica prisoners.[194]

The paper posed the question, "Should prisons be abolished?" The answer was not the resounding "yes" of the AHC, but a more cautious "maybe." The authors recognized that punishment was "a psychologically immature and uncivilized response that mankind should learn to overcome," and that we have seduced ourselves into believing that punishment is acceptable if done for deterrence. In the end they ducked the question by recommending that those concerned with reform should focus on "the relation of punishment to both custody and correction."[195]

The MCA addressed the full gamut of problems in the penal system and, ultimately, supported prison reform—even radical reform—because "it was the decent thing to do."[196] By and large, the paper adopted a correctional treatment methodology with a goal of returning prisoners to a state of normalcy. The AHC and the NPRA were opposed to all treatment that was not demanded, developed, and self-selected by the prisoners, recognizing that "normal" could also mean enforced compliance with societal ideals. The MCA's report concluded by directly referring to Walpole, about which it proclaimed, "It is not possible for us to keep some of society's erring members in a deliberately contrived legal slum without accepting responsibility for what it does to them and to those we hire to keep them there."[197]

FROM DONNELLY TO PORELLE

The NPRA was formally established on September 1, 1972, as was BANTU. Shortly after the election, Superintendent Robert Donnelly's resignation took effect. Walpole had developed a national reputation as an extraordinarily hard prison to administer, and it was difficult for Boone to find a permanent replacement. Over the next few months, Walpole was run by a series of interim superintendents, with Joe Higgins, Boone's deputy commissioner, pinch hitting for them all from time to time. During this period, Boone focused on finding a person with a strong background in prison security to bring Walpole under control. Ultimately, without Boone's approval, Raymond E. Porelle, who had been Boone's assistant for security at Lorton, was tapped for the job.[198] James Isenberg reports that the appointment was not anticipated by others on the staff.

> Initially, Boone brought Porelle to Massachusetts to interview for a deputy superintendent position. Just then, Donnelly was leaving. There was a hiring committee and none of us were on it. They liked him in the interview so they hired him as the warden for Walpole. We were surprised when this happened.[199]

On November 13, Porelle was appointed superintendent of Walpole. This was the first time that Porelle was to head an institution; Boone hoped he could bring discipline to the prison. Yet Porelle's approach was the antithesis of democratic, and the prisoners did not react to him well. Things got hot really fast, giving the media ample grist for the mill. Three days after Porelle was hired, a prisoner was murdered at Walpole. On December 4, another Walpole prisoner died, and on December 20, a guard was held hostage by prisoners for several hours and then released.[200]

From any perspective, Porelle could not have been a worse choice. His arrival threatened the delicate balance achieved in the negotiated truce. Donnelly was known for his ability to broker agreements with prisoners. Porelle was a "strong-arm" man, accustomed to a very different style of leadership. He was also a white southerner—which put the Black population on edge. Accustomed to working in prisons where the majority population was Black, he relied on a divide-and-conquer strategy to maintain control of a population he considered racially inferior. At Walpole, Porelle attempted to discover which Black prisoners could be controlled. When that failed, he appeared to discount them—perhaps because their numbers were relatively small. This decision would be his undoing. Black prisoners may have been in the minority in Walpole, but through the organization of BANTU, through the NPRA and Hamm's particular role within it, these men had successfully negotiated real power among their peers. Ever conscious of their diverse cultures, the prisoners had taken on a unified identity: they were blue together. Porelle never took into account the intellectual preparedness of men like Ralph Hamm and Solomon Brown, the chairman of BANTU, or how deeply Black Consciousness resonated among the prisoners. Hamm believed Porelle completely discounted the social relevancy of Black Consciousness and treated Black prisoners and Black community leaders with equal disdain. According to one NPRA member,

> Porelle was known as "Crazy Ray" by the prisoners. It was rumored that he used to carry two pistols. When he would come into the chow hall,

prisoners would begin to bang the table chanting, "Crazy Ray." He would get frustrated and leave. He was also reported to have come into the blocks and shot a shotgun into the air.[201]

Porelle's hiring severely undermined Boone's credibility and support among the prisoners. Hamm characterized Porelle as a "cracker" and to this day cannot understand how Boone trusted him. Moreover, as he reports it,

> Truth be told, I never really trusted Commissioner Boone in those days. Bobby had to continually tell me to give him some slack. I believed that he was simply using the leadership of the NPRA for his own political agenda, and we would be thrown to the wolves in the aftermath. My fears were reinforced when he hired ex-superintendent Robert Moore as security and management for the DOC, as Moore was a devout racist and supporter of the guards' "goon squad" in Walpole while he was superintendent, and also, when Boone gave us Raymond Porelle as Superintendent in Walpole.[202]

In my discussions about this with Boone, he said that he had known Porelle to be severe but fair. When Porelle arrived in Massachusetts, a strange tension arose. It was rumored that Porelle thought that if he succeeded in controlling Walpole, he might be able to take over as commissioner. A decade later, Boone recalled that "Some said he wanted to be a blond-haired, blue-eyed John Boone."[203] Still, Boone never publicly challenged Porelle up to the day he tendered his resignation.

SELF-DETERMINATION IN ACTION

A single spark can start a prairie fire.
—Weather Underground

Despite the problems within the institution, Porelle gave permission for all the inmate self-help groups to celebrate the holidays. For BANTU, this was to be the first celebration of Kwanzaa, a ceremony intended to recall and revive traditional African values.

The significance was more than symbolic. One of the principles of Kwanzaa is self-determination. Another is collective work and responsibility. David Dance, Obalaji Rust, and Bob Heard had helped the prisoners raise money for the event. The prisoners had bought and prepared food. Kwanzaa, which had not yet been celebrated for a full decade, was to be the Black prisoners' chance to teach their friends and family members the values they'd been studying, and an opportunity to showcase the new level of responsibility they had embraced—for their own lives, and for the lives of those who remained in their communities. But the celebration was short-circuited before the celebrants even arrived inside. Hamm recalls the evening well.

> On December 29, 1972, when Porelle ordered Walpole Prison locked down for his major shakedown, he did it an hour or so be-

fore BANTU was to hold its first Kwanzaa Celebration in the prison's visiting room.

The members of BANTU had spent hundreds of dollars ($1,600 and change) in collected funds for the event, and our families, friends, community supporters, and entertainment were invited. We even chartered buses to bring our guests from the Boston and Springfield areas. We had spent most of that day in the prison kitchen preparing/cooking the food that we had bought for the Kwanzaa feast, as well as cleaning and preparing the visiting room to receive our guests.

The Irish-American Heritage group, the Italian American Heritage Group, and the predominately white (only three black members) Christian Action group, had previously been allowed by the administration to hold Christmas celebrations in the visiting room for their families and guests.

The morning after the shakedown began on [the] 30th, guards could be heard yelling into the cellblocks thanking us for the food and laughing. When Porelle was later questioned why he chose that particular evening to lock down for his shakedown, he replied that he had received information that a motorcycle gang was going to attack the prison.

He and his guards had blatantly disrespected every Black prisoner in Walpole, as well as our families. Our invited guests were left out in the cold wondering what was going on, and being interviewed by television media—which we viewed on the evening news. We were furious, to say the least.

We were unanimously determined to prevent him from ever reopening Walpole and remaining its superintendent. Up until December 29, 1972, the Black prisoners were reluctant to join the NPRA, but afterward you can say he was the single profound catalyst that pushed the Black prisoner population to form the NPRA Alliance with the predominantly white, exceedingly violent, prison population ... and further alienated me from Boone, because he put that "cracker" in charge of the prison and supported him to the bitter end.

We, the Black prisoner population, hated Raymond Porelle more than we did Robert Moore. The fact that Porelle had allowed the white organizations to have their holiday festivities without hindrance and then curtailed ours did not go unnoticed. It was business as usual as far as racist practices in the prison was concerned; but this time the Black prisoner population was united in not going to take it anymore.[204]

Porelle ordered the prisoners confined to their cells 24 hours a day throughout the shakedown. After watching their families in the snow, their children crying, the Black prisoners resolved that even though Porelle started it, they would end it. The Kwanzaa lockdown would continue until Porelle was gone. They were joined by the white prisoners and together, in Dellelo's words, they "went to war." Prisoners remained locked in their cells from December 29, 1972, to March 7, 1973. To ensure that prisoners were isolated from their support networks, Porelle canceled all visits and suspended phone privileges. Porelle claimed to have confiscated 300 items of contraband. When Porelle tried to open the prison, the prisoners refused to leave their cells; they instituted an inmate strike. All runners—the prisoners responsible for cleaning the blocks and running errands for the staff—not only refused to do their jobs, but refused to even leave their cells. No garbage was picked up; no floors were mopped—nothing happened unless the corrections staff decided to do it. The prisoners hurled the gauntlet to the floor and were content to let it lie, a smoldering, stinking challenge. Walpole prison's Kwanzaa lockdown became the focal point of prisoners and advocates across the nation.[205]

THE BATTLEGROUND

Within a week of the lockdown, the prison became an unsafe and unhealthy environment. The prisoners' refusal to cooperate led to beatings and repression which, in turn, caused more solidarity and non-cooperation. Food, trash, and excrement piled up in the blocks. The conditions inside Walpole prison were squalid.

Walpole had become the front line in the struggle for prisoners' rights. The prisoners at Walpole saw themselves as actors in the ongoing, ever-changing corrections-reform project. Through utter non-cooperation with the guards, they were laying claim to their agency, as they had with work stoppages. Boone, on the other hand, saw the prisoners only as actors within the DOC's predetermined reform scheme.

Compromise with the DOC was out of the question for the prisoners. Porelle had insulted every Black prisoner. The Black prisoners had decided there was only one solution: his removal. Since all of the prisoners' allies expected strong interracial organizing, if the white prisoners broke ranks with the Black prisoners, they would jeopardize their public support. Furthermore, Porelle's policies flew in the face of the administration's claim that its goal was prison reform and demonstrated that the DOC was prepared to punish anyone who expressed dissent. As Dellelo once put it, "I need to say, the NPRA never broke any agreement that we made with the DOC. The DOC broke every agreement it ever made with us."[206] The Kwanzaa lockdown at Walpole was brutal. Prisoners subsisted on cornflakes with powdered milk and bologna-and-cheese sandwiches. Guards beat them. They fought back, throwing excrement and food at their captors, and, again, refusing to clean up the mess. Isolated and in despair, some prisoners hanged themselves.[207]

The AHC expected Boone to condemn the actions of the superintendent. Instead, initially he resisted all pressure to intervene in the crisis.[208] Meanwhile, the AHC received letters telling them that things behind the wall were profoundly wrong.

7

THE STRUGGLE FOR VOICE AND SOVEREIGNTY

the npra negotiates power

> One inmate spoke of his beating last Wednesday which
> he received (recorded in the March 9 Boston Globe)
> for telling Commissioner Boone and Anderson about the
> "goon" squad. He then explained to me the institution of
> "10:30 lugs" or "10:30 gassings" or "10:30 macings,"
> all of which refer to a troublesome inmate getting the shit
> beat out of him by a number of guards (5 and up) at night
> when it can be done more quietly, without causing a great
> commotion among the general population. He also spoke
> of the blue room in Block 9 where recalcitrant inmates
> are left naked without a mattress on a bed, with a hole in
> the floor to use as a toilet. Later, when I asked the guards
> about the story of this inmate, they did not deny the story
> of the beating or his reason for being in segregation.
>
> —Observer 107[209]

EVEN THOUGH THE EVENTS OF DECEMBER 29, 1972, SIGNALED
both the depth of the institutional crisis and the ground that had to be covered before

sustainable prison reform was possible, it is important to take note of the achievements that had already been made under John O. Boone. In one short year, the Department of Correction had made significant, if not monumental, strides toward community corrections.

In little more than a year, Boone's policies had dropped the prison population by 14 percent in the state prisons and 15 percent in the county facilities. In February 1973, there were 50 prisoners holding jobs outside the wall and 30 more attending classes at nearby colleges. During this first year, Boone had used the LEAA monies to triple the number of Black employees within the DOC, partially through the hiring of a new set of guards known as cadets, who would be trained in conflict resolution and mediation. He also implemented mandatory training for all guards in human relations, contraband control, and riot control.[210]

Boone's initial budget request for fiscal year 1974 would decrease by $1.1 million.[211] Boone planned to save money by reducing staff. Aware that the collective-bargaining agreements precluded a layoff, Boone froze hiring throughout the DOC, with an exception for minority recruitment. He projected an annual attrition of 100 staffers through retirement, resignation, and death.[212] The announcement of the new budget and the hiring freeze was poorly received by DOC staff, who expected family members and friends could count on DOC jobs. They were enraged by the thought of "their jobs" going to Black men and women.[213]

Boone had also developed a new classification system, which was now ready to be implemented. LEAA funds had been approved for the project. This system would be the heart of the community-based corrections program. A central diagnostic center, scheduled to open later that year, would be located at Norfolk. By March 1973, the DOC had already opened two pre-release centers with accommodations for 50 adults, and another center, structured for young prisoners who had been confined at Concord, was opened in Shirley. Three small centers were planned for other parts of the state. These centers were far less expensive and would decrease overall operating costs for the department. Boone expected to begin placing prisoners in the community correction centers by late spring.

A profoundly successful furlough program had been instituted. From November 1972 to March of the following year, 2,966 furloughs were granted to 968 prisoners. Only 38 "no returns" were reported. However, a "no return" does not necessarily mean an escape—it could simply designate a late return. Tina Williams, formerly incarcerated at Framingham, has described returning to the prison after a successful home visit.[214]

The Framingham State Prison for Women had been turned into a co-ed community-reintegration center, and the department had released its plans to make the Shirley halfway house co-ed by April 1973. And of course, Boone had closed the Bridgewater DSU and the ancient east wing of Concord prison.

BROKERING DIGNITY

On January 4, 1973, nine Walpole prisoners were transferred out of state. Advocates for prisoners' rights moved for an injunction to return the prisoners, and three weeks later, the courts ruled the men's constitutional rights to due process were indeed violated. They were returned to Massachusetts. But in the meantime, on January 9, Walpole prisoner Joseph Chesnulvich Jr. killed himself. Chesnulvich was mentally ill; the staff had denied him psychiatric treatment, and had been frequently harassing him as well.

On January 15, the AHC met privately with Boone. The agenda included an investigation of alleged beatings, access to the prison, an end to the lockdown, and a request to meet directly with Porelle.[215] Two weeks later, Porelle tried to open the prison to visits, but—maintaining solidarity with BANTU—most of the prisoners refused to accept visits from their families or loved ones. It took another three weeks—47 days into the Kwanzaa lockdown—for the AHC to secure another meeting, this time with Porelle as well as Boone. The meeting must not have satisfied its members. On February 4, the AHC made its first public challenge to the commissioner. In an open letter to all its supporters, the members expressed their anger about the lockdown and the crawling pace of prison reform.[216]

UNION CERTIFICATION

In the midst of this chaos, on January 31, the NPRA's petition for recognition as a collective-bargaining unit was referred to the State Labor Relations Commission (SLRC). According to Phyllis Ryan, the decision would turn both on whether the SLRC had jurisdiction, and whether a representative group of inmates could be considered a union.[217] For the first time in US history, a labor board had agreed to consider whether prisoners were actually employees. Recognizing prisoners as workers ran contrary to the provision of the Thirteenth Amendment that allowed the involuntary servitude of those convicted of crime. Because of the constitutional implication of the prisoners' request, the National Labor Relations Board (NLRB) was closely following the NPRA's petition. According to Hamm, the Walpole NPRA argued that, regardless of their respective convictions for crimes, this provision of the amendment was overridden by the indisputable fact that the prisoners did perform work, for which they were paid by the state. The state had made them de facto employees, but withheld all contractual and statutory protections.

The SLRC scheduled a hearing for February 26. The only opposing brief came from the Walpole Guards Union, which held that there was no statutory formulation in Massachusetts that, in fact or intent, conferred the status of "employee" to prisoners.

PRISONERS CONTINUE THE KWANZAA LOCKDOWN

During this time, the only contact the prisoners had with the outside was an occasional letter and an even more occasional phone call. Yet, the Ad Hoc Committee was receiving information from prison employees who were sympathetic to the prisoners' plight. Throughout our story, Ed Rodman would visit the Episcopal churches near Walpole and talk with the guards who worshipped there. Rodman, Obalaji Rust, and Phyllis Ryan decided they had to serve as the public face of the prisoners' concealed struggle. After Chesnulvich's death, Rodman requested a meeting with Boone. Because Boone wanted the support of the advocates, he agreed. On February 4, Rodman came out to Walpole.[218]

While Boone's focus was reform, for Rodman, the rhetoric of reform was simply another tool to use to end the slavery of prisons. At his meeting with Boone and Porelle, Rodman made sure that both understood that his commitment to the project of prison reform was inextricable from his commitment to self-determination for the men within those prisons. Porelle and Boone agreed to the AHC visiting the prison the next day. Yet when the AHC members and other allies arrived, guards refused to admit them because there were ex-prisoners in the group. In order to disrupt AHC advocacy, Porelle had instituted a policy of prohibiting ex-prisoners from entering the prison. He announced this new policy as the AHC was waiting in the visiting room. However, the AHC rebuffed this effort to destabilize it, publicly reiterating its position: "*We* are a group which *always* includes ex-offenders."[219] And the members stayed there, waiting for Porelle to grant them entrance.

While they waited, the group held an impromptu strategy meeting. Bobby Dellelo had been describing the conditions at Walpole through letters to individual AHC members. This information was passed on to the group as a whole. Knowing that the debris had reached a height of 15 feet in 8 Block, and that the stench inside the maximum-security end of the prison was overpowering, they decided to threaten Porelle. Members would demand to be allowed to meet with the NPRA within three days, and if Porelle refused, they would call a press conference and challenge the media to go into the prison, cameras in hand. The entire group also agreed to support the NPRA by calling themselves the "external board of the NPRA." The AHC retained its own name and identity, but the use of this new name legitimized their place at the heart of the dispute.

> The official body elected by the Walpole residents to represent them is the internal board of the National Prison Reform Association. The group designed by the prisoners themselves as their community counterparts is the external board of the NPRA. These two bodies—the internal and external boards—must now meet and communicate so that inmate views can be properly heard and represented. Our top priority is to facilitate such a meeting and we stand ready to assist the prisoners and the Department of Correction to achieve this end.[220]

The AHC's strategy did leverage a meeting—but it was to be with Boone and Porelle—not the NPRA. The February 6 meeting at Walpole was attended by 40 advocates and the "external NPRA," with Representative Bill Owens accompanying them.[221] Boone arrived, alone. When Porelle arrived, he told the AHC and the external NPRA that the prisoners had refused to meet with them.[222] However, Massachusetts legislators can enter prisons at will. Representative Bill Owens exercised his right of access to verify the prisoners' refusal.[223] He wasn't able to speak to the prisoners, so he never found out if they had refused the meeting, but he did walk through the entire prison, bearing shocked witness. When Owens returned, he told Boone and the advocates that he was appalled by the conditions within the prison. Porelle tried to evade the criticism by shifting the focus. He explained that he was dealing with many problems within the institution, paramount among them prostitution, the laundry side business, and corruption among both the guards and the inmates.

Three hours into the meeting, Boone affirmed his recognition of the NPRA as the group he needed to negotiate with, saying, "I want all of us to work together to make things work out."[224] Finally, there appeared to be an opening. However, the AHC decided it was best to maintain some kind of presence at the prison until its members were permitted to meet with the prisoners. Despite the brutal winter weather, the advocates stood outside the prison in the cold, ice, and snow off and on for that entire month and into the next.

Despite Boone's affirmation of the NPRA, he had already supported Porelle, in word and deed, creating an awkward tension for Black leaders. As long as Boone stood behind the superintendent, it was difficult for them to demand Porelle's dismissal without undermining Boone. Since Porelle had destroyed the Black prisoners' Kwanzaa celebration and left community members standing literally out in the cold, Boone had become the target of unmitigated racial attacks in the *Herald*. Black leadership was forced to walk an increasingly narrow path, trying to protect the prisoners from the superintendent, and the commissioner from white supremacists. Complicating matters, Boone continued to back Porelle's initiatives even though Obalaji Rust, Ed Rodman, and David Dance, as members of the BANTU external board, were presenting him with increasingly desperate communications from Black prisoners. BANTU's supporters were united with the prisoners in their commitment to remove the superintendent.

The AHC, with Rodman in the lead, agreed to keep the lines of communication with the administration open. The Black United Front (BUF) and the BANTU external board agreed to express their justifiable rage. Rodman leveraged power through his membership in both the AHC and BANTU: he openly confronted unabashed racism, bolstered by his position of leadership within the largely white AHC, and from the backing of his own community. Rodman explained, "We had come so far, I couldn't just let it go at this crisis to save Boone. Because he was Black, I was careful in what I did, but my commitment was to the prisoners."[225] Boone became increasingly uncomfortable with Rodman's anger over the treatment of the prisoners and the advocates, and thus more wary of both Rodman and the AHC. Eventually, Boone would attempt to bar Rodman from Walpole.[226]

According to Ryan, the members of the BUF were enraged by the AHC's strategy of maintaining communication with the DOC. They accused the AHC of stalling to give Boone and Porelle more time.[227] Of all the groups, the BUF was clearest about its own position. Its members were not taken in by any of the reform rhetoric; they knew that prisons could not be reformed and called for the closure of Walpole. They were comfortable with their own militancy and unquestioningly supported the prisoners.[228] They not only wanted Porelle removed; they wanted Walpole closed.

On February 7, Citizens and Relatives Concerned About Prisons (CARCAP), composed mainly of the families and girlfriends of the prisoners, joined the BUF and the AHC in a display of support in front of Walpole prison. During the demonstration, Rust and Rodman engaged in heated discussion over the next steps. Rodman later explained that the public confrontation between the two Black leaders was staged to push the more cautious AHC toward action. Chuck Turner, then a member of the BUF, has said that the Front often used this technique to advance action. The BUF knew that if it waited calmly, the oppression would continue unabated.

On February 8, advocates met with Porelle to negotiate the end of the Kwanzaa lockdown, which had been in place for 42 days by then. Afterward, the DOC held a press conference, at which Porelle announced that the lockdown had officially ended, with the exception of the segregation units in 9 and 10 Blocks. He informed the public that "the recent inmate lockup and search for contraband was part of a larger plan to create a secure environment in which rehabilitative programs can begin to prepare inmates for reintegration into the community." At the end of the press conference, Porelle announced that the lockdown had served its purpose and was now over. Yet, it was far from over; Porelle was still in place.

INSTITUTING INSECURITY

The next day, February 9, the *Herald* ran a story supportive of Porelle, focusing on Porelle's staged performance in front of the media condemning administrative staff and corrections officers who were running a prostitution ring at Walpole. It quoted him exclaiming, "I couldn't believe it when I heard about it. The people in the community even knew about it." Porelle publicly urged his employees to come forward and talk with him "if they were involved in organized crime." Porelle also used the opportunity to vilify prisoners who ran a "laundry scheme where prisoners were paying to have laundry done."[229] This public "truth telling" increased Porelle's stature with the reactionary opposition. He was depicted as a strong, fair man doing a hard job under a commissioner who had lost control of the institution. Yet when the search of the institution turned up contraband and money in guards' lockers, the guards involved were not fired; they were transferred to "another institution." And despite the large amount of money that exchanged hands through the so-called laundry scheme, it was hardly the racket Porelle made it out to be. As Dellelo describes it,

These guys who worked in the laundry, they would, for a fee, a few bucks, sort, fold, and press your laundry. If they lost your stuff, they would replace it. Prisoners did not have to take advantage of this service, but most did because it was a good service.

When you agreed to have your laundry done, the person would request a transfer of money to the laundry avocation. The deputy, Fred Butterworth, would have to sign off on each transfer. There was nothing hidden about it. [Porelle's accusation] was just a smoke screen to make it look like prisoners were ripping other prisoners off and getting rich in the process.[230]

While the *Herald* was lauding Porelle's actions, Golden Frinks, a representative of the Southern Christian Leadership Conference (SCLC), had asked to meet with Boone.[231] John O. Boone and his brother, the Reverend Joseph Boone, had been leading figures in the Southern Christian Leadership Conference in Atlanta. Desperately needing support, Boone readily agreed to meet with Frinks. Nonetheless, after the meeting, Frinks released a statement on behalf of the SCLC condemning Boone's treatment of the prisoners. Though some of the Massachusetts Black leadership may have agreed with the criticism, they all vehemently opposed any public statement against the commissioner.[232] The Massachusetts chapter of the SCLC immediately disassociated itself from the statement.[233] Boone contacted his brother, who arranged for the SCLC to retract the press release. Ralph Abernathy called the Frinks attack "regrettable" and withdrew Frinks's authority to speak on behalf of the SCLC. But the damage was done. The SCLC statement had fractured the apparent public unity of the Black community.

BRINGING IN THE GOON SQUAD

Eventually admitting that the guards, as much as the prisoners, were responsible for the security problems, Porelle instituted new regulations, requiring guards and visitors to pass through a metal detector before entering the prison.[234] Guards were prohibited from bringing "superfluous equipment" (left undefined) into the prison. Porelle mandated strip searches of all prisoners after each visit and set up protocols for searching all vehicles that entered the prison.[235] Lastly, the superintendent created a five-man team of corrections officers, called the Security Team. Its job was to search the institution for contraband seven days a week. The Security Team was the prototype for today's Inner Perimeter Security (IPS).

The Security Team was a fallback for Porelle. Since his area of expertise was internal prison security, he responded to the ever-increasing prisoner resistance with a "security plan." Throughout his tenure, he amply demonstrated that he was unable to think outside of this box. Even when given creative support from DOC administration and prisoners' rights advocates, he consistently came back with repressive law-enforcement solutions. Porelle's attempts to create a controlled atmosphere inside the prison only exacerbated an already volatile situation, because he relied on the same corrupt guards who were already terrorizing the prisoners and their families. The guards who were bringing drugs and prostitutes into the prison were unlikely to be deterred by the new protocols. The Security Team quickly became a "goon squad" with ultimate authority over the prisoners. Dellelo remembers the first time the Security Team entered the blocks.

> You heard this *shi, shi, shi* noise and you said, "What was that?" I took a mirror and angled it so I could see down the corridor. There were about twenty screws standing two abreast. They were shaking so much that you could hear the shells in the shotguns. They were rattling. Porelle was walking up and down saying, "Don't let them see that you are scared."
> They wouldn't come into the blocks. They were so scared that they did not enter the blocks. I was scared that they would lose those guns, that prisoners would take them away from them. They were scared to death to come into the blocks with guns.[236]

TRAINING THE GUARDS ON THE JOB

Boone and Isenberg were all too aware that the Walpole guards were poorly trained and totally unprepared to do their jobs. However, the Walpole guards' labor contract did not allow the administration to replace the staff. Instead, Boone and Isenberg announced the second aspect of Porelle's security plan—that the Walpole guards would undergo "on-the-job training." The administration was involved in a complicated dance with a partner it did not choose: its own employees. Boone and Isenberg fervently hoped they could learn the new steps. But the prisoners were far beyond dancing; *they* were engaged in a war fought from within their locked-down prison cells. By resisting every aspect of Porelle's law-and-order plan, and utterly refusing to cooperate with his staff, they were determined to prolong the lockdown until Porelle and the DOC were exposed and the ill-chosen superintendent was fired.

The on-the-job training plan was full of ironies. For one, it proposed to teach the guards who were trafficking contraband to recognize and discover contraband. Further, they were to learn to conduct shakedowns and lockups, to deal with prisoners and visitors in a courteous way, to prepare and submit written reports, to handle firearms properly, and to control riots effectively.[237] Isenberg set up the program for the guards, and beginning in February, the administration planned to put all Walpole guards through the training process, the focal point of which was teaching nonviolent conflict resolution and written and verbal communication skills. Many of the prisoners had suspected that the guards were illiterate because they signed papers with an *X*. Rodman recognized the guards' educational limitations, but he believed guards used the anonymous mark to hide their identity, and hence escape accountability.

DIVIDING THE CONVICTS: THE CREATION OF CADRES

The last part of Porelle's security plan, a new classification system created specifically for Walpole prison, was the most controversial. A prisoner's location within the prison was to be "based on the level of confinement and treatment deemed appropriate in each case."[238] Rather than the programming needed to rehabilitate prisoners that was called for in Chapter 777, "treatment" was punishment by segregation. Under the new system, prisoners who demonstrated their willingness to follow Porelle's rules were given "cadre" status. The cadres were assigned to A-1 Block and were expected to "assist the superintendent in running the prison." The second part of Porelle's classification scheme was a system of "phases." Phase 2 was segregation. Prisoners who cooperated with the guards would be moved from Phase 2 to Phase 1, general population, where they would be able to get furloughs. The prisoners recognized this phase system for what it was: behavior modification. The prisoners who were in segregation maintained solidarity by refusing to work toward classification to Phase 1. The prisoners in Phase 1 refused to accept furloughs. In the words of Jerry Sousa, they told the administration to "stick it."[239]

Nowhere was this program more divisive than among the Black prisoners. At Lorton and at Terre Haute, Boone had relied on Nation of Islam members to maintain order within the prison. Because the NOI was a sizable group in the federal system, and because their own discipline was so rigorous, the NOI had been able to create a support system around Boone, advancing both his ability to control the prison and his policies. Other prisoners respected them, so they followed their lead. But in Massachusetts, the situation was radically different. The Black population was small but it was growing. Black prisoners were resisting throughout the system and being shipped to Walpole. By this time, there were over 100 Black prisoners in population, and around 40 of them were Muslim.[240] The NOI members used the cadre system to gain privileges. According to Hamm,

> NOI members [were] scabs to break our strikes.... At times, the NOI would be the *only* prisoners out of Walpole leaving on furloughs ... even when the prison was locked down, for their cooperation with the prison administration, in opposition to the prisoner population.
>
> When Porelle locked down Walpole prison he transferred prisoners between the minimum and maximum sections, as well as had others he deemed "troublemakers" taken to Isolation Block 9 and Segregation Block 10 to be housed. The transfers were principally undertaken in order to instill what he hoped would be fear and uncertainty in the psyche of the collective prisoner population, to facilitate the creation of his "Cadre Block" in minimum section cellblock # A-1, which was the cellblock at the furthest end of the corridor, closest to Segregation Block 10. The bulk of the newly formed cadre cellblock was composed of the entire membership of the Nation of Islam, with fillers consisting of transferees from the rest of the prison population who were classified as "trustees" (those determined by the prison administration as prisoners who could be trusted and relied upon to run vital areas of the prison— i.e. laundry, kitchen, sanitation or trash collection, general maintenance, electrical—in the event of a lockdown and/or general prisoner strike).[241]

Porelle's creation of "cadres" after the imposition of the phase system in mid-February was of great significance to BANTU. The men in the cadre were offered the avocations (voluntarily undertaken money-making endeavors like the laundry, haircutting) that the various groups within the prison had been using to make money to send home to their families. The avocations had been run by different groupings within the prison. The "hard core" white prisoners were enraged when their businesses were offered to Black prisoners. Hamm intervened for two reasons. Since the core of the cadre was the NOI, this break in the ranks of the Black prisoners complicated BANTU's ability to negotiate with the NPRA. The privileged cadre status of a number of Black prisoners, combined with the already virulent racism in the prison, had the potential to destabilize the tentative cross-racial unity that was the foundation of the NPRA. Hamm and the other leadership of BANTU also knew the only way to force Porelle's removal was to make it impossible for him to run the prison. Since the cadre's primary function was to do the jobs NPRA members refused to do, its presence weakened the NPRA's strategy of non-cooperation. Hamm and the other members of BANTU put pressure on those designated as "cadres," with some success. Hamm writes:

> Whenever the prisoners from the cadre block would move through the prison they did so mostly under guard escort, and their journey to the dining hall had them moving through the main corridor of the prison by cellblocks # A-3 (where I was housed) and #A-2 to the jeers and insults of those of us living in those two cellblocks. The verbal harassment of the prisoners in the cadre block, and my personal admonition of the leadership of the Nation of Islam ... that BANTU would no longer support or protect them from the ire and wrath of the general prisoner population because of their strike breaking and cadre position, had the effect of causing a rebellion in the cadre block itself and shutting it down before it had the chance of truly opening up.[242]

The leadership of the NOI remained in cadre status but many of the rank and file understood their position within the cadre made them vulnerable, and they refused to do the jobs that Porelle assigned them. It was clear that BANTU and the NPRA were not going to cave. However, it was not at all clear who would prevail in the end.

FIRING UP SUPPORT

The prison was barely open for one day before the prisoners shut it down again. The majority of prisoners refused to leave their cells; those who left them created chaos. On February 9, Deputy Superintendent Leon Corsini was in charge of the prison while Porelle was elsewhere.[243] When the prisoners refused to leave their cells, Corsini ordered a new lockdown of the prison. Later that day, when Porelle returned to Walpole, he attempted to reopen the prison. Determined that Porelle would not succeed, the prisoners set fires throughout the institution and notified their allies of the chaos. Members of the Black legislative caucus rushed to the prison. They were refused admittance.[244] When more fires were set, Porelle brought in the state police onto Walpole grounds to initiate a new lockdown. The next day, Porelle did not show up for work. When he was finally located, he informed the administration he was taking a leave of absence on his doctor's recommendation.[245]

A day later the state police unleashed a new form of horror into the blocks. Dellelo describes how the police took the prison.

> On February 12, I was in 6 Block. They dropped out of the gallery window what they call a triple chaser. It looks like a beer barrel, one of those kegs. The two ends fly off when it hits the floor. It hits you with force—it could break your leg. The center piece had gas coming out, going up. The two ends went to each end of the block with gas pouring out of them. I don't know how many of those dropped into the block. There are two tiers in 6 Block, with three banisters. The gas was so thick you could only barely see the first banister. You could not survive on second tier. You had to be on the ground floor.
>
> The news media said they were one hundred fifty feet outside the prison and the gas was unbearable. They had to back off. It was hurting their eyes.[246]

The prisoners did their best to support each other through the terrifying ordeal. Hamm recounts:

> There was solidarity in the prison through all of this. We tried to take care of each other. Something would happen at the max end of the prison and we would hear it. Those guys had been locked down since December 29—almost 50 days. We would hear it and we knew they were going to get gassed. We also knew that their windows did not open, so we would start something in the minimum end to draw attention and the tear gas our way so that the prisoners in the max end could be spared. We could at least open our windows and breathe. They could only put a wet towel over their faces and hope for the best. They never checked or removed anyone who had asthma or any kind of lung problem.[247]

On February 13, prisoners' wives and ex-prisoners who were part of the Ad Hoc Committee visited the legislature's Committee on Social Welfare. They urged the legislators to go into the prison so they could witness the conditions there firsthand. Ultimately, the legislators agreed to visit Walpole and judge for themselves rather than rely upon the divergent reports they were receiving from the DOC and the AHC. They were not prepared for what they would find. Committee members reported that their eyes teared from the lingering gas even though the windows of the prison were left open day and night to clear the air. It was mid-February—the weather was freezing, and temperatures inside the prison were bone-chillingly cold. Later that day,

Senator Jack Backman responded to the horrifying discovery by filing the first bill in Massachusetts that would guarantee prisoners' rights.[248] Dellelo recalls:

> That night, they let off four hundred eighteen canisters of tear gas in the prison. It was so bad that you could smell it all the way in the town of Walpole.... When the legislators arrived they were crying— they could not breathe. They were walking over garbage and they could not breathe.[249]

When the legislative committee visited the prison, Boone knew there would be no more room for political maneuvering and accommodation. The legislators' report would lend credence to the prisoners' complaints and action would have to be taken. Finally, Boone called Rodman and asked for assistance.[250] In response, the AHC immediately mobilized for what ended up being a daylong vigil at the prison. The political climate had shifted. The public report from the Committee on Social Welfare had severely compromised Boone. Yet, the advocates knew that any hope for prison reform was tied to Boone's ability to maintain his position, so, as bad as things were in Walpole, the AHC held back from making any kind of public statement. The commissioner had asked for their help and they had agreed to negotiate. They wanted entrance to the prison. They wanted the brutality to stop. Having followed the legislators to the prison, the AHC assembled outside the gate. After their tour, the legislators and the AHC spoke with Boone. Rodman postured, telling Boone that the legislators were prepared to go public. Boone called Rodman's bluff, saying, "If I ever thought I was preventing you from going public, I would be very sorry."[251] Despite exposure to scrutiny, Boone continued to support Porelle.

SPEAKING TRUTH TO POWER

On February 14, Representative Tom Colo held a public hearing on the progress of prison reform.[252] The hearing, long and passionate, focused on Walpole. Senator Jack Backman, chair of the Committee on Social Welfare and a member of the Colo Commission, challenged George Burke, the Norfolk DA who had been so critical of John Boone, to investigate the "gross neglect" of the prisoners at Walpole. In his testimony, Backman reported that prisoners were locked in their cells without water for flushing toilets, feces smeared the walls of the maximum security end of the prison, soap powder had been found in food, some men were in dire need of medical care, and some men had been locked in their cells for 59 straight days.[253]

Again, Rodman testified on behalf of the AHC. "Last year I came before the legislature asking for prison reform legislation, this year I come asking for reform in fact."[254] Rodman went on to declare that Porelle was violating Chapter 777, many other Massachusetts statutes, and the US Constitution. Calling Porelle the "Czar of Walpole," Rodman explained, "He holds himself responsible and accountable to no one—not to the taxpayers, not to citizen groups, not even to the representatives of the government of this commonwealth."

Boone was tired; the AHC was tired. As for the prisoners, for nearly 18 months, since September 1971, they had engaged in nonviolent civil disobedience.[255] The consequences were brutal. Over a dozen men had been killed, committed suicide, or died from "natural" causes. Hamm explained the way it felt:

> It is really difficult to talk about what happened during this time. It really hurts. It was such a difficult time and so many guys were suffering. You knew every day was going to be difficult and you were not sure if you all were going to make it through alive. A lot of people died. It is hard to go back in your mind and talk about it.[256]

And still, the Kwanzaa lockdown continued.

On February 15, the Ad Hoc Committee was before John Boone again.[257] This time it had more credibility and power. Boone had relied on its members to focus the Walpole investigation toward the prison staff and away from the commissioner's office. It was apparent to the AHC that Boone was going to have to remove Porelle, yet his silence had amply demonstrated that he was unwilling to do so. The meeting centered on clarifying how the widely touted community-based correctional model could be realized. Then, the AHC steered the discussion to the commissioner's views on the role and function of ex-offenders in the rehabilitative process, as well as the role of citizens in general.

Rodman did not attend the meeting. His relationship with Boone had suffered over the previous two weeks, but he was trying to keep all the balls in play. He had used his strong connections in the Black community to challenge Porelle's policies, he had used his political connections to ameliorate the damage that the commissioner could have sustained when the conditions inside Walpole were made public, he had continually supported the prisoners no matter how crazy it got inside Walpole, and all the while, he told Boone the hard truth. Boone feared that Rodman would support the prisoners and leave Boone to pick up the pieces. Boone ended up being correct in his assessment, but failed to understand that Rodman would have done everything in his power to protect the NPRA, while protecting Boone as well. Rodman believed that to achieve both required strategic use of inflammatory rhetoric. Boone took this rhetoric personally.

TESTIFYING ON INHUMANITY

In the latter half of February, the NPRA released a "Manifesto of Dehumanization," signed by the group's secretary, Solomon L. Brown. Brown, according to Hamm, was college educated, a member of the Black history course facilitated by David Dance, and chairman of the BANTU board of directors. Brown's importance to the NPRA and to BANTU cannot be overstated. Brown was older than many of the other prisoners. He developed many of the educational programs and self-development programs, first for BANTU and later for the NPRA. He was a mentor to Hamm, and challenged the young, passionate leader. Hamm says, "Solomon did most of the talking during the [BANTU] board meetings and community volunteer sessions when it came to laying out the program material that we devised as I was too extremist and radical in my approach."[258]

That Brown signed the manifesto demonstrated that BANTU had taken over leadership of both organizations. BANTU had to step into the leadership role to counter Porelle's efforts to destroy unity among the prisoners. Because he had transferred all white prisoners to the maximum end of the prison and all Black prisoners to minimum in 2 Block, distinct from the cadre, Black prisoners could meet among themselves and strategize. They could get word to the white prisoners and vice versa, but they could not meet directly. This reality would compromise trust and strain relationships, but—due to the work of Dellelo—the prisoners stayed unified. The white prisoners took the brunt of the oppression handed down by Porelle. The Black prisoners took the responsibility for waging the campaign of non-cooperation in order to force Porelle's resignation. Every time Porelle moved to open the prison, the Black prisoners would do something to lock it down again, while the white prisoners refused to cooperate with the phase system or accept furloughs.[259]

The manifesto clearly described the conditions inside Walpole during the last two weeks of February, detailing book burning, the phase system, beatings, starvation, and the destruction of the prisoners' hope for prison reform. It was this utter negation of the humanity of the Walpole prisoners that pushed the AHC to stand in the snow and ice to end the lockdown.

> There is a great shame in what I am about to put here in print. A shame because no form of correspondence can bring the true impact of the emotions felt by this respondent. Time has proven over and over again that only a minimum amount of certainty and truthful consideration is ever given to the statement of a man or woman who is confined to any institution for any reason whatever. We are also aware that we could face the legal actions of libel for false statements given without the substance of facts. Society has to judge all that we say with a closer ear, a keener eye, and an extra grain of salt, since we are the convicted, the guilty, whether by fate or by choice. But that is not the issue. In this statement I reach back into the files of my mind and gather all the pure, the innocent and the God-fearing memories of my youth to say that I shall say in truth—so help me God.
>
> For some time now, since December 28, 1972, people of this state have asked what is going on in here. There has been a blanket put over this place. We, the men of Walpole, have been under this blanket for a long time—far longer than since December recently past. We had to deal with Superintendent Moore, who left the place in a very confusing state of inner af-

fairs, Superintendent Donnelly, who did likewise, and Superintendent Higgins, who confused, confused, confused, and confused us all with a well-planned method of creating questions but never an avenue for answers. Then before us all stood Mr. John O. Boone, the man we thought would answer these questions and bring about a better avenue of future approach in such matters. What we didn't know then, but now know, is that Mr. John O. Boone, through the overt actions of Raymond Porelle, his superintendent, has instituted what amounts to a manifesto of dehumanization.

Society knows very little about what goes on behind the bars, and so we here record the 24 points of this manifesto of dehumanization. Whoever doubts what is here recorded need only make the simple trip to Walpole to confirm these shocking facts.

A Plea for Understanding and Help!! (Excerpts)

Manifesto of Dehumanization—Walpole

The maximum area of the prison has been completely cut off from the minimum area, even though men from both ends were deeply involved with the few progressive programs that did exist in the prison before Porelle came into office. These two sections are now not able to meet, except by chance, and if any conversation or attempt at reestablishing ties are detected by any correction officer, the parties involved can be punished.

1. All men who have shown great individual initiative, whether constructive or non-constructive, have either been taken out of population, transferred to another prison, or have felt the direct and overt pressure of new policy.
2. In establishing a cadre block (Cadre: a nucleus, esp. of trained personnel (inmates) capable of assuming control and training others) the administration has created an atmosphere in which inmate is pitted against inmate. The result can be violence such as never has been seen or imagined by men in prison. This block (cadre block) is cellblock area No. 1 in the minimum section. It houses 72 men who are employed in the clerical areas or other areas which are the envy of other prisoners.[260]
3. All 39 self-help programs have been disbanded: the Lifers Program based upon new prison reform actions, providing hope for the hopeless. BANTU, a minority program, which after long hard struggle, is win-

ning community support, and developing a concern for many men who have never known such bliss in the past. This is a program that has proved to be sound and alert in its human obligations to help one another overcome shortcomings of a sometimes cold and heartless society. Their doors were open to all ... for "concern" was their goal. The Christian Action Study Group, which had concerned religious people coming up every week and corresponding with their members in an effort to restore their faith in their fellow man. The Nation of Islam, a group of concerned black men who in their unity displayed a unique reflection of dignity. Educational programs, drug programs, community relations programs, job and home placement programs and many others.

4. Placing informers in the cellblock areas that don't fit into the new policy. Finding such men is not hard to do, when they are promised a sure parole, or sentence reduction etc. These informers have been placed in grave danger for their lives. These men are numbered at the present, but have only suffered minor harassment from the population as they themselves have not conformed with Porelle's ideas.

5. Hand picking of inmates to go to all the prisoners trying to persuade them about fruitless ideas and plans. But these men never speak about the present fact that Porelle is unhumane in all that he has done here in Walpole.

6. Placing in danger of their lives those men who have pledged their support for Porelle's new program is without doubt an exploitation of inmates of the worst sort.

7. Men are taken out of their cells as late as midnight and one AM and brought to the 10 block or 9 block without any questions or answers given. It is very frightening. Usually you assume that the last inmate you saw speaking to an officer was the informant.

8. Cadre block can have visits seven days a week, and they are promised to be first in line for institutional consideration, such as furloughs, paroles, honor camp.

9. A new confinement system has been set up. There are detention cellblocks arranged as a step system, starting with ten block. Good behavior there gets you into 9 block, etc. until you can join the rest of the population.

10. All of our mail has been delayed as far into a given week as Monday is to Friday. Legal mail has

been opened; pages of personal mail have not been delivered in their original envelopes. We've been over taxed for postage at will; newspapers have been delayed up to three days.

11. The Community of concerned people other than families is prevented from coming up to the prison and finding out what is going on....[261]

17. All books that have been donated to groups and prison programs—as well as books in the library—have been taken away and their whereabouts are unknown. According to the rumors that the books were burned.

18. All of the prisoners in dead lock for more than 60 days. [Now] is probably the most vicious era in this prison's history. We have had to rely on information received on our T.V.'s and radios to those who have none, and who are very much in the dark as to what is happening in here. Ever since Porelle has been in here there has been nothing but word of mouth rumors to go on.

19. Sporadically men are taken out of the maximum section and placed in the minimum to give the impression that the Dehumanization plan is working.

20. Men are locked in their cells 24 hours a day without food served at proper intervals or the proper amount. We've been without showers for weeks at a time. Have been made to work but then returned to our cells for lock up again, without recreation. We have not been able to buy needed items to keep clean, such as soap, toothpaste. We've lived with nothing but the constant threat of being taken to 10, 9, 8 disciplinary blocks if we don't agree with the evaluation.

21. The entire block is locked up for infraction committed by one or more persons. Tear gas is sent into the cells without reason. Then the doors are opened to make sure that every man has been gassed....

In conclusion we the men of Walpole submit to you our plea for your concern and assistance in preventing this cruel, inhumane, and immoral conspiracy of the administration which is experimenting on human beings in this day and age. We are not the most perfect when weighed by society's standards of right and wrong. We are not the strongest, and the environments of our upbringing have not equipped us well, nor do we profess to be men with deep felt religious or moral feelings. But this we say with deep conviction, "My god we are human; please don't let men with their machines of mental death come upon us in the dark of night at

> a time when [our] lives are already so much without
> light. O Lord, there is not justification for what is
> being done to the minds and bodies of the imprisoned.
> There must be another way."[262]

OPENING THE DOOR, BUT NOT THE PRISON

In the early morning hours on February 19, the AHC entered into negotiations with Boone and Isenberg that went on until after day broke. The primary issue they addressed was how to open the prison and avoid a riot; secondarily, they were negotiating public access to the prison.[263] Because of his connection to BANTU leadership, Rodman was aware that allowing the prison to open would undercut the prisoners' strategy—demonstrating the power they could wield to disrupt the prison's operation, if conditions weren't changed. The AHC leadership seemed to focus on the end of the lockdown, not the resolution of the problems that caused it. The next morning, still on "medical leave," Porelle simply announced that the lockdown had ended. In reality, the prison was still, for the most part, locked down. Rodman drew Boone into negotiations over allowing civilian observers into the prison.[264] Although the relationship between the two men had soured, Boone understood that it was valuable to be in conversation with this powerful ally of the prisoners. Rodman proposed that the civilians act as neutral observers and report on events that took place inside the prison. Rodman hoped observers would be able to explain the prison's problems to the public in a way that would increase support for reform. Boone saw that their presence could deter the guards and prisoners from engaging in further conflict.[265]

Rodman, under the auspices of the Ad Hoc Committee, planned to place a neutral group of people, the majority of whom were white and middle class, in the middle of the conflict.[266] He would train them to simply observe, letting whatever conflict remained to unfold around them.

The DOC saw the benefit of having impartial observers, but it stipulated that ex-prisoners not be allowed entrance as observers. Rodman's response was quick and consistent.

> Ex-offenders must be given equal access and there must be a negotiation process by which the points of dissension between inmates and administrators can be worked out. We cannot in good conscience be used as an interim measure to reduce tension without there being a plan to work out the problems over the long term.[267]

While the AHC was formalizing its agreement with the DOC, Senator Backman and Representative Colo called a press conference to release more information about what was happening inside the prison. This time, Rodman and Ryan did not participate; they did not want to destabilize the AHC's negotiations with the DOC.[268]

The AHC's all-night negotiations paid off; they won their second objective: public access, effective immediately. Despite his medical leave, Porelle showed up at the prison to meet with the AHC and issued a special schedule for the day that allowed for community people and staff to circulate inside the prison. Lunch was to be served in the dining hall, and the guests were to eat with the prisoners.[269] But "prisoners" turned out to be one: Bobby Dellelo.

> I was in 8 Block. It was horrible in there. We were locked in 24/7 and we were mad. We didn't have anything to fight back with so we used bullfrogs. A bullfrog was a pile of shit. We would throw it at the control room. If you caught your bullfrog on a piece of paper, it was a bullfrog on a lily pad; in a milk container, it was a steamer. We spit at everyone who came onto the blocks. We threw our food out of the cells. And then we refused to clean it up. Our runners went on strike. The guards wouldn't clean it and so it built up. The place, well, smelled like shit.
>
> Then Leo Bissonnette comes up. He shackles me and cuffs me up. I think: I'm off to Marion again. The guys are shouting, "Bye, Bobby—have a good time—ha, ha—see you soon," you know. Bissonnette, he takes me out to the front and brings me through the trap out to the visiting room. And he uncuffs me and takes the shackles off and I say, "What's going on?" He says, "Go in. Go on." I looked ahead to see the outer-control-room area and there are civilians in there; I am the only prisoner. I say, "Oh, shit, they set me up." The tables are piled high with food. Now, we've been starving on the blocks. I was really wary.
>
> I see the man, he says, "Sit here." So I sit next to him. This was the first time I actually met Rodman, though I don't know who he is at the time. I knew of him because he always met with BANTU. Ray Porelle gets up. He's talking a lot of trash and saying he's going to do this and that. I am getting pissed off because I know it's not true. And then he says, "We are going to bring work in the prison. Prisoners are going to be stuffing envelopes for five dollars an hour." I lean to Ed Rodman, not sure who I was talking to, and say, "Did you hear that?" Ed smiled, laughed, and leaned over and said, "Isn't that what you want?" I said, "Shit, the minimum wage is about a buck something. People are going to be breaking down the doors to get in here to make five—free room, free board, and five!"
>
> I interrupted Porelle, saying as much. The AHC asked what should happen. I says you have to tour 8 Block, today. But, I says, I got to go back first so no one throws nothing on you. So I go back to the block and I tell everyone that these civilians are coming up and they are not to be spit on or anything.
>
> I wish you could have seen it. All these folks in their street clothes trying to step around the shit. And Walter Williams[270] saying, "This is outrageous. We are going to close this block down immediately." Like they did not know what was happening.[271]

GAINING ACCESS TO WALPOLE

The state legislature's Committee on Social Welfare met with the advocates who had toured the prison the same day.[272] The AHC described the conditions inside the blocks. Colo responded by calling Porelle, even though he was on sick leave, to answer to the entire Legislative Commission on Corrections the next day.

Porelle and the Colo Commission focused on their areas of agreement, and brokered a solution.[273] The commission made a public statement after the meeting, supporting Porelle while denouncing the conditions inside Walpole and demanding immediate redress. The commission declared that the December 29 Kwanzaa lockup and shakedown at Walpole to uncover "excessive amounts of contraband, knives and weapons material" was necessary. Yet, it clarified, "It is also understood by all that the lock-up was too long, and the effort to re-open Walpole became increasingly difficult." Then Colo quoted a prisoner representative, who said, "Success is based on good-faith efforts from this place onward." These good-faith efforts would begin with a commitment to explore every means to return Walpole to a more "normal" situation. Putting the players on notice, the legislators cautioned, "Cooperation must be a mutual responsibility of the Walpole staff, the inmates, and those members of the legislature and general public who are informed and concerned." Porelle agreed to meet with the commission in the near future to discuss allegations of corruption in the prison laundry, prostitution, and any improprieties or wrongdoing by any correctional personnel. The commission closed by commending a spokesman for the guards' union who emphasized a clear commitment to continue the implementation of the rehabilitative programs authorized by the Omnibus Correctional Reform Act.

This public announcement did not come across as good news to the AHC or the prisoners. It was "politics as usual." The Colo Commission had pandered to Porelle, who was clearly responsible for creating utter hell in Walpole. As public officials are wont to do, the commission focused on finding a solution, without addressing the reality that some of those designing it were themselves the problem. AHC members finally understood that Porelle would never succeed in opening Walpole. Porelle and all the guards who had implemented his policies had to go. They also knew that Porelle, given this public support, could very possibly react with sustained violence against the men under the guise of "exploring every means possible" to bring the prison back to "normalcy." The AHC set up another vigil at the prison. Its members were very concerned that Porelle would again go in with tear gas, shotguns, and the state police.[274]

He did not disappoint them. The next day, February 22, Porelle officially returned from medical leave. Immediately, the NPRA demanded his removal. Boone responded with a letter to the prisoners. In the letter, he appealed directly to the prisoners, asking them to negotiate in good faith and end the chaos.

The guards used the letter against him, releasing it to the press and claiming that the commissioner was reduced to begging the prisoners to cooperate. Boone responded by saying that, since the guards were gaming him, "I've got to run out here and do everything myself."[275]

Porelle had gone too far and the prisoners had resisted too long to consider any form of negotiation with the administration. Boone's letter to the prisoners indicated that he had turned a corner. He knew that if he proved unable to control Walpole, he was unlikely to survive as commissioner in Massachusetts. His staff had ceased any semblance of cooperation. The only thing he could do was appeal to the decency of the men inside Walpole to preserve the prison-reform project that was already bearing fruit in all of the other state correctional institutions.

Porelle's first action upon his return was an attempt to undercut the NPRA. Dellelo tells the story.

> Porelle came back and he calls me in for a meeting. The chairs are all set up in an oval. And I get there and it is not the NPRA board. It's a bunch of other guys. I said, "What are they doing here?" Porelle says this is the new Inmate Advisory Council, so I turned to the first guy and I say, "What is going on here?" He says, "I don't know." I say, "Who represents you?" He says, "You know, Bobby. The NPRA represents me." Each guy says the same thing. I say, "This meeting is over."[276]

When Dellelo walked out of the meeting, Porelle declared another state of emergency in the prison. He claimed that the NPRA "broke off" negotiations. The prisoners all responded by dumping their food on the floor. The NPRA sent word to the advocates to remind the press that the prisoners would not clean the cellblocks or return to work as long as Porelle stayed.

Deputy Superintendent Walter Anderson categorized the resistance as simple prison loyalty.

> There's a code in this society in here. It's not to let anyone divide you. I think there are guys who'd go back to work tomorrow if we gave them a chance. It's camaraderie. They've been loners all their lives and they've banded together as a unit and realized in unity there is strength.[277]

But Anderson had missed the mark. Hope had swept into Walpole with all the power of a tidal wave. For nearly half of the prisoners, Walpole was it; they were never going to see the other side of the wall. Furthermore, many of the prison leaders who were elected to the NPRA had scant trust that anything planned by the government, the prison administration, or any other kind of "authority" would be in their favor. They had recognized the cadre/furlough program for what it was: behavior modification. And they had the practical experience that told them that unifying the prisoners and using their labor power as a lever got results.

After the state of emergency was declared, Backman and Representative Bill Owens went to assess the conditions at Walpole. They accused guards of "deliberately sabotaging" the Boone administration. Parts of the prison were open and prisoners were moving around the blocks but none of them were working. The guards tried to justify the lockdown by reporting that 198 inmates had refused to enter their cellblocks for a noon head count. However, when the legislators checked with cellblock officers, the report proved to be false.[278]

Boone brought a group of women who had administrative positions within the DOC into Walpole. These women had volunteered to take on some of the work the prisoners had spurned as part of their strategy of non-cooperation. Given that no hot food was being offered the prisoners, Hamm remembers, the prisoners were relieved to see these volunteers. "They related to the prisoners with much more respect than the male guards. And they got more respect back. They were very professional and their presence served to inhibit the usually brutal guards."[279] The guards seized upon the presence of women in an all-male correctional institution to suggest impropriety. Eventually, Boone would acquiesce to pressure, deciding that having women working inside the prison in any capacity was problematic.

On February 23, the Massachusetts legislature's Black caucus lent its support to the AHC by sending a letter to Boone requesting a meeting with the external and internal NPRA boards, with him, and with Porelle. Three days later, the meeting took place. Yet only Colo and Jack Backman showed up.[280] Despite the progress made during the fall, Porelle's lockdown had challenged the prisoners' racial unity. Dellelo explains,

> [Porelle] took white prisoners from the min end and lugged them to max end. Took Black prisoners and put them in the minimum end. The nine Black leaders went to minimum and the nine white leaders went to maximum. Then he took 8 and grabbed the hard core, and put them there. I got stuck in 8 Block, where we resisted by [throwing] bullfrogs.
>
> There was a breakdown between the Black and white prisoners because the white prisoners thought that the Black prisoners had sold them out.
>
> When I finally got the whole board together, after the civilians had left, the guys faced off. There was a lot of shit going down. People were talking a lot of trash. It got really hot and guys were calling each other a lot of racist shit. Ralph Hamm gets up and says, "I didn't ask to go to fucking minimum. They just took me out." Other guys describe what happened.
>
> And I says, "Okay, all of you shut up." I run it down for them. "This was done to break our unity. We didn't do this to each other. They did it to us." They get it. They're like, "It's okay, we're straight." Everybody was pissed off and we were back as one solid movement. We went back to kicking ass.
>
> It was good this happened because we learned how they would use us against each other. That never happened again. We got right to work outlining our demands.[281]

From this point on, the prisoners considered themselves to be at war. The AHC members were never again referred to as "allies" or "advocates"—they were now "civilians." By February 26, the NPRA had settled upon 12 "grievances," later characterized as "demands."

1. Visits: No shake-downs of visits (skin shakes of outside visitors), eliminating odd and even day visits, outside lawn visits, outside lawn open year around, re-instating all barred visits, the allowance of visits regardless of relationship to inmate: e.g., friends; stop harassment of outside visitors: re-instating the policy that visits be allowed to bring in clothing and other articles, e.g. boots, shoes, pants, shirts, books, instruments, typewriters, underwear, etcetera, to be left by visits.

2. Amnesty: Amnesty for any and all disciplinary action taken in the duration of the shake-down up to present date, e.g. tickets, segregation, etc. that all personal items taken during the shake-down be returned, and that inmates be allowed to re-decorate their rooms as was the case before the shake-down of the 29th. Charges that have been referred to the district attorney excluded.

3. Avocation: that men with avocation be allowed to conduct their avocational business: that the laundry avocation be allowed to run as it did prior to the 29th.

4. Groups: that all groups have the right to assemble and have meetings as before; e.g. Lifers, Revitalization, B.A.N.T.U., Christian Action, Wild Life, S.N.A.P., etc.

5. Canteen: Expand and operate same with (1) institutional representative and several inmates.

6. Privileges: Telephone privileges be re-instated for the maximum and minimum sections.

7. New Men: That new men be allowed to purchase radios and televisions immediately upon their entrance into the institution.

8. Death Row: Return all personal belongings back to the men on death row, and return open yard policy on recreation for same.

9. Restore: Eight block back to the original status, return the radios and T.V.'s back to the men in isolation: restore the status of the nine and ten block committee as it was before December 29, 1972, that they be allowed to enter said blocks at the request of the men in isolation. Restore the status of the canteen purchases for the men in nine and ten block: that max and minimum be allowed to integrate as prior to the 29th, e.g. block visitation.

10. Press: Free access to the news media and the right to call the press into the institution.

11. Counts: That lock-up counts be at 7:00 AM and 10:00
    PM only, with no standing count.
12. Bulletins: Re-instate   commissioners   bulletin
    72a regarding disciplinary, rules, regulations,
    and procedures.[282]

The Reverend John Foley, Walpole's Catholic chaplain, worked closely with the NPRA throughout the lockdown. He also visited with the men in 9 and 10 Blocks, who had been locked down for some two months. As the prisoners were preparing to release their demands, Foley voiced scathing criticism of the Walpole prison officials and their actions, saying that "Human, civil, religious and constitutional rights have been flagrantly violated.... The alleged 'shakedown' became in fact a general house cleaning.... Contraband was defined three weeks after the lockup began. Promised regulations have never been published. Methods used were savage, irresponsible, vindictive, inhumane." Foley informed the media that there were "serious" questions about the origins of the contraband that they were being shown, and said prisoners had been left "bitter, angry, hostile, vengeful—and with good reason." Foley also challenged the media, declaring them "sadly negligent.... The men truly felt that 'no one really cares.'"[283]

Despite their previous failure to show on February 28, Black caucus members urged Boone to take "immediate steps to alleviate present conditions [and to] restore the confidence of the inmates and the administration." In the strongest statement they would ever make, they laid full responsibility at Boone's feet. They accused Boone of protecting Porelle and evading the charges of brutality made during testimony before the legislature's Committee on Social Welfare, and they called for an end to the lockdown and "amnesty for all men accused of indiscretions during the lockdown." Knowing the labor issues confronting the commissioner, they also asked for additional negotiations involving Boone, the NPRA, and the guards' union.[284]

Even though the prisoners refused to negotiate an end to their resistance, Porelle finally opened Walpole to the press. On March 1, the prisoners told the public they wanted Porelle to resign.[285] Dellelo accused Porelle of "allowing severe beatings of prisoners and of planning a behavior modification program at the prison." He also explained how Porelle's cadre program had destabilized the prison by giving certain prisoners special treatment.[286] The *Herald* quoted Dellelo as saying,

> We are trying to keep things cool, we're trying to keep the lid down. And you'll see when you tour the cellblocks that there is paper and debris on the floors. The debris is a non-violent protest and it is our only form of protest short of violence. We feel it's better than taking guards as hostages.[287]

After the press conference, 50 community representatives from legislative groups and penal-reform organizations stayed in the prison. They met with prisoners and prison administrators to try to resolve the stalemate caused as much by Porelle's presence as by his policies.[288] The groups that participated were the state legislature's

Committee on Social Welfare, the Black caucus, the Massachusetts Council on Crime and Correction, the AHC, and the NPRA. The negotiations continued into the next day. While they agreed on some of the issues, they did not reach agreement on the two most crucial points: amnesty for the prisoners who participated in the resistance and Porelle's removal.

The negotiated points fell far short of the prisoners' demands. Representative Colo, apparently satisfied, told the press, "70 to 80 people got together in a rational manner and discussed our concerns."[289] Yet, the conceded points did not come close to answering the prisoners' demands. Rather, they outlined an outwardly fair process that gave a nod to due-process protections. The legislators hoped that if prisoners could see that procedures were fair, they would begin to work with the administration. This expectation was far from reality. The prisoners *were* concerned about due process, but first they wanted actual power and the capacity to be real participants in the design of any reform project.

After the legislators had left the prison, the NPRA went to work again. The prisoners saw the conceded points as a start. The NPRA board drafted another list of grievances to present to their membership. The list echoed the concerns they'd already presented, boiled down to the essentials.

List of Grievances

1. Get rid of Porelle.
2. Inhumane treatment by Porelle. In instituting an eight week lockup/lock-out.
3. Porelle is/was not obeying the law.
4. Failure to comply with the Department of Corrections Policy.
5. Inability of Porelle to supervise staff of officers in Blocks 9-10, which has resulted in repeated macings, gassings, and beatings, and total denial of their constitutional Rights; such as, limiting visits to one and two a month, refusal to provide clean linen and underwear and clothes, skin searches after visits, refusal to clean up the Tiers, which results in totally unsanitary conditions, where men are required to live, denial of adequate exercise, and arbitrary denial of showers, confiscation of all personal property including necessities of life, refusal to provide medical treatment on a regular basis: e.g. Frank Martin has therapeutic shoes that were taken away from him, George Harrison was refused by the guards to be taken to the infirmary to have his bandages changed.
6. Refusal of Porelle to establish and require personnel to follow any disciplinary policy before transferring any people into segregation.
7. Tear gassing population for no reason.

8. Insults to men and families during visits, including personally insulting people in the public visiting room, skin searches of women and babies, and arbitrary denial of visitation rights of families and friends.

9. Arbitrary denial of access to Attorneys and the news media. On one occasion officers told Attorneys that an inmate who had been recently beaten could not be visited on his Attorney's request, and investigation showed that there was no attorney that had ever requested that.

10. With Porelle's knowledge many men have been beaten, and no action has been taken to discipline the responsible parties.

11. At Walpole, under Superintendent Porelle, this prison has been preparing for negative Behavioral Modification. The end result being Neuro-Surgery and Lobotomies, and we know if behavioral modification is to be a reality here at Walpole, we will be the ones subject to the experimentations on our minds and bodies.

12. Porelle has prevented the much needed community involvement which Mr. Boone says was needed. Porelle believes that all of our problems can be dealt with, with shotguns, tear gas and storm troopers. This is an intimidation to inmates, and adds only more fuel to the fire.

13. Totally irrational ship outs of nine men during the middle of the night in Gestapo-like fashion. These ship outs were declared totally illegal by the Courts. Men shipped from Concord were put into 9-10 Blocks without hearings. For months they wrote letters to Porelle to see him, and he did not come to see them until a hostage was taken.

Again, the prisoners presented their grievances to the public.[290] Some guards formed an informal alliance with the prisoners and let the legislature know they too wanted Porelle removed. Dellelo explains, "Ever since the night when they dropped the tear gas, the guards were nervous about Porelle. He showed that he would risk their lives, too. Sometimes we were on the same page with some of the guards. We knew who we could go to."[291]

The legislature, eager to end the standoff, proposed a solution: they finally requested that Raymond Porelle resign. Despite his emphatic refusal, the next day, March 2, "Crazy Ray" Porelle did resign. He blamed the guards for the problems at Walpole, saying they had been "deliberately misinterpreting his orders and allowing, or sometime creating potentially dangerous situations."[292] Almost immediately, the guards began a work slowdown. They reported to work, but did little, or clocked in, then left the prison, returning only to clock out.[293]

The prisoners, on the other hand, were prepared to fill in any gaps in leadership or service. As soon as Porelle resigned, the NPRA called off the strike they had instituted on December 29. Collectively, leaders working alongside members, the union set to work cleaning the prison. The NPRA also began negotiations with Kenneth Bishop, who had been appointed acting superintendent. The line staff watched warily as Bishop negotiated with the prisoners; they saw his willingness to consider the prisoners' demands as weakness and betrayal. While the negotiations went forward, Boone, the cadet trainee guards hired with LEAA money,[294] and Ed Rodman went to the segregation units and opened the solid steel doors in 9 and 10 Blocks; for the first time in 72 days, these men were able to take showers, shave, change into clean clothes, and eat hot food. With Porelle's resignation, the NPRA had its first concrete win and an opportunity to gain substantial power.

The allies had given substantial support to the prisoners during the long three months that Walpole was locked down and the NPRA was grateful. But while the civilians were an important part of the NPRA's strategy, the NPRA board decided that the very crucial next steps would need to be taken by the union, without consulting with the advocates. The results would also determine whether the NPRA would have the power to actually act in its capacity as the recognized representative of the Walpole prisoners.

The NPRA had learned an important lesson during the lockdown: it was possible to prevail as long as they were deliberate and clear about their strategy and, most important, as long as they remained unified. The prisoners were all too aware that Boone was under intense political pressure and needed things to calm down at Walpole. They did not hold the keys to the prison, but they could force the locks to turn—and outside support would help them do it. As the NPRA positioned itself to negotiate, strong support came from an important and powerful quarter: the Catholic Church. On March 2, the day Porelle had resigned, Cardinal Medeiros announced the creation of a permanent commission on penal reform. Later that day, the Priests' Senate of the Archdiocese of Boston called for prison abolition:

> It is time to consider forthrightly as immoral the treatment of any individual in a manner that lessens, denies or ignores that person's innate dignity and worth as a child of God and a member of the human family, a brother of Our Lord Jesus Christ and our brother.... It is clearly and demonstrably shown that imprisonment is totally ineffective as a tool in the correctional process.... As such, it tends to brutalize, dehumanize, degrade and embitter the suffering prisoner.... For these reasons, prisons as currently conceived and administered should be abolished. The religious community should work with others toward this end.[295]

Community and legislative pressure mounted quickly after the Catholic Church added its voice to the public discussion. Emboldened by this support, the next day the prisoners at Walpole held their first independent press conference since the prison was locked down in late December. Ralph Hamm read a brief statement:

> In response to the departure of Superintendent Porelle, and the assurance that there will be immediate systematic review and hearings of all the cases of the men who have been in 24 hour lockup in Blocks 9 and 10 since December 29, 1972, we of the NPRA representing the inmate population at Walpole as a show of good faith, agree to
>
> *   Clean up our living area.
> *   Return to "help assure the smooth operation of the kitchen."
> *   Immediately enter into "good-faith negotiations with the commissioner or any person authorized by the commissioner to resolve our grievances."
>
> We have demonstrated through a coalition of the men inside Walpole and concerned members of the community that peaceful protest can bring about peaceful change. We hope this process can result in meaningful and humane changes in Walpole and in other prisons across this country. We wish to thank the External board of the NPRA, The Black United Front, CARCAP, the Ad Hoc Committee on Prison Reform, the Black Caucus, Rep. Colo and his Commission on Corrections, Sen Backman and the Social Welfare Committee, Speak Out, the Health and Welfare Committee and the Delancy Street Foundation and many other concerned groups and individuals.
>
> Our show of good faith is a beginning. We will depend on the good faith and cooperation of everyone to achieve success in our efforts.[296]

8

STEALING TIME

the npra takes over

*The old way does not work, has not worked for years,
will not work in the years ahead.... The old way should
not work, for we are dealing not with animals born to be
caged, but human beings born to be better. Security and
rehabilitation: We can have neither one without the other.
[Walpole] takes locks and keys and rules and regulations
and it has a level of security second to none. But neither
is it a concentration camp where the name of the game
is suffering and violence and endless human misery.*[297]
    —Governor Francis Sargent

AFTER WALPOLE'S CHAPLAIN, JOHN FOLEY, MADE HIS BOLD
statements, the Catholic archdiocese of Boston focused its energy and considerable
power on the conditions within Walpole prison. As we saw in the previous chapter,
on March 2, Cardinal Medeiros had announced the creation of a permanent commission on penal reform. Later that day, the Priests' Senate of the Archdiocese had called
for the abolishment of prisons "as currently conceived and administered."[298]

The impact of the support of the Priests' Senate on the prisoners should not be
underestimated; the majority of prisoners in Walpole were Catholic. When the most
conservative body of their church announced that the treatment of the prisoners was
immoral, prisoners, ex-cons, and their families experienced a greater sense of self-

worth and political possibility. Indeed the statement made headlines in the *Boston Globe* and the *Boston Herald American.*

The successes of the campaign of non-cooperation made it clear that neither guards nor administrators could control the prison, while the prisoners' first press statement demonstrated that the National Prisoners Reform Association had stepped into the breach. With the list of grievances they presented publicly, the captives had already determined the framework for the new relationship with their captors. After the press conference, Kenneth Bishop, the interim warden, his administrators, and the NPRA entered into serious negotiations, starting with the issues of most concern to the prisoners.

The NPRA won from Bishop all the demands embedded in the list of grievances. Bobby Dellelo reports:

> DOC had us negotiating with [Deputy Superintendent Walter] Anderson. After we walked out on him once—he was the guy who negotiated with the grape pickers,[299] for the other side—well, we negotiated for 16 hours straight. And we negotiated all the stuff we wanted. And then Anderson says, "Now, if we give you all of this, what are you going to give us?"
>
> I could have kissed Ralph that day. He crosses his legs and leans back in the chair and says to Anderson, "We'll take out the garbage." 16 hours and he got the trash barrels emptied. He threw up his papers in the air and he ran out of the room. We had all of his papers. We were just laughing.
>
> Later, Bishop calls us in. He says, "This is what you got." I look over the list, and it is everything we wanted. I say, "What do you want from us?" He says, "Nothing, this is just what you got."[300]

Bishop's assignment was to defuse the tension at Walpole and end the labor strike. For Governor Sargent, an end to the strike was imperative. He was walking a fraught line—he had to demonstrate that his administrators could control the volatile maximum-security prison. Furthermore, the cumulative effects of the work stoppages begun in September of 1971 were being felt in the state and local economies, clearly demonstrating the commonwealth's reliance on prison labor. All license plates for the state were produced at Walpole. The work stoppage meant that no automobile license plates had been produced for three months, compounding the already spotty production of the previous 18 months. With no new plates, it was becoming increasingly difficult to register cars. This, in turn, decreased the amount of excise taxes that towns could claim. In a recent interview, Dellelo reflected on this realization, saying, "You know, everybody laughs, 'only prisoners make license plates'—well think about it; what would happen in the United States if prisoners all together just stopped making plates? Talk about power."[301]

Responding to mounting demands that it resume producing plates, the Department of Correction attempted to mitigate the power of the NPRA's strike and reduce its impact on outside communities by ordering the Walpole guards to work the presses. In other words, the guards were ordered to do the prisoners' work. Ultimately, when Walpole guards refused to accept the assignment, Boone transferred in guards from Bridgewater. However, the Walpole Guards Union won a temporary restraining order against the DOC that resulted in the closure of the plate shop and the return of the Bridgewater guards to their primary jobs. After this, the DOC unsuccessfully tried to find a subcontractor willing to take on the job. Conditions were so dire that Walter Anderson, in the earliest negotiations after Porelle's resignation, tried to bribe the NPRA with an offer to close the cadre block if the prisoners went back to work in the plate shop. The offer insulted the prisoners, and they walked out on Anderson.[302]

Once the NPRA had won major concessions from the administration, via Bishop, the prisoners did return to their jobs on a part-time basis. The prisoners gained the right to choose to work four to five hours a day so they had time to attend classes or work at their avocations. Ultimately, the NPRA, not the AHC, negotiated the crucial right of access to the prison for the allies and transparency for the public. Outside pressure alone would not have yielded these results. Boone knew he controlled neither of the prison's two workforces: the custodial staff and the prisoner employees.

At this moment, the Walpole Guards Union lost sight of the fact that they were a labor union with specific responsibilities to the members of their collective-bargaining unit. They became embroiled in an ideological battle, not a labor dispute, and refused to communicate let alone negotiate. The prisoners did not fall into this trap: they always came to the negotiating table—even when the administration and the guards did not show.

PRYING WALPOLE OPEN

Finally, on March 7, after nearly ten weeks when prisoners were locked down and visitors were locked out, the "civilians" entered the prison. When the AHC and the external board of the NPRA, including the Black United Front (BUF) and Citizens and Relatives Concerned About Prisons (CARCAP), went into Walpole, they were able to see the prisoners, assess their health, and hear directly from the prisoners exactly what the conditions had been inside the prison.[303] Ed Rodman and Phyllis Ryan were invited to attend the negotiations that were scheduled for the following day. In advance of these negotiations, the prisoners agreed to extend their commitment to clean the blocks and run the kitchen. They offered to formally end their strike in return for "citizen observers" and continued good-faith negotiations.

That day's headline in the *Herald* announced the prisoners' victory—"Walpole Inmate Demands Granted, Porelle Replacement Yields." The guards saw the settlement and the privileges negotiated by the men as a serious failure of the administration. Henceforth, Bishop's requests for support from the Walpole guards were answered with animosity and vocal protest.

Ryan credited the new access to the prolonged presence of large numbers of family members and the publicly voiced anger of the Black United Front. This public pressure played a significant role in toppling Porelle; the AHC never allowed the media to avert its attention from the prisoners. However, in her notes, Ryan, like many prisoner advocates, did not even acknowledge the critical role of the prisoners' own agency. The reason the AHC was able to enter the prison was that prisoners had determined that direct access to civilians was crucial to their success, and they refused to cooperate with the authorities until civilian observers were inside the prison. Furthermore, they did not begin to clean up the blocks until the commitment was manifest.

Ryan and Rodman attended the March 8 negotiations as "outside negotiators"; Ryan took copious notes. Boone was not present at the meeting. Instead, he sent Joe Higgins, his deputy, and Deputy Superintendent Anderson as his representatives. The entire NPRA board was present, as was Representative Colo. The following descriptions of the conditions are excerpted from Ryan's notes.

Peter Wilson, who represented the "hard core" prisoners, testified,

> In Block 10, both in phases one and two—there were no showers, no exercise, and no clean clothes since December 29. The press was refused [access] to see phase one and two of 10 Block. Nothing could be done until Porelle was gone. I advise you, don't picket Boone's office, picket Sargent. Money is wasted on extra guards and the taxpayers will pay. The prisoners here at Walpole are 550 men filled with bitterness and hate.

Wilson was followed by the NPRA's president, Bobby Dellelo.

> The NPRA does not have access to 9 and 10 Blocks. In isolation there are only two meals. You are handcuffed when you have visits. [Ryan notes to check this.] During the lockdown, guards broke Larry Rooney's arm. William Hurst is in [10] block, with 14 officers to 32 men. He is locked up twenty-four hours a day, behind both doors.[304] Who is paying that bill? Ten Block is the new DSU. Mike Taibe asked to go to phase one in 2 Block—he was refused. We have to do something soon. We will, even though we don't want to make trouble. Right now they are staggering visiting so there is no time to visit. Visits are only in the afternoon from 1 to 3:30. We had a meeting with Porelle before he left and the kitchen guys were to go back to work. The NPRA was to provide security. We will go back to work making license plates in exchange for night visits.

At the end of the meeting, the prisoners and advocates agreed to offer a "package" to the DOC detailing their demands and the mechanisms for putting them in place. The NPRA had already negotiated classification hearings for all of the men who had been placed in punitive segregation in 9 and 10 Blocks during the course of the lockdown. Ralph Hamm pushed the envelope. He told Anderson:

> To trust you, we need the following proof that we are together in this: release every man from 9 and 10, renew the blood program with ten days off your sentence instead of five, put the one-third

law back in place allowing parole eligibility at one-third of your sentence, allow fifteen days good time for forestry work (automatic twelve days), permit one private visit per man, and recommend a ten-year parole eligibility for lifers.[305]

Later, Hamm would explain that the NPRA had given him the role of making demands that could not be met—some were even beyond the DOC's power to grant. This time the DOC only had jurisdiction over two of his demands: the release of the men from 9 and 10 Blocks and the expansion of the blood program. Hamm describes his strategy:

> What you need to understand is that all this stuff was scripted. We knew that people were scared of me. I was very big, really muscular, very tall and Black. Bobby had the long hair—he was the "pretty face." I would pound the table and make demands. I would usually follow up with something like, "A Black man can't get anything in here." Then I would get up and all of BANTU would get up with me. Bobby would come in and say, "Wait a minute, Ralph, let's talk this out." He would make the demand we really wanted. It would look tame after mine. They would do anything to negotiate with him rather than me. It worked every time.[306]

Using this strategy, the NPRA usually gained the concessions it was really concerned about. This day, Anderson tried to divide the negotiators by taking the demands one point at a time. Ryan recorded Hamm's angry reaction to Anderson's strategy.

> You have broken family ties, tried to make babbling buffoons of us, fried carrots, vegetables out of us. [In Walpole] they try to treat you like a gentleman while you are slowly driven to insanity. I was telling you weeks ago about 9 and 10 Blocks.

After the negotiating session, a general meeting of the prisoners was held in the auditorium at Walpole. Frank Kelly from Packard Manse offered this description of the proceedings:

> When the general population, some probably three or four hundred inmates, assembled into the auditorium, several very well-spoken and cool and collected impressive members of the committee spoke favorably towards the objective of having the inmates vote in favor of returning to work, on the condition that observers be maintained for 24 hours and that negotiations in good faith with the administration concerning the grievances of the inmates be begun immediately. There were two other inmates, I believe, who spoke in opposition to this direction. The amount of applause they received for their comments was so overwhelming that I felt certain that the cooler heads would not prevail and that there would be no return to work.... One of their spokesmen ... spoke in opposition to the return to work because of seven years of discouraging results from

many efforts of negotiations with previous administrations [but] evidently he was encouraged to change his mind; he later spoke in favor of returning to work on a one-week basis, while negotiations continued and observers were present. Following this a vote was taken. A vast majority of the inmates did agree.... There was discussion as to whether or not the observers were to begin that night.[307]

Hamm and Dellelo both said that little surprised the NPRA leadership in this meeting with the general population. The leadership knew that it was crucial, in every meeting, that all the perspectives be expressed. Without this transparency, the normally suspicious population could become paranoid and turn upon the leadership. Yet this inclusive approach differs from many organizing cultures, where the leadership decides a general course of action and then works to control any opposition to the strategy as decisions are presented to the wider group for approval. Kelly's description, which may also reflect his own anxiety about open dissent, clearly represents his own assessment of the negotiated decision to return to work as the "right" decision. Public opposition and public resolution of conflict were key to the NPRA's strategy. As Hamm puts it,

> One of the most important things that you need to understand about all of our meetings and our negotiations was that every meeting of the board and every negotiation session was tape-recorded. At night, we would transcribe those tapes. That was really important for me because some of the time during the day, I was running around the prison doing conflict resolution, stopping stuff from jumping off. That was me and Larry Rooney. If I missed a meeting or a part of a meeting, I could listen to it as it was being transcribed and I could give input or make sure I was at the next meeting. But, and this is important, the transcripts of the meetings would be handed out at general meetings of the whole population. We held these meetings in the auditorium. There was complete transparency and all the prisoners knew what their representatives were saying on their behalf. It was in the night, when we were going over these tapes, that Ed [Rodman] would be there. That was when he taught me how to manage my role as a leader.[308]

Hamm went on to explain how Bobby Dellelo was a unique leader. At night, before the executive board meetings, Dellelo and Hamm would agree on what Dellelo's line would be on a particular issue. To his credit, Dellelo never let Hamm down. Even if Hamm were not there, Dellelo could keep with the agreed-upon decision framework should Peter Wilson disagree with him. Wilson was the only other white prisoner on the executive board. They had four votes against Wilson on any issue. Dellelo was also very committed to racial equity. He was also very stubborn. Hamm said the only problem was that Dellelo was able to run best with his own ideas. Hamm and Rodman spent a lot of time convincing Dellelo that certain ideas were indeed "his." Because they fought it out openly challenging each other, once Bobby agreed he never backed down. He never let BANTU down. He promised he would make sure they had equity and parity. He never wavered from this.[309]

Later, Hamm would more carefully define his own leadership role within the NPRA.

It was the role of *all* of the twenty-one members to keep the prison calm during the course of our negotiations with the prison guards' union, the Department of Correction, and the executive branch of the state government; and during those early times a couple of us stood out as the best suited for the job. The fact that Larry Rooney and I were often called upon to quell a prisoner disturbance, especially one that involved the explosive factions of black and white prisoner population, points to our influence over our respective ethnic groups due to the respect we garnered from our peers, and the fact that we could each call up a large contingency of support from the prisoner population to bolster any effort. Let there be no mistake about it: the NPRA was a collective of various ethnic groups and gang affiliations working toward a common goal most of the time [and] sharing equal voice. NPRA relied heavily upon BANTU's community-oriented structure to devise and formulate its programs and long-range goal strategies (enter Solomon Brown), because we had the expertise and we were good at it. We, the executive board of the NPRA, met everyday to discuss our agendas and strategies for the next day's meetings; I met everyday with the board of BANTU for the same purpose.

It was an extremely rare occasion when NPRA negotiators had to ad lib a situation, as most of our responses were foreseen and rehearsed, as well as thoroughly thought out. Upon those occasions when we had to act spontaneously, we knew each other so well (having a clear vision of our goals) that even those rare instances seemed planned—as we could, without hesitation, feed off of the others' lead and bolster a given direction.

The NPRA was lucky to have a highly gifted, intellectual, talented, and visionary external board of directors, mostly drawn from BANTU's external board and the Boston community—people like the Reverend Ed Rodman, Arnie Coles, Russ Carmichael, Amina Green, John McGrath, and Obalaji Rust, just to name a few. These individuals had been movers and shakers in their respective communities for years and lent us their organizational skills and voices. It could be safe to say that most of the NPRA's program direction was rooted within the Black Consciousness Movement of the time. The roles that we prisoners played in an effort to maintain order in the prison, and to best represent ourselves to the media (hence, the public), were carefully selected based upon a given prisoner's skill level and then orchestrated. We were afforded a lot of role models from the outside community to pattern ourselves after.

There was no such animal as a Black chief of security in the late 1960s and 1970s. [Nor did I] consider myself one with the

NPRA. There was the Black Panther Party and the Nation of Islam, and we—I—drew heavily from those models. Pulling security,
so to speak, was no snub or demeaning task—everyone did it from
time to time, even the block representatives. Security was one of
the most important jobs in the organization because all of our lives
and futures depended upon it, ... and it was surely the hardest job.
Try to prevent 500 repressed, angry, racist, and extremely violent
prisoners from rioting and tearing each other apart at any given
moment of every day utilizing the only tool that you've been afforded—the promise of hope. It is not easy.

It can be said about the bulk of the white prisoner population
in Walpole (who were the overwhelming majority in the prison)
that there was an appearance that they were opportunists looking
only for what they could get "now." On the other hand, the Black
prisoner population (i.e., BANTU) had far-reaching expectations
that took us from behind the prison walls, having entered as the
proverbial pariahs; back to our respective communities, as educated and contributing members of the Consciousness Movement. We
sought meaningful vocational and educational programs to transform us into productive human beings; where we saw our white
counterparts as already accepted in society by virtue of their skin
color, focusing upon momentary pleasures and good time credits.
Robert Dellelo was seen as one of the exceptions to that rule, as
he had the most difficult task of balancing the prospective goals of
the NPRA (i.e., seeing the need for career-oriented educational and
vocational programs for all) with the "gratification now" attitude
of his constituency or the white prisoner population, all the while
having to keep the majority, extremely volatile prisoner population in check. He, more so than any of us, may have understood the
fine line upon which we all walked, as he was placed in the position
as the spokesperson for the NPRA's community-based corrections
format.[310]

Yet, even though the NPRA was doing everything in its power to keep the
prison population under control, after the meeting in the auditorium, a prisoner
stabbed a guard. To his credit, rather than blaming the prisoners for the stabbing,
Boone blamed the guard culture. The *Herald* responded by publishing an article describing the crimes and convictions of Dellelo, Hamm, and Miguel Trinidad, the
board representative of the Latino prisoners.[311] The paper included cartoons of the
three men with placards hanging from their necks, labeling them cop killer, rapist,
and drug dealer.

WITNESSING REFORM: THE ROLE OF CIVILIAN OBSERVERS

Boone finally acquiesced to the prisoners' demands for civilian observers because the
guards were increasingly hostile to the administration and increasingly slothful on the
job. Rodman invited Boone out to discuss how well-trained citizens watching and

documenting the actions of prisoners and guards could be a catalyst for stability. According to Rodman, after this discussion, Boone decided he could trust him.

Once Boone accepted the idea of civilian observers, Rodman had to produce them. He assembled a small group of trusted volunteers who became the core of the AHC's Observer Program (OP). Among them were a number of dedicated ex-cons: John McGrath and Arnie Coles from the External NPRA, and Russ Carmichael and John Ramos from Ex Cons Helping Others (ECHO). Rodman also recruited John Osler, a divinity student; Obalaji Rust from the Black United Front; Douglas Butler, a highly respected labor organizer in the Black community; Frank Kelly from Packard Manse; and David Dance, the Harvard student running the Black history class at Walpole. When the AHC announced that the observers were to be permitted in the prison, many of the women from CARCAP showed up at the prison to volunteer. Boone's assistant, Walter Williams, told Rodman that no women would be allowed to enter the prison as observers. Rodman recalls:

> I didn't really disagree with him, but I knew this would be a difficult conversation because these women had spent months outside the prison protesting the conditions their husbands and loved ones were enduring. I said, "Sure, but who is going to tell them?" Then I opened the door and turned to face them; Williams closed the door behind me and left me out there alone to tell them. They were none too happy, but there was a lot of work to do, and they coordinated the volunteers and made phone calls keeping the lines of communication open.[312]

On March 8, the first observers from the OP entered the prison with the 7 AM guards' shift. The Kwanzaa lockdown had ended; the men in 9 and 10 Blocks had been locked down for 70 days. That day, Obalaji Rust began political-awareness classes. Over the next 12 days, Rust would stay inside the prison continuously, only leaving for one break.[313]

FROM GUARDS' UNION TO PRISONERS' UNION: THE INSTITUTION CHANGES HANDS

On March 9, after the first observers took their posts, 50 guards refused to punch in at the three o'clock shift change. Those who did report to work tried to turn an already scheduled meeting with the commissioner into a press conference by bringing the press with them. Refusing to play along, Boone left the prison. As he walked out, the guards who were assembled on the lawn began to "boo, hiss, and shout, eventually spitting racial slurs at the Commissioner. 'Get out of here you bum' and 'Pack your bags you carpet bagger.' They also chanted 'Boone the coon.'"[314] "Boone the Coon" was the headline in the *Herald* that day. The guards' union released a statement saying they were disturbed by Boone's interference in running the prison.[315] The liberal white North had been unmasked, revealing the ugly face of overt racial hatred.

After Boone got into his car, the entire three o'clock shift—in front of the assembled media representatives—walked off the job, leaving the prison in the hands of the AHC's Observer Program and the prisoners. Ed Rodman remembers:

> That morning, I had set up a table after the first shift of observers went in. We let the second shift in at three and I was sitting at the table. One of the guards came up to me with a big manila envelope. He dropped it on the desk with a big clunk, saying, "I think these belong to you." In the envelope was every key to the prison. I got up and took the keys over to the office the state police had just set up in the prison that morning. I placed it on [the state police officer's] desk and said, "I think these belong to you!"[316]

That afternoon, there were no guards in the prison. The NPRA had already determined what its role would be. Dellelo remembers: "When the guards went on strike, we were prepared. We had everything in place. We could not afford to miss a beat."[317]

Within a week, Bishop withdrew DOC support for the Inmate Advisory Council and quickly recognized the NPRA as the prisoners' bargaining unit.[318] This acknowledgment affected the State Labor Relations Commission's process. In fact, the SLRC had already reached the decision that it could not certify the union. The SLRC notified DOC attorney Robert Bell, who asked the SLRC to delay the release of its decision, since the guards were on strike and the commissioner had just recognized the bargaining power of the prisoners' union. The SLRC complied; it would be well into September before the commission released its opinion. The NPRA and its allies would proceed with the conviction that the organization had a strong chance at recognition as long as the NPRA could demonstrate its ability to perform the functions of a labor union.

The NPRA set about demonstrating just that. Hamm explained the structure the NPRA adopted as it assumed responsibility for running the prison:

> Each member of the internal board of directors for the NPRA was assigned as overseer of at least one committee. The committee itself was usually headed by a cellblock representative or his assistant, with the board member as the chair. The committee head was accountable to the chair, the chair was accountable to the board of directors, and the board of directors was accountable to the general prisoner population (membership of the NPRA). The committee chairman and his designee had total access to his area of concern (e.g., school, hospital, 9 Block, 10 Block, chapel) any time within reason, day or night. A committee report had to be typed and submitted to the board of directors twice a week, except in cases of emergency when matters had to be decided upon and dealt with immediately. The education, furlough, vocational training, legal, and visiting committees were oriented toward research and program implementation.
>
> It was these specific committees' task to develop feasible programs for the prison population's benefit and to submit these pro-

gram formats to the legal committee for verification ... to be formulated into proposals, submitted to the board of directors for review and a vote, and if approved by the board then forwarded to the Department of Correction or the prison superintendent [Bishop] for consideration. The findings of the committees once submitted to and signed off by the board of directors were sent to the prison superintendent, the commissioner of correction [Boone], the external board of directors [NPRA], and the correctional officer union representative, and released to the general prisoner population via the block representative and the monthly general prisoner population meetings held in the prison auditorium. Emergency meetings with the general population could be held any time, especially if we of the board needed a vote from the membership concerning proposed policy.[319]

Dellelo's description of the NPRA's structure, developed in the fall well before the Kwanzaa lockdown, contributes further to our understanding of how the prison was run under its authority.

There was an army of committees in the formal structure of the NPRA. Because there were so few Latino prisoners, Miguel Trinidad took care of the Spanish; there was a Spanish Committee, but it wasn't as formal. The Hospital Committee worked with hospital staff and made sure medical and dental treatment was decent, all the prisoners were taken care of, and that the hospital was running in a humane manner. If a doctor wasn't there, they would record it. We had some really great paramedics working in the prison. They were Vietnam vets; they were used to trauma, and they were used to dealing with drug addicts.

Guys who knew the hospital would get assigned there; guys that worked in the kitchen would get assigned there. What we did with the committees, what I tried to do, was find the guys who were sincerely interested in the area and put them in the area. For example, Jimmy Pena did not give a fuck about prison reform; he wanted to get a good meal and to be treated like a decent human being. He was on the Kitchen Committee.

Industries encompassed the laundry, the brush shop, et cetera. The Sports Recreation committee made sure all the equipment was available. The canteen was the property of the inmates. When Recreation needed basketballs, et cetera, they would make out a request to us and we would purchase the equipment. We did not stop with recreational equipment for the prisoner population. The Rec. Committee built a playground for their children. The avocations pitched in and built picnic tables.

There was a lot of internal house stuff: work that was necessary to make the institution functional. We negotiated control of the canteen and its profit was to be used to support additional NPRA initiatives. We took things a step further because we wanted to open a store that sold sandwiches, sodas, hot dogs, and hamburgers so that the money went back to be used for halfway houses.[320] We wanted NPRA halfway houses. They would be supported by selling product inside of Walpole prison. The NPRA philosophy of prisoner self-determination would be the philosophy. We wanted the NPRA expand to other institutions. We are talking good money in those times.

We could have developed three halfway houses and paid for them ourselves and charged guys a minimum amount to live there—that way they could hit the street with money in their pocket. Prisoners who had shown leadership while they were in the prison and had experience developing programs would run the houses. John McGrath and Russ Carmichael were already doing this in Cambridge. This would give guys a job on the outside and build our external network.

We didn't control industries—they were controlled by DOC—but we had committees about safety conditions and making sure guys didn't get screwed. We didn't have jobs to pay everyone so we wanted to make sure it was a fair process. There was some equitable forum to get employment, like a working list.

It was important that those of us in leadership did not appear to be benefiting from our positions. I didn't move to minimum end—I stayed in the maximum end. I didn't take any perks. I wasn't doing anything to benefit myself, which was another reason they feared me.

The observers did not have any keys. But the NPRA block leaders did. The prisoners had keys to all the cells, but no keys to the outside. Didn't want them. That was the insanity of the situation. We even passed out meds, which was against the law. And no one got ripped off. Everyone got their pills—even the assholes.

What almost happened is that we almost got a union, and the concepts that we laid out, they are still talking about today, thirty years later: rehabilitation, vocational training, providing rehabilitation tools, and halfway houses. The notion of making a prisoner a law-abiding person who goes out better than when he came in. Unfortunately, the system has gone in the opposite direction. For example, the BU college program resulted in a zero recidivism rate. Education is a viable tool. People became law–abiding, productive persons. You have to give a guy a trade to make a living.[321]

There was no denying that Walpole prison was a community of laborers. According to the SLRC opinion, delivered later that year, of the 575 prisoners, 400 were working. The opinion lists 31 specific work assignments, ranging from the industrial jobs in the foundry and the print shop to custodial jobs such as corridor maintenance. In December, when the NPRA had applied for certification, two prisoners were even employed to orient new arrivals. Within Walpole, the pay ranged from 25 cents to $1.25 a day; the NPRA was negotiating for minimum wage, then at around $1.75 an hour.

Despite the strikes and work stoppages, $443,835 worth of goods were produced at Walpole in fiscal year 1973. The Boone administration was far along in negotiations with private industry to provide job training and jobs that would follow the prisoners after release. The SLRC opinion also referred to a computer-programming service, and to a Walpole contract with Mail Group, Inc., that was prepared to start prisoners at $30 to $60 a week.[322]

WHO IS MINDING THE PRISONERS?

CIVILIAN OBSERVERS OR CITIZEN GUARDS?

When the afternoon-shift guards walked out on March 9, Rodman knew that he was involved in something much bigger than he had originally conceived. Initially, the observers were to enter the prison to observe, not to act. Their presence was intended to bring balance to the environment. With the line guards gone, though, the observers had an even more crucial role to play. It was essential that all of the observers fully understand that their proper function was not replacing the guards, but rather witnessing how the NPRA ran the prison in their absence. They were to be the eyes and ears of their communities, relaying accurate information to the press to counterbalance the reports guards had clearly fabricated from air, given that they weren't even in the prison at the time. At the end of each shift, observers would leave a report for Phyllis Ryan to review before she released her daily summary to the media.

MAKING OBSERVERS OUT OF ALLIES

Almost immediately, it became obvious that a larger group of volunteers would be needed to meet the AHC's commitment to the prisoners and the administration. Phyllis Ryan and Mary Norris from the American Friends Service Committee (AFSC) went to work contacting all of the organizations that supported prison reform. Then they contacted all the individuals who had signed the postcards sent to the governor in December 1971. The AFSC Criminal Justice Program became the coordinating center for the Observer Program. Within a few days it had hundreds of volunteers.

Ed Rodman adapted training lessons originally designed for volunteers witnessing civil-disobedience actions undertaken by CORE and SNCC to prepare the civilian observers. Rodman's first concern was that dedicated volunteers who spent too much time on the blocks might begin to consider themselves responsible for the prison. Because they were primarily middle-class church people, he feared they would identify with the role of guard or custodian. Ultimately, Rodman turned to an unexpected source to prepare the observers. Sunny Robinson, who was part of the medical team at Norfolk prison, recommended approaching George Moore, a guard who sat in on the Inmate Advisory Council at Norfolk prison. Moore, who had also been a member of the Elam Committee, agreed to work with Rodman to train the observers. Rodman remembered, "Without Moore's advice and participation, we would not have been as successful. He understood the dynamic at Walpole and the seduction of power."[323]

At Moore's suggestion, the AHC reduced the shifts from eight hours to six hours and limited the number of shifts a volunteer was permitted to take per week. Years later, Rodman reflected, "I think about this all the time. Guards who log even a thirty-hour work week, well, they start looking at control as their job and as the prison as 'their prison.' Imagine how this plays itself out when there is no AHC to debrief you or say, 'Watch it—power is getting to you.'"[324]

Certain observers were key to this project, and despite Moore's guidelines, they worked long hours inside the prison. Osler, Butler, Rust, and Kelly were the core volunteers, with Rodman and Doug Butler taking most of the night shifts. Butler was a middle-aged Black man who had been a prize-winning body builder in his younger years. He withstood the rigors of the Observer Program better than many of the other volunteers. His name appears on the log for the night shift as many as five times a week. On many occasions he did double shifts. His copious notes evince a disciplined man who never lost sight of his purpose.

The work with the prisoners became a commitment for Rodman's whole family. Many recently released prisoners were already making their transition to the community at the Rodman home under the careful mentorship of Gladys, Ed's wife. White ex-cons who lived with them had all of their stereotypes challenged. "When they found out that Gladys's mother was a school principal and they realized that many of the adults in our family were educated, professional, and respected people, well, you could see that they were thinking about it," Ed Rodman recalled. "Gladys and her mother didn't really cut them any slack either. They challenged them whenever possible. And they did regular household chores just like the rest of us."[325] On weekends, the reverend's young daughters would accompany him to the prison and help the observers file papers and make phone calls in the waiting room.

Guards Out, NPRA In

On March 10, the *Boston Globe* reported on the guards' walkout the previous day, explaining that it was the prisoners who were actually responsible for the relative calm within the institution. The paper relied extensively on information provided by the AHC members and ex-cons who were observers. Rodman's statements focused on the irresponsible behavior of the guards who

> instead of being on the job ... are at the governor's office and the State House trying to get Commissioner Boone fired. The prisoners with the help of the Ad Hoc Committee on Prison Reform and the NPRA are trying to get the institution under control and running in an orderly fashion. [The guards] are resisting the process.... There will come a point when it will be necessary for them to be reprimanded for not following the orders of Ken Bishop, acting superintendent, and I think we are very near that point right now.[326]

Arnie Coles, an ex-con, chair of the external NPRA, and a former member of BANTU, described the NPRA's work during this critical time.

What the men are basically doing in there is holding the institution to-gether. What prisoners want is relevant programs and the return of the institution to what it was before the lockup, when men were not pitted against each other. They want relevant job training and programs and this harassment from the officers to cease. It is a correctional institution and not a concentration camp, and it's been run like a concentration camp since the lockup.[327]

The prisoners counted on Ryan to manage the media and use the observers' reports to inform the public about conditions in Walpole. The guards' union's public-relations strategy relied on a fabricated and alternative story line. The *Herald* printed these fabrications as fact—daily, relentlessly, spitting out baseless, venomous attacks on the commissioner and the NPRA.

HONORING AGREEMENTS, INSPIRING CHANGE

On March 11, two days after the guard walkout, the prisoners finally went back to work for the agreed-upon one-week trial. Walter Anderson, Walpole's deputy super-intendent, publicly disputed the one-week stipulation, but the AHC and the external NPRA members backed the prisoners' memory of the agreement.[328] The prisoners planned to meet in committees and as a whole after a week to assess the progress of negotiations and determine whether they would continue to work.

Later that day, there was a rebellion at the Concord State Prison in New Hamp-shire. Prisoners there broke furniture and allegedly assaulted officers, though no guard injuries were actually reported. In the end, four of the prisoners were put in solitary confinement.[329] The *Herald* raised the specter of chaos spreading across New England prisons as a result of the activities of the NPRA at Walpole. There was some substance to the paper's fears: the Attica rebellion had offered Massachusetts prison-ers the opportunity to bring fresh public attention to their yearlong protest against the conditions of their own confinement. Now the Walpole prisoners' resistance had become an inspiration to other prisoners across the country, albeit minus the chaos the *Herald* invoked. Dellelo remembers,

> When the guys from the California prisoners' union came to Wal-pole, we asked them, "How do we stack up against what other pris-oners are doing across the country?" They said, "Are you kidding? Everybody is watching you guys; you are leading the way. Every-one is waiting to see what is going to happen in Massachusetts."[330]

The NPRA was not alone in claiming prisoners' right to self-determination. Prisoners in many states were forming unions; however, most simply used prisoner unity to fight for the extension of certain rights, or entitlements, to prisoners. In ad-dition, these organizations often relied upon the leadership of formerly incarcerated men and women who had contacts within the prison. The NPRA in Massachusetts was unique in that it was composed entirely of incarcerated prisoners and used a workers' rights framework buttressed by bargaining-unit recognition given by the Department of Correction.

The travesty at Attica and the influx of LEAA monies ushered in a new wave of correctional reform. For prisoners and advocates across the country, this was seen as a time of possibility. At the same time, there were indications that the criminal justice system was prepared to tighten up. On March 14, President Nixon called for the reimposition of the federal death penalty—just as death-row prisoners were being released from 9 Block at the insistence of the NPRA.

STEALING TIME

The AHC met with Boone and members of his staff early on March 12 to discuss procedures for continuing a 24-hour observer protocol. Ryan noted that the commissioner was "pleased" with the success of the program.[331] Boone's support was crucial. So supporting Boone in turn was imperative. The AHC recognized that it needed to keep Boone in his position as long as possible. Rodman and Hamm fully understood that the remarkable amount of prisoner agency that the NPRA was able to negotiate was tenuous. Hamm recalled:

> We knew this could not last forever. We were committed to getting everything we could before the door closed. Each night I would look at Ed Rodman and say, "Well, we did another day." We knew we were stealing time. A day, an hour, a minute at a time.[332]

At Ryan's request, Herbert H. Hershfang, on behalf of the regional office of the American Jewish Congress, sent a letter to Governor Sargent supporting Boone. The letter reflected sentiments shared by all those who supported prison reform.

> The real objective of the guards at Walpole is not an increase in salary or improvement in working conditions, objectives that are well within the rights of unions and laboring people to pursue. Instead, they are attempting in the guise of seeking security in the prison to make policy, a function which is not theirs to perform and one for which they cannot and ought not to be held responsible. In addition, what they see is essentially security without justice, a set of conditions which is inimical to our democratic institutions and which in the long run will provide for no security at all.[333]

The conflict between the guards and the commissioner was finally given full, public voice on March 14, during a highly publicized hearing on a bill that would transfer control of the DOC from the Office of Health and Human Services to the Office of Public Safety. The auditorium at the State House was filled with guards venting their anger against Boone, Goldmark, and the governor. Shortly before noon, Sargent was informed by telegram that the guards' union had issued a strike ultimatum, demanding Boone's removal before guards would return to work.[334]

Sargent responded that he would order the state police—who were monitoring the prison from an office, but not patrolling the halls—to advance into the prison interior to take control of the prison if, indeed, the guards did strike. Asserting explicitly that Boone, not the guards, was charged with Walpole's operation, Sargent declared, "I will not succumb to whatever threats of violence inmates pose to gain unreasonable demands. I will not succumb to threats of a strike by guards to win the demand that they, and not the Correction Department, run Walpole."[335]

At the three o'clock shift, some guards reported to work. The guards complained about the presence of civilian observers in the prison 24 hours a day. They resented the fact that citizens were on hand to report retaliatory acts against prisoners and violations of prison regulations. The guards were especially angry because some of the observers monitoring their job performance were men who had been released from prison less than a year before.[336] Dominic Presti, head of the Walpole Guards Union, proclaimed, "The inmates are now running the institution; I don't think the institution can get back to normal as long as Boone is commissioner."[337]

Yet according to Ryan's notes, the reason the institution was not "normal" was that the guards continued to disrupt it:

> Problem is described as guards refusing to go along with the program which has been worked out. The reason there are no rules and regulations is because the guards refuse to sit down with the inmates and the administration and work them out.[338]

That night, after the hearing, the guards who had returned expressed their anger by severely beating a prisoner who had complained to the commissioner. Ryan's notes read, "The men want security, afraid of the guards. Want administration of prison to live up to the agreements."[339]

STRIKE AND LOCKOUT

The following day, March 15, eleven men were released from 10 Block after going before a classification review board. As these men entered the general population, the official guard strike began. Two hundred guards, the entire force of line guards, walked out of Walpole prison and a state of emergency was declared.[340] The state police were mobilized and the National Guard was alerted. The guards' union demanded that the commissioner "pack his bags."[341] Boone decided that the time had come to fight for control of the Department of Correction. Tired of continually fighting his employees, he wanted to use the guards' strike to break the back of their union, which, unlike the NPRA, was standing in the way of his reform project, his top priority.[342] He announced that he would fire every guard who walked away from his job. In response, the guards' union threatened to "pull all state workers" from their jobs. This was not an idle threat, because some of the guards in Massachusetts, including those in the Walpole Guards Union, were represented by AFSCME, which also represented all other Massachusetts state workers. Boone was ready to fight for control of the institutions, but Goldmark intervened.

Goldmark believed that the prisons were a lost cause. He wanted Boone's energy to be focused on establishing community corrections, not battling guards at one or another institution. Boone, on the other hand, knew that he had to have staff who respected him to do his job at all. He had been cursed at, threatened, and targeted for racist speech and action for over a year. For John O. Boone, the attacks were made not only on his own integrity and personal dignity; they impinged on the dignity of all Black men and women. He would not tolerate any more racist abuse. If this meant going to war with the guards, he was prepared to do it.[343] Boone and Goldmark had come to a philosophical breaking point. Isenberg stayed close to Boone, supporting all his decisions, but Goldmark began to pull away. He described the split this way:

> I always felt a little bit alone in what I thought reform should mean and what I wanted to do. What I wanted to do was basically to build a community correction system and decrease the reliance on the old institutional approach.... Strategically, I did not want to fight in the institutions. By fight, I mean I did not want to fight the reform battle there.
>
>   And ... that's where Boone and I parted ways.... Conceptually he felt he had to fight there. [It was] a matter of his integrity and it was a matter of what were human, deep, moral issues that go on in a place like this. I felt it was a loser.
>
>   I wanted somebody in charge of Walpole. I wanted that guy to be given the head to run it and I didn't want a fight there. I wanted to leave it alone. I wanted to find a way out. A compromise, I didn't care what. I didn't see the great human issue at stake in Walpole that John did. I felt both the inmates and the guards were full of bullshit. Both groups.... I felt that was the only way for John to survive as commissioner. He wanted to change Walpole. He wanted the guards to behave. I think he wanted a much greater deal of inmate say in running the prison.... What I wanted was to get somebody in who could run Walpole, calm it down, get things back on the track. I wanted him to leave Walpole alone and let someone else—Mr. Strong—run it.[344]

This assessment came a year after Raymond Porelle—the quintessential "Mr. Strong"—had been forced to resign and nine months after Boone had been fired. It illuminates how slowly lessons are sometimes learned.

Although Goldmark appeared to support the commissioner, they had definitively parted ways. Goldmark hoped that Boone would sacrifice his own integrity in order to achieve the department's goal of community corrections. But for the moment, Goldmark and Boone came to a compromise: instead of firing the striking guards, which he was allowed to do because state law prohibits public employees from striking, Boone suspended 150 of them for five days without pay.[345] And Goldmark made a public statement indicating his continued support of Boone and "his policies."[346]

By March 15, the state police were manning the wall boxes and outer control of the prison, while Boone recruited 40 cadet trainee guards and combined them with 40 observers to keep the institution functioning. Visitors to the prison described the situation within as calm.[347] The same could not be said of the State House. Several hundred guards and their families had jammed into the State House's Gardiner Auditorium for another day of hearings on proposed corrections bills. Robert Moore, the former Walpole superintendent, testified that Boone and Goldmark had given control to the "scum of the inmate population, … a small group of extremely dangerous violent and unpredictable inmates, … the most treacherous men I have met in 30 years of corrections."[348] On the basis of such testimony, the guards issued their own set of demands. They asked for an increase in the use of segregation and lockups, more control by the guards over the movement of prisoners, the removal of all observers, and the firing of Commissioner Boone.[349]

COURT ORDERS GUARDS TO RETURN TO WORK

Despite the improved functioning of the prison without the guards, on March 19, the Massachusetts supreme court ordered the guards to return to their posts.[350] The guards who had been on strike returned to the prison, but not to the blocks. They stayed on the observation deck, talking to prisoners through the prison's two-way PA system, which also allowed them to monitor what the prisoners were saying.[351] The NPRA retained responsibility for program, industry, culture, and conflict resolution. The cadet trainee guards worked the blocks, holding the keys and observing counts. Each block had at least one, and usually two, civilian observers assigned to monitor and report on conditions and issues. During the time the NPRA both functioned as the elected representative of the prisoners, and took responsibility for the actual running of the institution, from March 15 to May 18, there were no outbreaks of violence, no murders, and no rapes. The reports all described a calm prison.

After the court order was handed down, Boone issued a memo to Walpole superintendent Kenneth Bishop detailing the phased return of the guards to the prison. Because the NPRA, the cadet trainee guards, and the civilian observers were able to create a calm and productive environment inside the prison, Boone was able to be flexible in returning the old guards to their posts. They were ordered to attend a "retraining program" held at the Framingham State Police Training Academy and the DOC Training Academy. The memo explained that "an integral part of the phased supervised reentry will be an official reeducation program. All officers will be expected to read and understand Department of Correction policy and institutional procedures."[352] However, despite the DOC's intention to keep guards out of the prison until they were retrained, a number of problem guards had returned to work after the public hearing on March 14—with the intention of destabilizing a prison that was running smoothly without them.

As Dellelo assessed the guards' motivation,

When the guards went out on strike, they expected the prison to explode. And we held it together. It was peaceful in there. There was no tension in the prison. As soon as the guards came back, all the tension came back with them. The guards started where they left off. The thing is, the guards weren't going to let Boone succeed; they weren't going to let any of his or our programs succeed. The guards were totally embarrassed because we showed that the prison could run without them and they had to destroy that.

The inmates were always the inmates, the administration was always the administration, and the guards were always the guards. When the guards left, it was apparent that the problem was not the administration; it was not the inmates. Not all the guards stayed out the whole strike, some crossed the picket line. The first guards that crossed the line were the dogs. They were out to destroy us from the beginning. Here's the thing, they were embarrassed and they had to come back in and destroy the notion that they were the problem. The truth was thrown out on the table and they were intent on cleaning up the table. Everyone, the newspapers, everyone was picking up on it. They had an agenda to get into the prison and destroy it quickly. We had to be the bad guys.[353]

The AHC and the allies knew that, ultimately, the prison staff would be reinstated. They were well aware that Boone had gone "further than any prison administrator ever had or ever would."[354] As an administrator, he had exceeded their expectations. At this moment, the prisoners were completely engaged in their project. They chose to use the precious time they had won to develop and test their model of self-determination and self-government. Walpole prisoners had unlocked the door of a maximum security prison to anyone who was willing to be trained and volunteer as an observer—not as an administrator or facilitator—of the NPRA-designed program. That's the opposite of most "prison reform," where volunteers come in and offer direction to the imprisoned.

NPRA'S PROGRAMMING

Solomon Brown began to develop additional curricula for BANTU. Under the auspices of the NPRA, he created a remedial learning program, located across the hall from the barren prison school. The difference in the learning environments was like night and day. Brown understood the needs of his peers and developed a meaningful, practical curriculum. The men could learn to read, write, and do math, but the learning process started with examining their own experience. The students had many barriers to overcome; the majority had not finished grade school, let alone high school. Because many of them had spent their adolescence in custody, they had many negative associations with learning.

The Phillips Brooks House at Harvard, a students' community-service organization, ensured that the men had the educational material that they needed, providing books, paper, chalk, maps, and many other necessary classroom materials. Some of the observers provided typewriters, adding machines, curtains, microscopes, and chairs. Curry College was setting up a college-preparatory course at Walpole, but the NPRA leadership knew that Brown's basic educational program was the foundation.

As Dellelo has put it,

> When I was in Walpole, I got my college degree. You can't do that in Walpole anymore. But for most of us who were capable of earning a college degree, we were going to have a better chance at success. Most of the prisoners, they needed elementary education. That is the first step to giving a guy a chance to succeed.[355]

And the men achieved much under the program. Hamm remembers,

> There was this guy in our block—he could not read.... All the brothers took turns working with him. It was slow, but he learned to read. That was a remarkable achievement. For me, this is where it is at. I had the job of keeping order in the prison, but I really love teaching. I would walk by a bunch of guys playing "killer chess" and I would throw a book on the board, scattering the pieces. They would say, "Why'd you do that?" I'd reply, "Read it and find out." Later, we took what we learned and created the Adult Basic Education Program.[356]

The prisoners also developed a real structure to replace the arbitrary "discipline" of the guards. It was up to the prisoners to settle all disputes and create an agreed-upon code of behavior. The NPRA proved quite adept at developing accepted rules. Its code was founded on the principle of idealized brotherhood: "We are all brothers. Don't do anything that you would not do to your brother." This included theft, assault, and murder. During this time, Ralph Hamm and Larry Rooney took responsibility for teaching the code to the general population. Because of his conflict-resolution skills, Hamm was called upon to settle most disputes within the prison. He relied upon his knowledge of the men to reach and maintain agreements. He did carry his famous two-and-a-half-foot machete strapped to his side under the three-quarter-length army-fatigue jacket. However, he never used it. His ability, as a young Black man in a majority-white prison, to mediate peaceably demonstrated the success of the crossracial organizing that the NPRA had done. Hamm's reputation for expertise in martial arts only served to a point. The white prisoners had guns; they could easily have taken him out. Hamm describes the work he undertook with his friend Larry Rooney.

> Our main responsibility was teaching the prisoners how to live with each other across differences and across racial polarity. It was our job to keep the lid on. Bobby did some of this work but he also concentrated on maintaining our outside support base and presenting our views to the media. These are roles we chose to take. Together, Larry and I were good at resolving racialized conflict. I did not resolve conflict among the white prisoners. That was Bobby's job. In the beginning, while we were negotiating with Bishop, I was constantly given reports at meetings concerning potential problems

inside and had to rush out to find Larry (if he wasn't with me at the meeting) and we were off to quell something or another. This was a 24-hour a day undertaking, or so it seemed then, and was foremost in my mind. Often I had to be brought up to date in the evenings by Bobby as to what had taken place at meetings with outsiders, and we would discuss our strategy then for the next day. I spent most of my waking hours distracted by thoughts of potential rivalries in the prison.... Larry Rooney is one of the unsung heroes in the NPRA story.[357]

In a later letter, Hamm continues his analysis of the work of the NPRA, and the role played by Rooney.

Rooney possibly had one of, if not the, hardest jobs of an internal NPRA board member. His primary job was to maintain order in a riot-torn, extremely volatile, majority-white prisoner population. I remember him as a humorous, slim, tall, relatively quiet individual (compared to the loud and boisterous individuals one tends to find in prison), as well as street smart and fearless. He could enter a chaotic, highly charged, situation in the prison where prisoner violence was either occurring or on the brink, and once his presence was noticed by prisoners (white, black, or Hispanic), the turmoil would cease. When both of us had to be summoned to quell a disturbance, it was done. It would be easy for me to say that the cessation of hostilities was due to both of us being present, but I believe it to have been due to the respect he commanded. He was a great no-questions-asked friend when he considered you his friend, but a person you immediately and instinctively knew that you did not want for an enemy. He had a great understanding of group or mob dynamics, as well as the psychology of pecking orders and peer pressure, which I believe many overlooked in him.

I believe that his political savvy was something tutored by Bobby D., as was the case with many of us (which is probably why we all fit together like links in a chain) when it came to understanding the dynamics and politics of prison, and I afforded him the same respect as I did Bobby, and considered him a friend. If not for Larry Rooney, I believe that the prisoner population would have imploded and erupted into violence born of frustration many times during the course of the NPRA's negotiations with the DOC and the union, as who he was and what he represented maintained the uneasy calm the board enjoyed during those months in 1973.

However, I don't fully attribute my own survival during this tumultuous period to my laurels, wits, or martial arts prowess. To this day, I remain uncertain, but believe that Bobby Dellelo may have placed me under a protective order within the white prisoner population—a hands-off policy that would be met with dire retribution if violated. I was more valuable to the white prisoners alive than dead because of my leadership in BANTU and the outside support that afforded the NPRA, and because of my ability to negotiate with the prison administration.[358]

With Bishop as acting superintendent and the NPRA developing programs, it seemed Goldmark finally had what he wanted: the well-run prison necessary to allow Boone to concentrate on reforming the whole system. Because Boone was willing to think outside of the institutional framework, he was able to negotiate control of this institution. Given court-ordered power to retrain his staff, he finally had the latitude to develop the correctional program necessary to depopulate the prison. Yet, these gains were not good enough for Goldmark. From his viewpoint, some large problems remained: control of the institution was clearly in the hands of the prisoners; the staff could not enter the prison; volunteers had demonstrated that impartial observers were more effective than the guards themselves; and the NPRA—not the DOC—was developing programming. The prison ran smoothly essentially because the prisoners were in charge of the day-to-day mechanics of the prison, and they wanted it to run smoothly. Goldmark knew this could change at any moment; despite Bishop's good work and Boone's well-reasoned strategy, the prisoners, not the department, controlled the climate of the prison.

CERTIFYING THE UNION

On March 22, while the public was still wrangling with the key questions inherent in this conflict—Were the prisoners really the "bad guys"? Were the guards responsible for the violence within the prisons? Was prison reform necessary or was it a costly, ruinous misadventure?—the *Boston Globe* finally—albeit incorrectly—reported on the NPRA struggle with the National Labor Relations Board for union certification. In fact, the NLRB was involved only as an interested observer wary of the SLRC's impending decision. Prisoners were quoted as explaining that since they worked for and were paid by the state, to produce goods or to operate the institutions, they were de facto state employees and therefore entitled to union recognition.[359] Suddenly new questions were added to the list: The imprisoned were employees? Entitled to minimum wage? The prison was full of laborers simply asking for recognition and a fair wage? The fact that they were convicted criminals was secondary to the reality that they were workers? Engagement of the "average" citizen in a conversation about prison reform was central to the NPRA strategy. By applying for SLRC certification, the NPRA had opened the window on another whole set of possibilities the public had not yet considered.

DIVISIONS DEEPEN

The United States was slipping further and further into a crippling recession. President Nixon had slashed the budget for the federal summer-jobs program for youth, and cuts to Comprehensive Employment Training Act (CETA) funds resulted in the unemployment of 5,000 youth across the country.[360] The Model Cities Program in Boston was cut by 52 percent. Jobs were scarce. As many young people faced the probability they'd be without much-needed employment the coming summer,

Commissioner Boone began disciplinary hearings for guards involved in the walkout on March 9.[361]

On March 21, responding to the state supreme court ruling two days before, more of the DOC staff had reported to work. If they had expected to return to their jobs, they were disappointed. None of the guards were allowed to have direct contact with prisoners, and only one out of four was allowed to work at all. All of the guards were mandated to undergo retraining, in which they would be expected to learn the newly published rules and regulations. Some of the staff were reassigned away from Walpole. Out of the 250 guards who stayed out on strike, 111 had been notified that they would be summoned before Boone for the disciplinary hearings. Since Boone had the power to fire staff, the guards' union president, Howard Doyle, had warned, "If they fire one employee, there will be a new day in Massachusetts for public employees. We'll show them what's going to happen." This time Goldmark defended the commissioner, explaining, "There is great resentment on both sides, and it is going to take a carefully phased supervised, step by step building process to enable the guard force to return."[362]

Even though Goldmark defended Boone, the division within the Sargent administration deepened. Sargent remained loyal to Boone, but others, particularly Goldmark, felt that the highly publicized volatility of the prisons was a great liability to the administration.[363] Goldmark struggled under the tension between what was good for the administration and what was necessary for prison reform. Since Porelle's resignation, Goldmark had turned down four candidates for the Walpole superintendent position and Boone had rejected the only candidate Goldmark had approved.[364] Goldmark decided he could no longer support Boone: "His judgment was gone. Again I come back to the superintendent issue. Very important for me. Nominating four turkeys and lost the guy who could do it."[365] Boone had a substantially different take on the issue.

> I never seriously entertained hiring this favorite candidate of Goldmark's, because he wanted more money than I was able to pay. The reason that I did not nominate the fellow was because it was not realistic to believe that I could pay his salary, which was substantially more than the salary I was being paid as Commissioner. Goldmark was anxious for me to arrange to pay him, through some combination of the statutory salary and funds from the LEAA, and possibly private funds. There were several reasons why I was unwilling to do this. One was that I was dubious about the legality of the scheme. Another was that I knew that the media and the guard union were just waiting for me to make a mistake like that, in order to try to blow me out of the water with one shot.[366]

Boone had been called a carpetbagger, a nigger, and a coon. Some of his staff had refused to work for him because he was Black, and now it seemed as if Goldmark wanted Boone to arrange for someone on staff to receive an illegally paid salary nearly double his own, which could give the governor the pretext to fire him. Goldmark wanted a "way out" while demonstrating that his community corrections plan was viable. No longer believing that Boone could deliver, Goldmark and others pressured Sargent to fire him.

The Massachusetts legislature was in session throughout the lockdown and the NPRA tenure at Walpole. When the guards walked off the job, the conservative legislators began to maneuver support to repeal Chapter 777. The bill had barely been enacted; the implementation plan was still in its developmental phase; and the legislature had not approved funding for prison reform; yet, the legislators pointed to the guard-fabricated *Herald* articles as evidence that prison reform was a failure. If the legislature voted to repeal, Sargent would be forced to use his veto. He might have prevailed, but the fight in the legislature would probably have involved chipping away at the bill with harassing amendments.[367]

CHANGE OF THE GUARD

Fifteen of the former Walpole guards were cleared to return to work beginning March 24. They refused to accept their assignments, claiming that prisoners had threatened them. Following their lead, 18 civilian employees (teachers, social workers, administrative support) refused to go to work because they, too, were afraid.[368] Rebutting the *Herald*'s emerging portrait of the predator prisoner, the *Globe* quoted the prisoners' response—part reassurance and part warning: "It's nice and quiet now and nothing will happen until they let the guards back in. This place has been running smoothly without them."[369]

The guards had reason to be nervous about returning. The prison was very different. Since the DOC had recognized the NPRA as the representative of the prisoners, the guards' union was no longer the only union to be reckoned with. Complicating matters, the NPRA was running aspects of the prison that the guards had never been responsible for, such as the school, conflict resolution, counseling, and conditions of confinement. Thus, the prisoners' capabilities demonstrated how inadequate the current "correctional" workforce was. The NPRA board hoped that the guards would engage in antiunion activities against the NPRA and prepared to file union-busting complaints against the guards' union. To avoid the same charges, the NPRA never took on custodial or "security" work. They focused on service provision, government, health, education, conflict resolution, and communication.

The NPRA's success increased the pressure on the guards. Adding to that pressure, there were now civilian observers on hand. Many of the returning staff had abused their power during the lockdown, and they were keenly aware of the implications of the prisoners' newly enacted agency. Offering a multitude of excuses, the guards stalled, refusing to return to their posts until the NPRA was dismantled. Again, because of the protections of their union contract, Boone could not easily fire these guards. This created a paradox for Boone. If the commissioner were to be taken seriously, he had to be able to name his staff and control the prison. With the NPRA running the prison, staff could not take their posts, and when the guards were at their posts, the prison was in chaos.

CASE STUDIES IN SABOTAGE: HURST AND SUBILOSKY

Two incidents occurred at Walpole during the NPRA's tenure that reflected badly on the DOC and focused negative media attention on Commissioner Boone. Neither involved the NPRA, but both gave opponents of prison reform additional ammunition to question Boone's correctional philosophy. The first incident involved the transfer of a federal prisoner, William Hurst. The second was the escape of Joseph Subilosky while on furlough.

William "Whitey" Hurst had just been convicted of murder in Massachusetts, but was awaiting transfer to a federal prison to serve an outstanding federal sentence before he could begin his Massachusetts sentence. Hurst had a long history of escapes and was considered a flight risk.[370] On March 24, Frank Kelly was the afternoon-shift coordinator for the OP.[371] He informed all the observers who would be in 10 Block that William Hurst was in bed with a herniated disk.

David Gagne, one of the observers, reported that guards had come through the block and removed all brooms and mops from the unit as if they were expecting trouble and did not want any potential weapons around. Later, a federal marshal, a cadet trainee, and four other guards entered the unit. The marshal was carrying handcuffs and chains. The cadet trainee and one guard cleared the corridor of observers while the marshal entered Hurst's cell. Hurst was indeed lying on his bed. The observers and prisoners who could see into the cell testified that the marshal informed Hurst that he was being transferred to USP Danbury, in Connecticut. Hurst explained that he could not get up; one prisoner reported that he asked for a stretcher to take him out. The marshal had one of the guards call for medical clearance. Clearance was obtained; the marshal asked Hurst to get up again and Hurst refused. A guard was heard calling for gas; he was told that none was available. Then the observers heard five minutes of punching and moaning. Prisoners reported that the marshal beat Hurst across the face with the chains. The other guards entered Hurst's cell and joined in the beating. The prisoners began throwing things from their cells to get the attention of the observers and to distract the guards from beating William Hurst. When it was over, Hurst was led out in his boxer shorts, bleeding from his head and face. According to observer reports, the guards were covered with Hurst's blood; one guard's fist and arm dripped with blood. Bloodstains spattered the bed sheets, blankets, and wall.

The observers called for the commissioner, who happened to be in the prison. Boone arrived immediately, called the state police, and asked them to intercept the transportation van to check on the status of the prisoner and get him medical attention, but his order was disregarded. The next day the *Globe* reported that a state police spokesman had explained that the van had not been stopped because Hurst's injuries were minor.[372] This incident reflected poorly on Boone. He was in the prison but not present when Hurst was brutalized, even though his long experience in corrections would have indicated that guards often took advantage of such "routine" transfers to assault prisoners, and with Hurst considered a flight risk, it was all the more likely. And as a demonstration of law enforcement's disrespect for the commissioner, his concern for the prisoner and his direct orders to intercept the transportation vehicle were ignored.

Neither the *Globe* nor the *Herald* focused on the extensive injuries Hurst sustained. Rather, both papers reported that three corrections officers were treated at Norwood Hospital for injuries after a "scuffle." The three guards who claimed injury in Hurst's beating were among those who clocked in each day but refused to take their posts inside the prison.[373] Norfolk County DA George Burke capitalized on the guards' injuries, using them to support the claim that the entire prison workforce needed to return to work as a unit: "The guards have talked to me and said they would feel secure only if the whole shift could go in. They said they can operate as a shift because that's what they're used to."[374]

The Hurst beating had a profound effect on all the observers present. In a sense, they lost their innocence. They could not forget the terrifying dull thuds of the blows on Hurst's body. They were outraged, concerned for Hurst's well-being, and angry that the guards got away with it. Determined to do something about it, they all wrote affidavits about the incident, which were then fashioned into a report by Dyche Freeman, an Episcopal priest and the archivist for the OP.[375] One of the observers, William Homans, was a lawyer; he asserted that a crime had occurred.

The next day, Ryan's husband, William, sent Burke a telegram urging that the "bloody bedding and towels in the cell of William Hurst cell 25 block 10 should be secured as evidence immediately." Referring to Homans's assessment of the beating, he concluded that the cell was a crime scene and should be preserved as such.[376]

Boone reacted to the assault by disciplining the offending officers. Walter Waitkevich had replaced Bishop as Walpole's acting superintendent on March 22, two days before the incident. This was a huge loss to the NPRA. Bishop understood that working with the NPRA was the most efficient solution to Walpole's problems. Waitkevich, on the other hand, was inexperienced at leadership and sympathetic to the guards' union. Boone sent him the following memo:

> At approximately 5 PM on Saturday March 24, 1973, an incident occurred in Block 10 at MCI Walpole which causes me to take the following action. In addition to the disciplinary charges already pending, I am sending a letter to ... Jesse Motta, Robert Euarts, [and] Rene Saulnier which indicates that they are also subject to disciplinary action because of their alleged involvement in an assault on a federal prisoner that was being held in Block 10 at MCI Walpole. I have instructed these officers to submit a report to my office by the end of the day of March 26, 1973, which describes in detail the events which took place during the transfer of inmate William

Hurst to a federal institution and the part which each of them played in those events. Further, I have made the US federal marshal for the eastern district aware of this action and have asked him to investigate the involvement of Federal Marshal Henry Lopez III. Finally, I have notified the DA of Norfolk County of this incident because of possible criminal violation.

cc. Officers Motta, Saulnier, Euarts, Chief Federal Marshal and DA Norfolk County.[377]

A copy of this memo is in Ryan's file. If Ryan had a copy, so did the NPRA leadership. Boone's response was swift, but it still fell short of advocates' expectations. They had hoped that the commissioner would call for an independent inquiry; instead, he had requested action from parties who would clearly not act against the guards' union. Neither the district attorney's office nor the federal marshal looked into the incident at all. The observers had gained important experience: they learned that prison authorities could engage in criminal activity with scant repercussions. The guards were suspended for a few days, but they did not lose their jobs, nor did they face prosecution; instead they were portrayed as injured in the line of duty. The observers could file their copious reports and talk endlessly to the press, but even the statement of a respected lawyer could not force accountability.

While William Ryan was sending his telegram and the observers were compiling their statements, Joseph Subilosky failed to return from furlough.[378] Subilosky had been convicted of murder, but that did not make him ineligible for furlough. Raymond Porelle had recommended Subilosky for a furlough because he had worked in Porelle's home and had "always been responsible." The furlough board had approved him in December 1972, before the lockdown. Both Bishop and Boone had signed off on the furlough. Bishop received a letter on March 21 from Sheriff Buckley in Worcester County asking the DOC to deny Subilosky's furlough, but he decided to approve it anyway, presumably because Bishop believed it was the furlough board who should control the furlough process, not the sheriff or the DA. When Walter Anderson drew Boone's attention to the sheriff's letter, Boone faced a very real conflict. He fundamentally opposed using the furlough program as a means of behavior modification. For Boone, such programs were meant to reduce crime through rehabilitation, not reward institutional behavior. The decoupling of program accessibility from classification underpinned his correctional philosophy, which made his programs different from others around the country.

Nonetheless, Boone decided that, given the pressure he was under, he could not afford to override the Worcester County official's request. On March 24, the same day guards violently removed Hurst from Walpole, Boone had instructed Waitkevich to cancel the furlough. Yet Waitkevich did not remove Subilosky's papers from the envelope of approved furloughs. Compounding the error, Anderson then failed to review the papers. On March 25, Subilosky was allowed to leave.[379]

Subilosky had always cooperated with Porelle, and he was not involved with the NPRA. Many prisoners thought that his approval for furlough in December was a bribe for continued cooperation with the prison administration. The NPRA leadership suspected that the officials who "overlooked" his paperwork were aware that he would not return and allowed the furlough anyway. If this analysis is correct, it is important for two reasons: Waitkevich demonstrated within two days of his appointment that he was willing to sacrifice Boone, and it was not until 1974, while being interviewed for the Kennedy School of Government report, that he accepted responsibility.[380] With full knowledge that he had not followed the commissioner's directions, he allowed Boone to twist in the wind, suffering public scorn in the media. As they would 15 years later with Willie Horton, the press honed in on the escape, talking only about this one failure, rather than about the success of this broadly applied program.

At the time, however, the commissioner did not notice where the chain of command had broken, putting at risk not just Boone's tenure, but also his correctional philosophy: prison depopulation. A furlough program was central to any depopulation plan.

But at Walpole, furloughs also signified cooperation with the administration. Many years later, Ralph Hamm reflected on how the furlough program operated at Walpole prison.

When John O. Boone introduced the concept of furloughs to the Massachusetts Department of Correction through chapter 777, I looked upon them with skepticism. On the one hand I saw them as an opportunity for prisoners to maintain ties with their families, as well as a great reintegration tool. On the other hand, I also saw them as a coercive administration tool to break the collective bargaining back of the NPRA (i.e., as a lure and incentive to pull prisoners away from the philosophy of the NPRA, and break the unity and collective resistance of the program). But being of the frame of mind not to dissuade prisoners from taking advantage of a perceived opportunity, I supported the furlough program. I never asked for a furlough because of my belief that if I did so it would co-opt my integrity. This belief later found support when F_____ was afforded a furlough, and gained the notoriety of being an informant for the guards' union, and the prison administration (this perception of him was exacerbated by the fact that on several occasions immediately after NPRA board meetings, he had to be physically extracted from the deputy superintendent's office or from the presence of guard union reps where he was overheard discussing the immediate NPRA business). Both the F_____ and the Subilosky furloughs were looked upon by myself, and unanimously by the BANTU board of directors, as a setup to undermine Commissioner Boone by the established white prison administration in collusion with the white guards' union, on the hope that they would escape, or at least generate adverse publicity in the media (*Boston Herald*, in particular) once the [escapes] were leaked.[381]

On April 4, Sargent asked Lieutenant Governor Donald Dwight to tour Walpole. Dwight met with prison officials and spent most of the time discussing the controversial furlough program. The NPRA also met with Dwight, and its leaders voiced their concern that Subilosky's failure to return from furlough might jeopardize not only the furlough program, but also the burgeoning success of the prisoners' union. At the press conference held after his visit, Dwight addressed the furlough program. He was careful to note that he was "pleased by lack of tension inside of the prison."[382]

That day conservative legislators filed legislation that would curb the furlough program by prohibiting the participation of prisoners sentenced to life without the possibility of parole or probation. In response, Boone froze all furloughs from Walpole, pending a review of the approval process.

Governor Sargent, on the other hand, demonstrated his commitment to Boone and his thoughtful support of the reform project, calling the furlough program the state's most important correctional reform. He turned the safety argument around, declaring,

> The stakes, the risks to public safety are too high to abandon it.... On the whole it is clear that the furlough program is working and that the myth of failure is false.... When we speak of reform ... we are not out to coddle the criminal, to make his stay in our institutions an easy one. What we are trying to do is guarantee the public safety.... For every criminal who serves out his sentence unrehabilitated, up to five crimes can be committed on the public.... You cannot pen an individual up in isolation from society and then one day open the gate, end the isolation, and expect him to be able to cope with all the forces of society.[383]

Subilosky's escape gave Norfolk County district attorney George Burke just the opening he desired. He used his power to investigate the Subilosky escape to try to discredit the NPRA, the AHC, and the Observer Program. On April 10, Burke issued a brief report on the Subilosky escape. The investigators demonstrated that they were investigating Boone's correctional policies, not the failed furlough. They asked each administrator if he knew about and approved of the participation of each ex-con in the Observer Program, insinuating that it was their presence alone that resulted in Subilosky's escape. Burke's investigators also accused the women who headed CAR-CAP of performing illicit sexual acts on prisoners.[384] Furthermore, the report suggested that Walpole was an arsenal of prison-made and observer-trafficked weapons, guns, and drugs.

Burke held a press conference announcing that Walter Anderson and John Boone were responsible. In reviewing the published report, the *Boston Globe* made much of the fact that Burke had never interviewed Boone in the process of his investigation.[385]

The NPRA wasted no time in responding to Burke. The same day the report was released, prisoners held a press conference at Walpole, during which shotgun-toting guards stood outside the administration building. The NPRA leadership challenged Burke to shake down the prison. Speaking for the NPRA, Dellelo offered the following:

> We are now saying, as elected representatives of the inmate body, that we wish a lockup in our cells for a forty-eight hour period if District Attorney Burke, accompanied by correctional officers, third-party observers, and one member of the NPRA per shake-down team, would shake down for the alleged arms, drugs, food stashes, and other forms of contraband.[386]

Consciously baiting the DA, Dellelo went on to remind Burke that "Public officials have the obligation to protect the men of this prison from political subversion and erroneous allegations."[387]

As Dellelo remembers it,

> The prisoners went crazy when they heard we had offered to lock down. They were in an uproar. We had to go around and explain it to them. I knew Burke would never do a shakedown if we were "offering" to lock down. And it gave us great publicity. We looked credible and sane in the media.[388]

In fact, the *Globe* threw down the gauntlet with an editorial supporting the prisoners in their request for a voluntary shakedown, just after publishing the article questioning Burke's report on the Subilosky escape.[389] Burke rejoined, as if on cue:

> Any search that is conducted will be conducted by my office and the state police. The terms will not be set by the prisoners.... It would take a month's time to conduct a thorough shakedown at Walpole and the inmates would have to be confined during that period.

Burke even went so far as to refer to the Porelle-instituted shakedown that had resulted in the Kwanzaa lockdown and documented prisoner abuse—as a "model" of what was necessary. Hamm's response was brief: "I wish the politicians would get out of corrections."[390]

9

SOUL CONTRABAND

observers witness terror and change

> *Only a "soul search" will ever detect this powerful con-*
> *traband which so seriously threatens the security which*
> *society has demanded of its agents, the guards. The*
> *system we have devised to maintain security has so*
> *dehumanized the men and women to whom we have*
> *delegated this responsibility that they are rendered in-*
> *capable of detecting this hazardous commodity.*
>
> *Soul contraband, as I have come to see it, takes*
> *various forms and manifestations. 1) Love, the so-*
> *lidifying, unifying power enhanced as men acknowl-*
> *edge that they suffer from a common oppressor.*[391]
>
> —Frank Kelly, "A Confession"

FRANK KELLY, A GRADUATE OF BOSTON COLLEGE, CLASS OF 1950, owned a printing company and lived in a "typical" suburban community.[392] The year before the Ad Hoc Committee was formed, Kelly decided to sell a half share of his business so that he could be free to "direct concentrated effort into the field of improvements or changes in our society that I felt necessary."[393] Kelly, like many of the AHC volunteers, was white, middle-class, and college educated. He was also different from most in that he was middle-aged, while many of the other volunteers were either college students or retirees. A businessman, he showed up at the prison in a suit and tie. For the time the Observer Program existed, he dedicated his entire life to it, as did Ed Rodman, Lou Brinn, Obalaji Rust, and Doug Butler. Kelly's experiences at Walpole became the basis of his "Confession," a 62-page memoir of the period. He describes what happened inside Walpole, what he felt, and how the prisoners affected him. After his first two nights in the prison, he had breakfast with the prisoners, who shared a serious grievance with him.

> Since the lockup on the 29th day of December, they had not had access to either the shops or the avocation shops. The avocation shops, I have learned, provide a substantial source of income … earned from the production of products such as woodwork, leatherwork and jewelry. On their first admission to the avocation areas on the previous day they had found extensive damage to much material of their personal property, missing or destroyed.[394]

Kelly understood the avocations as small business ventures. He learned that the avocations allowed the prisoners to maintain their positions in their families. Even though these men were separated from their families, they were able to make vital contributions to their loved ones. The money they sent home relieved pressure on marriages strained by long incarcerations and was a direct, purposeful link to the lives they had been separated from.

As Black men steeped in the Black Consciousness movement, Obalaji Rust, Doug Butler, and Ed Rodman knew that the prison system was simply a nationalized version of slavery; they knew that the abolition of prisons in the United States was inextricably tied to the liberty of all Africans in the diaspora. They saw an opening at Walpole, a way to tangibly and, remarkably, challenge an overpoweringly oppressive system. They put their shoulders to the wall along with the prisoners in BANTU and the NPRA with the understanding that the wall, the prison itself, was the tangible manifestation of the same doctrine of white supremacy that underpinned the US Constitution that legalized their own enslavement. They had no interest in upholding the rules that maintained this oppressive institution.

Kelly, on the other hand, often sympathized with both the guards and the prisoners. When he was in Walpole, he saw the prisoners as law-abiding men trying to make the best of very dire circumstances. Conversely, he saw many of the guards as rule breakers and troublemakers. He wanted the rules adhered to, he wanted the reporting to be accurate, and he wanted to do a good job.

Like the majority of the observers, Kelly initially had no idea what his role in the prison might become, but Rodman's training and daily memos made it very clear what the observers were not to do. They were not to hold keys, they were not to discipline, they were not to argue with the guards or give orders to the prisoners, and they were not to talk to the press. Like many people who sign on to "help others," Kelly wanted a voice; he wanted his impressions of what was happening in the prison heard. But the members of the NPRA and CARCAP were going to have to live with the outcome of whatever happened in Walpole. Theirs were the voices that needed to be amplified and heard. So Ryan did not play along. All press statements were coordinated by the NPRA with the assistance of Phyllis Ryan. Dellelo remembers Ryan's dedication.

> I don't know how she did it because she was so sick. But I could call her any time of the day or night and get a statement out or get a legislator up here. Ryan was solid and you just couldn't get in her way. With a cigarette in her hand and a telephone, she was like a moving freight train. She was a great woman.[395]

When the first observers entered the prison, they listened to the pent-up frustration of a group of men who had endured three months of threats, abuse, and isolation from the outside world. Initially, the observers visited each block, talking to each prisoner. They spent considerable time in Blocks 9 and 10, where prisoners had been segregated for 72 days. Obalaji Rust entered the prison with the first shift and stayed inside almost all of the following two weeks.[396] During this time, he interviewed and recorded the condition of all the men in 9 and 10 Blocks. He reported:

> Not one man with whom I spoke had received a hearing [to determine their ultimate release from punitive segregation]; yet the official pretenses for placing men on the Block are highly suspect, particularly in the cases of so-called protective custody. Incredible abuses, described in these notes, took place during Porelle's lockup. The men are still being beaten, one man spent seven days in the Blue Room under 24-hour confinement. Almost all the men are under 24-hour confinement, deprived of even an hour a day or so of exercise. Perhaps most important, the men are receiving enormous amount of tranquilizers every day which they readily use to help sleep in order to retain their sanity.[397]

After their first week in the prison, the civilian observers compiled a list of the things they heard most often from the prisoners about the conditions there.[398] Top on the list were the "fear of being beaten or thrown into the 'hole'" and "failure of the guards to respond to their needs (such as toilet paper, a mattress for the bed, etc)." These two points of concern, violence and neglect, had defined Raymond Porelle's entire tenure. The prisoners voiced their desire for programs that promoted respect and dignity and ended in real jobs, not just "dead ends."

Although observers offered a caveat at the end of the list—"they did say that they were not talking about all the guards"—by far, the vast majority of complaints centered on the guards' behavior. The guards were not held accountable to any professional standards, they had no rules to follow, and they had ultimate authority to harass and torture the prisoners. Some of these guards continued working on the blocks and being paid even though Boone had suspended them. The prisoners described being sprayed with fire extinguishers and being left locked behind solid steel doors rather than the customary grates. Guards would cut off the electricity, leaving them in the dark for long periods of time; deny them showers; and put things in the food.

Undoubtedly, the guards' absence allowed for the development of a more creative atmosphere. Observer 203 quoted a prisoner in the maximum security section of Walpole as saying, "Can you believe this? A maximum security prison functioning without screws! And working better without them. When they left, most of the tension left with them."[399]

TELLING THE TERROR, RECORDING LIBERATION

As the observers acclimated to the environment of Walpole, they realized that the extent of abuse, the condition of the prison, the experiences reported first-hand by the prisoners, and their own impressions as observers needed to be documented and preserved. Three decades later, thanks to Phyllis Ryan and Ed Rodman, six large boxes of handwritten observer statements still preserve what they witnessed.

The early statements taken by the first 400 observers testify to inhuman depravity of a purely punitive environment. Dyche Freeman, the Observer Program's archivist, crafted them into a report documenting the events of the first few weeks of the OP and the testimony of the prisoners.

The observers were overwhelmed with the concrete reality of what they would describe as a "concentration camp." They spoke with men who were on the brink of starvation after nearly three months of one meager meal a day—often something as paltry as reconstituted dry milk with cornflakes. They walked through blocks where toilets had been turned off and human excrement mingled with blood on the walls. They saw men who had not showered in three months because they refused to enter the shower area in the cell at the end of the floor; it was common practice for guards to lock in the rest of the prisoners, leaving the showering prisoner naked, vulnerable, in the presence of guards, and out of view of any who might defend him.[400] One observer reports,

> The conditions of Block 9 can be described as deplorable and representative of all that is wrong in correctional institutions. Broken windows, human defecation on the floor, 4 feet of trash in the corridor and open fires in inmates cells represent a general lack of control. The highest priority in this institution should be to clean Block 9 to the point where a healthy living standard exists.[401]

The prisoners were forced to wash their clothes in their sinks and toilets. Each cell had both a solid steel door and a grate. The steel door was used to visually isolate a prisoner. They had spent days behind these solid steel doors, hearing the whispered voices of guards talking about them drifting in through the vents of the cells—almost intelligible. A walkway behind the cells offered prison personnel access to the plumbing and electrical hookups for each cell. Guards would move along this walkway, shutting off water and electricity and using the vents to spray water, fire extinguishers, and gas directly into the cells. The harassment, the use of darkness and chemical assault, took a severe psychological toll on many of the prisoners. When the doors were finally opened, angry, fearful, and hollow-eyed men emerged.

It took a couple of weeks for prisoners to tell the worst aspects of their experience. The observers were struck by the lack of hostility and the numbness of the prisoners and outraged by what they heard. Over 30 years later, many of these men reported they were still affected by post-traumatic stress disorder. "Yeah, it was bad. If you have questions, I can answer them—I just can't think about it. It hurts too much."

Many people had invested their hearts and intellect in the reform project. As profound as Boone's success was, the utter tragedy behind the walls of Walpole took its toll on all who were involved. These first 400 observers saw the prison at its worst. They saw the filth and the blood and they were challenged. On March 20, one observer produced a long statement that confirmed the worst reports received by the AHC.

> Inmate gg Maximum Block gave me the following: Guards (lists 13) and others beat him up so badly on January 28 1973 at 11:30 PM with blackjacks, nightsticks, feet and fists. As a result of this beating he had to be hospitalized for a week and a half.
>
> Federal prisoner gg was gassed with 2½ cans of mace, beaten and thrown naked into the blue room (the hole) for seven days.
>
> Inmate cc said that on Jan. 21, 73 officer A came up and said Prs cc you are going downstairs. The guards, OO, a Bridgewater guard, and I, threw Pris cc back onto his bed and pinned him down while guards PP and NN beat pris cc and then senior officer QQ was present when guard OO hit inmate cc 5 times on the left side of his face and he was also hit with a club from behind. Then senior officer A sprayed a can of mace into prisoner cc's face. They threw cc in the hole and the other inmates shouted to yell for a medic for cc. Approximately ½ hour later a medic whose nickname is RR came and treated cc's eyes. Officer A also refused to give cc either a mattress or a blanket.
>
> Inmate ccc was maced 3 weeks ago. Senior officer QQ sprayed ccc. [Four guards] were the other guards who beat cc and inmate gg.
>
> Inmate gg had his left hand baby finger nearly severed by a guard who slammed the 4" thick steel cell door on it. gg almost got his hand back in. It was 9 days before gg was seen by the prison doctor. If the doctor came into Block [X] the old line guard would close gg's cell door so he wouldn't be able to call to the doctor. This happened on 2/19/73 and the medics who looked at his finger said it was not broken. Yet 9 days later and many request slips later, requesting that he be seen by the doctor, inmate gg was finally X-rayed and the doctor found his finger broken and knocked him

unconscious and set his finger on March 1, 1973.... Senior officer U was in charge and did nothing to help gg.[402]

Reports similar to this fill the folders.

COMMENTS OF THE OBSERVERS: MARCH 8 TO MARCH 26

Over and over reports from the first two weeks describe the prison as "calm." The prisoners seized the opportunity to introduce the observers to their world. They told the observers what they were proud of.

> By far the most encouraging thing I saw was the computer program. The residents who explained this to me emphasized repeatedly that they devised and implemented this program themselves [in spring of 1972].... The residents describe a mere 4% recidivism rate among those who have participated.... Even the atmosphere of the computer rooms is different, since residents designed everything themselves to create a warm, human environment.... From what other residents and guards told me, the computer program should only be seen as a beginning. More money and more programs like it are needed. More full time teachers, residents, and outsiders alike are needed badly.[403]

They also gave physical form to the depravation of incarceration.

> The thought of facing a lifetime in these animal cages is staggering. If the punishment is being here, being deprived of freedom, then it's hard to justify the day to day harassment, uncertainty over rules and rights and the procedures that give guards authority over every aspect of a man's life. In such a format, abuse in inevitable.[404]

Rodman had wagered that if he prepared the observers to be objective and threw them in the middle of the conflict between the kept and the keepers, ordinary citizens would get it. As Rodman expected, the enforced neutrality politicized the volunteers. Most of the observers that I have interviewed continue to hold an anti-prison position. Many remain outright abolitionists.[405]

> The atmosphere was so relaxed—not at all what I expected. I find that my own thinking has been so conditioned by society and the media. These men are not animals, they are not dangerous maniacs. I found my own fears were really groundless.[406]

The observers expected bitterness and anger; instead, they found men whose primary concern was reconnecting with their families. As the prisoners began to tell the stories of the beatings and the starvation, the observers reacted, with one observer asserting, "It is imperative that none of the personnel formerly in Block 9 ever return. It's worth paying them to retire. The guards are the security problem."[407]

CADET TRAINEES: A NEW LABOR FORCE

When the guards were out on strike, the cadet trainees remained on the job because they were not covered in the guards' union contract. Boone decided these young men of color would work with the NPRA leadership. The observers also watched with interest as the cadet trainees entered the prison; these men had been prepared to assume their positions through Jim Isenberg's training program. They arrived prepared to treat the "residents" with dignity, and it made a huge difference. "Prisoners report that the new part-time guards are great, good guys, you can sit and talk with them and they treat you like gentlemen."[408] Isenberg credits the success of the cadet trainees to Gary Robinson, who was a special assistant to Boone. Robinson was born and raised in Roxbury, a borough of Boston that was then predominantly Black. He understood both the racial tension within the prison and the "peculiar" problem that prison itself presented. He worked with the cadet trainees, giving them an intellectual framework to understand the prisoners' struggle as well as the interpersonal and professional skills necessary to do their jobs.

A profile of some of the cadet trainee guards later published in the *Globe* reveals that the cadet trainees themselves were not typical prison guards. Warren Greene, who was 27 years old and lived in Cambridge, had never been inside a prison before mid-March. "I really felt I could do something to better the system," he said of his decision to take the job. "In the past there has been a problem between the officer and the inmate, but with care and custody, which will be my job, there is also having a good relationship with inmates." Scott Bishop, a 25-year-old graduate of Rhode Island College, had worked as a social worker in the Department of Youth Services. Bishop described his job as "giving constant service to the inmates. You can really see how society fails sometimes to provide adequate outlets for hostilities." Myles Lawton, a 28-year-old construction worker from the Dorchester neighborhood of Boston, discussed the role model that the corrections officer had to offer: "I have to let the inmate know I'm no better than he is but still keep proper custody, security and respect. I've got to be the type of individual who can get to know the inmate and be able to sit down with him and talk." Mark Richardson, a 26-year-old graduate of Holy Cross University who hailed from Worcester, showed how different the cadet trainee guards were from the line guards: "I have to be somebody an inmate can come to if he's got a problem. You are the intermediary who can get them to places where they can get the proper help." Finally, Willie Burks, a 26-year-old Boston resident, explained that the job transcended work on the blocks: "keeping an eye on things, breaking up fights, opening and closing doors and also helping the inmates on parole and furloughs and getting them involved in programs in and out of the institution."

Many of these men were drawn to the job by the promise of Boone's idealism and reforms. Tony Van Der Meer was another of the cadet trainees. Thirty years later, now an Africana Studies professor at the University of Massachusetts, he testified at Ralph Hamm's parole hearing, describing the important role that Hamm played in stabilizing the prison and the affect that being a cadet guard at Walpole had had on Van Der Meer's professional life.

The observers engaged the cadet trainees in conversation. They wanted to know what the cadet trainees' take was. "Were the prisoners exaggerating?" "Did they believe that the problem rested with the guards?" Over and over, the answer from cadet trainees as well as seasoned guards from other prisons was uncomplicated and direct.

> The two trainees (K and L) are relating to the prisoners without great difficulty and feel they have established a rapport with the inmates, despite the fact that they have been at Walpole but briefly. And that they are, substantially, without training. They do not feel that the prisoners are attempting to cause problems in the prison, and that much if not all of the problems are caused by Corrections Officers. They are not afraid for their physical safety. Despite the fact that a prisoner told K that the guards who were stabbed "deserved it," he understands what the prisoners mean by this and that if he simply treats them like human beings, there is no danger in "deserving it."[409]

Most of the cadet trainees were young men of color who were willing to establish a rapport with the prisoners. They saw this as a crucial moment in the prison, and themselves as actors in the reform project. From the time they entered the prison, they were firm supporters of the NPRA and the Observer Program.

> Puerto Rican trainee guards have been in Block [Y] for the past 5 days, and the old hard-line no-change screws were out on their illegal strike, that conditions have greatly improved. These minority guards have treated the inmates as men, not caged animals. There have been no beatings.[410]

The cadet trainees were not the only guards in the prison; corrections officers were also brought over from Bridgewater State Hospital. It had been less than a decade since the documentary film *Titicut Follies* had exposed the horrors of Bridgewater, so it's perhaps unexpected that both the prisoners and the observers felt that the Bridgewater guards were significantly more professional and better prepared to work within Walpole than their predecessors had been.

RUMORS: BOONE HAS RESIGNED

On March 18, the guards' union claimed that Boone had resigned. The day began with observers remarking on the transformations that had taken place at Walpole in the space of the few short days. One observer made the following note.

> Striking changes since Thursday, 15 March. The floors and walls were being cleaned of their two-months pile-up of filth and refuse; personal belongings had been brought to the inmates; Bridgewater trainees ("dynamite guys") were serving as guards and four inmates had been released. Another one had been freed as a block "runner," and several other prisoners

were walking about. The men had showers. One inmate gave the NPRA credit for all this.[411]

Another observer began the day eating breakfast with the prisoners. He recorded the following impressions of their conversation.

> The topic of conversation is still the same—the guards vs. the inmates and how well things are going without the guards. Toward the end a deputy joined us and the inmates were perfectly willing to talk with him (at least the few I was eating with). He seemed to be fairly straight with the inmates and they in turn gave him more respect than is normally given a guard.
>
> Some of the improvements are seemingly minor to an outsider, but are meaningful to the men. Last night's dinner was just hot dogs and beans, but the hot dogs were grilled instead of boiled. The inmates told me that it was the first time they'd seen grilled hot dogs in at least six months. In this place they seem to have removed almost all the pleasures of life. One of the few remaining is the pleasure of eating. If you remove this, too, a man has nothing left.[412]

After the prisoners caught wind of the rumor that the commissioner had resigned, tension began to build. The prisoners appreciated the job that the NPRA was doing but they knew that without Boone, all that they had gained would be lost. According to Dellelo,

> This is the most frustrating thing about corrections and why prisons must be abolished. You can make strides and you can have great reform. Programs that work very well can be developed and then the administration shifts and it is all out the window. You can never count on really developing anything. Nothing at all. I have seen really good programs be put in place and then just dumped right when they are working. Look at all the educational programs. All the good things started by Boone and the NPRA, they were gone as soon as Boone left. We have never given up. You can't give up. But you have to realize you can't depend on anything. This is really the best argument for prison abolition.[413]

The old guard was quick to take advantage of the tale of Boone's resignation. An observer recorded a horrific beating. The shorthand report documents the most blatant of the rare abuses of power that took place during the three months the NPRA was in charge.

> Prisoner ? still out of cell, guards shake cell down, skin search, redressed, shake hands to start things right; tell him to shut up, other guards come in and knock his teeth out (cell 9, lower tier): put him in deadlock and walk off tier. Bleeding for 6-7 hours before doctors come; guard refused to open door when doctor wanted to take him out for treatment (no light in cell); argument with guard (finally shackled into wheelchair and taken to the

hospital. Three-four butterfly stitches over right brow and teeth removed); leg irons and cuffs removed before getting into chair.[414]

By 2:30 PM, the DOC had notified the prisoners that the commissioner did not intend to resign. An observer noted:

> Hopes for sustaining the more humane treatment instituted by Commissioner Boone run almost disconcertingly high—the expectation level being almost too much. Return of Walpole corrections officers is not only greeted with anxiety; these men find it hard to understand relaxation of suspension for law enforcement officers who have violated law. Meanwhile pride in the responsible self-discipline now being evidenced in the inmate community is very high. They are out to demonstrate they are responsible men.[415]

THE RETURN OF THE GUARDS

Later that day, the first set of cadet trainees who had been through the entire preparation program arrived. One observer wrote,

> New corrections officers came on the job and went to each man's cell introducing themselves and explaining that they did in fact plan to treat each of the inmates as human beings.... This demanded treating the inmate with respect. The guards also said that they expected to be treated the same way. Inmates commented that this phenomenon was indeed unique—that they had been treated previously in any way but a respectful one. They welcomed the responsibilities and obligations that this entailed.
> Every corrections officer that I met on the block treated myself and the inmates as gentlemen. These corrections officers talked about how they saw their roles—helping men by providing a model that could be respected and followed.[416]

Two days later, many of the old line staff returned to their jobs and the observers paid careful attention to the many ways that the guards attempted to destabilize the prison.

> An officer named A has been in 10 Block for the past two days. He has a history of being a trouble maker and appears to be back to his old petty tricks. One inmate referred to him as a "walking heat wave." He is also giving the trainee cadets in 10 Block counter-productive indoctrination.[417]

On their first day on the job, the returning guards spread rumors that one of the cadet trainees was a homosexual, and they placed four prisoners who had a history of fighting with each other in adjacent cells.[418] An observer wrote:

> Whoever put those four men together should be found out and had. The guards on duty said it was the front control. The four men are frightened

of continued mind fucking and harassment by the guard A who returned from the walkout three days ago.[419]

Other examples of guard harassment included offering bread to the inmates and then 45 minutes later offering them peanut butter, which was then denied them on the basis that they had refused the bread. Guards would also serve breakfast cereal without a bowl, or offer the milk at a later time. Prisoners also reported that guards would turn off the lights while the inmates were conducting meetings with their block representatives.

The guards increased tension by playing with the prisoner count. Before the guards had returned to work, the prisoners and the cadet trainees were taking count themselves. The few guards who were allowed to return to the cellblocks were placed in the maximum end of the prison, and by delaying or complicating counts, were often able to hold men in their cells well into the evening meal.[420] Several observers reported on the disruption of this daily ritual.

> According to one of the guard trainees the count was not held up last night, as it was tonight; however in two of the blocks the doors did not open. By the time these men got to dinner—the hall was closed. The trainee added that the guards were trying to aggravate the prisoners every way possible.[421]

> The most significant incident of my shift was the length [of] count—more than 2 hours. From 4:30 to 6:35 PM rather than the scheduled 40 minutes. Every inmate felt this delay was a deliberate harassment on the part of the guards in "control." There was a noticeable increase in inmate tension by the end of the count. At supper, inmate ss sought me out and asked me to record this remark: "This has been going on all week. They want something to happen."[422]

The guards put pressure on and picked fights with the trainees in the parking lot of the prison, calling them names.[423] Guards harassed observers as they exited the prison.[424] Some observers had their tires slashed. Ed Childs, a labor organizer who was helping draft the NPRA union contract, recalled that one night, the guards demanded to search his car. They took the seats out, then took the tires off. Not finding anything, they left the car with the seats and axles on the ground. Childs hitchhiked back to Boston.[425]

MEDICAL CRISIS

The observers documented both the overmedication of the prisoners and the way the guards would deny prisoners medical attention. Observers described protracted waits—sometimes for days or weeks—for prisoners to be seen for bone breaks, epilepsy, eye infections, and so on. Routinely, hours would go by before a prisoner received critical medical attention. This was especially true if a prisoner was placed in the "blue room" for punishment. The observers backed up prisoners' claims that the only way to see a doctor is to slash one's wrists or to get stabbed. The observers' reports document that many prisoners did indeed slash their wrists when they needed medical care or medication. Their actions were exacerbated by the fact that much of the population had become addicted to the painkiller Talwin. On March 20, the AHC brought in a medical doctor to evaluate the medical care the prisoners were receiving. He left pages of notes on the kinds of drugs prescribed and the levels of dosage. An observer, a doctor himself, made the following assessment:

> As a physician, I am impressed most with the apparent widespread use of drugs, largely tranquilizers and/or sedatives, but also mood elevators. The extensive prevalence (14 of 16 in one unit and 32 of 38 in another) of prescribed use is matched by the size of daily dosage.
>
> The dosages used here are not large in the therapeutic toxic ratio, but for the steady use by men in good health, they are indeed excessive and can be adjudged sufficient to modify judgment, perception, and relation of the person so medicated. A number of the inmates have suggested that they had their first drug experience in this prison, became dependent here.
>
> Drug use makes a pathologic situation worse and the victim sicker. Tranquilizers are most effective and most therapeutic in alleviating neurotic (ill-founded) fears, and are justified in long-term use only in such circumstances.
>
> In additional reactive anxiety (distress and intolerable anxiety in response to reality) the treatment of choice is to reduce the stressful situation, and should be possible in the controlled environment of the total institution. To dampen normal stress reactions to stressful situations only aggravates the pathologic state and increases the patient's unpredictability.[426]

The next day, an observer made the following entry: "A seemingly excessive amount of drugs being dispensed: valium, sleeping pills etc. A guard remarked they should be dispensed by medics instead of guards."[427]

Observers documented the way guards manipulated the prisoners by either delaying or withholding medication; the observers had seen the meds there on the guards' desks, while guards claimed there were none. The observers also recorded grievances from prisoners. One note reads:

> This inmate had open-heart surgery in December of 1972. "I have no nitroglycerin pills, which I need every time I get a chest pain. I am supposed to have blood tests twice weekly and I have had none since I came here over two weeks ago from the street on a parole revoke.
>
> Observer's Remark
> This man looks like living death in my opinion and should promptly receive some first-class medical treatment.[428]

COMMON CAUSE: CIVILIANS AND PRISONERS

Despite the guards' harassment, the Observer Program was successful because the DOC did not dictate its terms. If the DOC moved to "formalize" the program or to set parameters on the work of the observers, Rodman would have closed it down.

By and large, the Observer Program ran without DOC interference, but toward the end, the Norfolk County district attorney's office got some spies into the program. Boone's administration was worried by the hostility of Burke's office: they feared that the prisoners might trust these plants, and inadvertently give Burke added ammunition with which to attack Boone. Dellelo remembers when he became aware of this situation.

> One day Joe Higgins [Boone's deputy] comes over to me, he says, "Bobby, your observer program has been infiltrated by DA Burke's office. You got state police in here as observers." I said, "Okay, so show me." He said, "Bobby—I don't want anybody getting killed."
>
> I had to explain it to him. "Look, you guys don't want these guys to see certain things and we don't want them to see certain things. We don't want to hurt anyone. We just want to, well, keep them out of the way."
>
> So the two of us took a walk. We'd walk down a corridor and Higgins would bump my arm and nod his head in the direction of the observer. I would make a mental note and we kept the cops under control. They never saw anything we didn't want them to see.[429]

And there was plenty to see—perhaps not the scandalous events the spies hoped to uncover, but likely much of what the prisoners planned but dared not expect. As one observer reported,

> In talking with men who were most concerned with the climate of the prison there was a very, very, large amount of dignified pride in what is happening at Walpole. They, in numbers have been in and out of many institutions of correction and believe that what they are proving themselves capable of being and doing, could set an existential precedent. They want, for their brothers in other prisons, to profit from the example they are setting by showing what they are and can do *when given the opportunity* to take responsibility.
>
> *My impression summarily is that many of the men have known what they could be, and do, but that the present Walpole situation has given them a unique chance to act out what they have dreamed of being able to show people on the outside.*[430]

On March 12, two observers had spent time with the prisoners and compiled lists of "complaints" and "gripes." These lists included complaints about general conditions: too much heat, lack of heat, problems in delivering food through poorly designed food traps, poor food, and lack of clothes—two pairs of underwear for a week.

They outlined procedural issues, like the due-process problems in the disciplinary process, the arbitrariness of enforcement of rules when no real rules exist. Recording the utter horror of the blue rooms, both observers described the beatings and the way the guards had seized and destroyed the personal property of the residents.

Over the following two and a half months that they were inside Walpole, the observers continued to chronicle the events within the prison as they unfolded. They were most moved when the men spoke with them about the simple realities of their lives. They were frustrated when prisoners shared their fears that they would not receive a furlough to visit a dying parent, or when a picture frame for a family photo was declared a weapon while a TV antenna was left undisturbed. The observers questioned the pay rate for prison jobs and the DOC practice of withholding pay and not paying interest on bank accounts.

Still, the most remarkable thing about the entire tenure of the NPRA was what did not happen. There were no murders, no rapes, and no thefts.[431] Still, the NPRA fell short of its goals. Rodman explained:

> The observer program was vital. It was unique and it provided a lens into a world that is deliberately closed to the society that created it. But the OP was only useful to the extent that it built opposition to prisons. I feel it created space where that opposition could emerge, but the temptation to "fix it" instead is very seductive. Many of the observers were there because they wanted to fix Walpole. A few dedicated individuals understood the NPRA as an abolition project, but we never really made the transition. We maybe got further along the path than most, but even the prisoners got swept up in "fixing the problems."[432]

10

READJUSTMENT AND RESISTANCE

the state police takeback

BETWEEN MARCH AND MAY, WHILE THE OBSERVERS WERE witnessing the changes in Walpole, all the Walpole guards completed the mandatory training program. This training, which included communication and conflict-resolution skills, was intended to be a first step in preparing guards to do more than custodial work, or, as Judge Elam had said, "to do meaningful work." This change from "custodial" to "meaningful" work was intrinsic to Boone's vision that each DOC employee have a role to play in the reform project. Up to this point, the guards had received scant enough preparation for their jobs as custodians. But training the guards to play a different role hardly created a substantial commitment among them to play it.

A SAY IN THE RUNNING?

Recognizing that the clock was winding down on their experiment, on May 5 the NPRA again wrote to the State Labor Relations Commission requesting an answer to their petition for recognition. Recognition would solidify the work they had already done and preserve their ability to continue. The prisoners held a press conference to draw attention to the petition. The NPRA was setting the stage to demand minimum wage. Bobby Dellelo said that the inmates "simply" wanted "a community prison with self-government, inmate participation, and working conditions like on the street." Knowing this was not a "simple" expectation, Robert Dussault, chair of the NPRA

Legal Committee, clarified, "We don't want to run the prison; we just want a say in how it's run. This is our home." The guards' reported response was derisive: Lawrence Siskind, the legal representative of the guards' union, scoffed, "They'll bargain for spaghetti instead of frankfurters and beans. What's going to prevent the possibility of bloodshed over a spaghetti dinner?" The SLRC stalled, announcing that it would take another month to resolve the prisoners' request for bargaining power.[433]

Once the prisoners pressed the SLRC for a definitive answer, the gears of state oppression began to move again. Bishop, acting for the DOC, had given the NPRA nominal recognition, but unbeknownst to the NPRA, actual recognition would be denied. Goldmark, knowing what the SLRC had decided, began putting pressure on Boone and the acting superintendent, Walter Waitkevich, to take the prison back from the NPRA.[434] Goldmark had never supported the NPRA concept, and he wanted the guards to be "in charge" before the opinion was released. The question was no longer whether the NPRA would be shut down, it was when and how.

After the first two weeks of the observer program, the prison appeared to settle itself into a working rhythm. The prisoner population was supportive of the NPRA program initiatives. The men at Walpole had unprecedented independence and a glimpse of hope. The presence of the observers gave credibility to the efforts of the NPRA and the commissioner. After the first two days at his job, Walter Waitkevich told the *Boston Herald*, "The prison appeared very calm, though it would be very foolish to believe it would continue."[435] Waitkevich was not a supporter of the NPRA or the reform effort. Ultimately, he would see to it that the NPRA was finished. All the while, the Norfolk County DA, George Burke, continued to allege that criminal activity was taking place "under the nose" of the Boone administration, claiming the prison was full of weapons and drugs.

Despite the *Boston Herald*'s relentless criticism of the commissioner and the reform project, by May 18 the prison was running smoothly, with no recorded "incidents" for well over six weeks. The NPRA had everything under control and was beginning to implement programs. Yet, while Boone was willing to work with the NPRA and the AHC, he only invested them with power when there was no other option. As much as he appreciated the prisoners for their work in Walpole, he was publicly embarrassed by the fact that he could not deploy his own staff: the pressure on Boone to be in complete control of Walpole was immense. All the administrators were clear: the guards had to be back at their posts, the NPRA had to be neutralized, and the role of civilian observers had to be determined by the prison administration.

TASK FORCE FOR TAKEBACK

To resolve these dilemmas, Boone developed a task force to plan the "transition" in early May. He did not invite participation from the Ad Hoc Committee or the NPRA. When the prisoners and advocates discovered what he had done, they were angry. Because of the racialized nature of the attacks against Boone by the *Herald* and the guards' union, Rodman restrained the advocates from directly attacking Boone themselves. But Ryan's notes were full of angry statements that reflect the extent of betrayal felt by the members of the AHC and the NPRA.

Yet Ralph Hamm also remembers fully understanding Boone's position; he had discussed the dilemma with Rodman on many occasions. Hamm had long suspected the moment would come when Boone would decide he needed to prove to Gold-mark, Sargent, and himself that he was in charge. Hamm was well aware that Boone endured particular pressure because he was Black, and had temporarily chosen to ally himself with another oppressed minority: prisoners. Hamm knew that Boone was grateful for the work of the NPRA. He understood that Boone respected Hamm's leadership and the investment Hamm had made in the reform project. But he also knew that Boone had a job to do, and the NPRA would have to accommodate that reality. Hamm expected the NPRA would lose some, if not all, of its liberty, but he hoped that SLRC recognition would preserve the prisoners' union's framework and ability to secure its members' rights.[436] If the union was indeed recognized, the prisoners would not only have the arsenal of protections afforded organized labor, they would have a framework to access institutional power. Through continuing the calm at Walpole, Hamm hoped to hold off the moment when Boone would have to shift allegiance.

Boone charged the newly appointed DOC task force with one responsibility: to develop a way for the guards to be brought back into Walpole and regain full control over the prison for the department. Little creativity was shown. Ultimately, task-force members decided upon a lockup and shakedown of the entire prison, followed by strict regulation of the prisoners' movement within the institution. This was exactly what the prisoners had expected and they were prepared to negotiate with the task force. The task force scheduled the shakedown for May 21. After the date was set, the task force hoped to win agreement from the NPRA leadership about the implementation plan.

The prisoners believed the administration was negotiating in good faith. The NPRA knew there were weapons throughout the prison and that the overprescription of Talwin had created an increasingly drug-addicted population. They were sure they had proven that they could control all of the major problems within the institution much better than the guards had: there was a voluntary truce in effect, so the weapons were not in use; and prisoner-designed substance-abuse programs were being put in place. The goal of the NPRA was to go into the lockdown and search with as much power as possible. This meant getting a few concessions from the task force in the negotiating process—and the leadership believed they would obtain them. They developed a three-pronged position: the lockdown would be accomplished block by block, thus keeping the prison "open"; the search would be conducted in the presence of outside observers and NPRA leadership; and there would be no interruptions of visits from their families.

Keeping the prison open and maintaining visits was crucial, given the amount of contraband the prisoners had amassed. The NPRA needed to be able to move some of this around during the lockdown. The prisoners who had voluntarily put down their weapons needed assurance they would not lose them. Under the NPRA, prisoners had assembled libraries on their blocks, they had decorated their cells, and they had brought in stereo systems with huge speakers—they had begun to transform the prison environment. Prisoners were indeed armed, but they also had assembled a school. The union had a working office, and it was using the print shop to produce program and public-relations material.

On Friday, May 18, the prison was running smoothly. Boone went out of state to visit his fiancée, leaving Joe Higgins to act as commissioner in his absence. And things began to go very wrong.[437]

TAKEBACK: MAY 18, 1973

Seven observers reported to the prison for their afternoon shift at around 3:30. Two men were assigned to 10 Block and five were sent to the general population. At 6 PM, the prisoners were given written notice that the long-expected lockup and shakedown would begin at 7 AM on Monday, May 21; the prison would be locked down for two days. The memo specified that there would be no visitors or showers, and that the lockdown would be followed by the reinstitution of a pass system.[438]

The prisoners knew a pass system would give the guards and the administration control of the prison: they would decide who could move where and when. With a pass system, even the NPRA's ability to hold meetings would be at the whim of the program coordinator of the institution.

A group of prisoners went to discuss the memo with Dellelo. It caught him by surprise. The NPRA board had not been consulted, and none of the NPRA's demands had been acknowledged. In fact, the very existence of the document undermined the integrity of the NPRA. Because he could not explain the memo to the men, they became, in his words, "confused and paranoid."[439] Dellelo called together the NPRA leadership. The conversation moved from the memo itself to a discussion of how to express their dissatisfaction with its mandate, including the possibility of "staying out" after count.[440] Dellelo cautioned calm.

The NPRA leadership convened an emergency meeting of the general population in the auditorium. Many of the men objected to the restrictive provisions in the shakedown plan. NPRA leaders established their position: they would not allow this sort of loss in the position of autonomy they had gained through arduous bargaining. This statement was greeted by a burst of applause, but the applause was followed by an angry demand for explanations. The meeting was tense. Knowing that public support for the NPRA depended on their maintaining the moral high ground, the NPRA leadership advised the prisoners to refrain from violence. A full-scale rebellion would compromise the good will the prisoners had achieved. The administration must have known this, too, and been counting on an extreme reaction to turn the tide of public opinion. Dellelo cautioned, "As long as there's no violence, we've got them where we want them." This statement was met with sustained applause.[441] Reporting on the meeting, observer Eric Howlett mused that he had spent half an hour listening to the most violent language he'd heard being used to exhort the prisoners to nonviolence.

In the end, the NPRA leadership assured the prisoners that they would meet with the administration about the contents of the memo and report back to them. With the help of a supervisor, Dellelo reached Waitkevich by phone. He explained the men's concerns and made him aware that some men might be "staying out" as a sign of protest. Waitkevich had what he needed. The prisoner's candid warning gave the superintendent a reason to put the state police on alert.

At first, Waitkevich resisted Dellelo's request that he return to the prison for a meeting, but by 8:30 that evening, he was discussing the memo with some of the NPRA leaders. Peter Wilson, Richard Devlin, Dellelo, and Hamm spoke for the NPRA. There were about ten other NPRA members present in the room. Two civilian observers, Ash Eames and Eric Howlett, joined them.[442] Howlett took careful notes during the meeting.

The NPRA leadership put forward three demands the men had articulated at the general meeting of the prisoner population. During the two-day shakedown, the prisoners wanted to retain their visiting privileges, avoid pass-control and a long lockdown, and be allowed to take showers. In the recent long lockdown, many of the prisoners had gone months without a shower and were unwilling to forego this simple, crucial dignity again. Getting concessions was imperative: without them, the NPRA would be no more than an inmate council and certainly not an effective collective-bargaining unit.

Peter Wilson patiently explained to Waitkevich how important it was to address the pass-in, pass-out procedure—the men saw this as the key to prisoner agency. He cautiously intimated that returning guards might suffer the consequences of a violent or disrespectful shakedown. Wilson restated the terms discussed in the negotiations between the NPRA and the administration. These were being worked out in consultation with the commissioner, regarding the logistics of the shakedown. Not knowing that the state police were already on notice, again the prisoners asserted that conducting the shakedown beyond the bounds of an agreement with the NPRA would open Pandora's box. They cautioned the administration that the mere presence of a guard in central control who was one of the more notorious "goons" would make him an obvious target for revenge. Waitkevich remained quiet while he listened to the prisoners. After they were finished, he calmly informed them that the terms of the shakedown were designed to allow for "the most feasible reintegration of the officers."[443]

Undaunted, the prisoners argued that the shakedown could be accomplished one block at a time, eliminating the necessity for a prison-wide lockdown. Such a shakedown was really no shakedown at all; Waitkevich refused, explaining, "We need to know where all the guys are." He assured the prisoners that the press would be invited into the prison on Monday at 1 PM and that the observers would indeed be present for the shakedown. They continued to argue about how big an area of the prison really needed to be locked down at any given time.

Wilson returned to the issue of visits and questioned the purpose of allowing guards who had been indicted for "goon squad activities" to work. The superintendent blandly replied, "Things are going better." The men reacted, expressing unified dissent. Wilson took exception to Waitkevich's assessment of the prison climate, quoting a guard as saying that during the mandated retraining the guards had undergone in preparation for returning to their jobs, he had "learned better ways to hurt inmates."

A prisoner named Murray interrupted the meeting with a message from the visiting room. The visitors wanted to know if they would be allowed to come in on Monday. Waitkevich responded by shaking his head, "No, I can't."

Hamm slapped the table, saying, "That's it!" and prepared to leave. All the other Black prisoners got ready to leave with him. Not wanting to alienate Hamm and the BANTU leadership, Waitkevich offered the names of the people who had actually determined the terms of the shakedown. Hearing these names for the first time, everyone in the room responded with rueful laughter—the list named only administrators. Hamm knew the time had come: Boone had switched tactics even if he had not switched allegiance. From this point on, Hamm's only concern was his primary constituency, the men of BANTU.[444]

Waitkevich began to leave the conference room and started moving into the central area. The NPRA leaders and the observers followed, asking Waitkevich why the NPRA had not been consulted. Waitkevich was holding all the cards. He responded, "Boone has his top people represented—can't go any higher. *We all agreed* we can't let the people out."[445] Waitkevich went on to evade any personal responsibility by saying that he had no power to change the decision of the task force.

The prisoners argued, "What do you mean you can't let people out? It's your institution, you can do anything you want."

Waitkevich replied, "It's not *my* institution, it's *your* institution."[446]

Realizing that Waitkevich had no interest in reducing the tension, the prisoners asked for Boone and were told that he was out of town. Part of the group followed Waitkevich into a smaller office. Dellelo, knowing that he had to emerge from the meeting with at least one concession, explained to Waitkevich that the biggest issue was really the visits. He suggested that the NPRA control the visiting process as they had in the past. Waitkevich replied, "It might be a hassle for the guards—rocks could be thrown. We have to know where people are. Anyway, this was a unanimous agreement of the task force." Someone from the NPRA asked what was wrong with the count system the NPRA had been using. Waitkevich didn't answer. The meeting was over. Waitkevich slowly walked to the door and left. This was the last face-to-face conversation he would have with any of the prisoners that weekend. The NPRA left empty-handed.

After Waitkevich's departure, the NPRA developed a strategy of resistance based on principles of non-cooperation, one designed to make Waitkevich more open to negotiations. Knowing that they were about to lose everything, the NPRA struggled with the fragility of their enterprise. The NPRA's control within the institution was the product of truces that were tied to personal agreements with individual prisoners. A tangible loss to the NPRA would inevitably shake the foundation of those agreements, and thus the organization of the prison. The leadership feared that the night could get ugly. In a last bid for power, they decided to have prisoners prop open the cell doors so that the guards could not close them by remote control.[447] BANTU decided to render their doors inoperable. They removed the large cover panels and stacked them on the third tier. The rest of the night would be a test of the NPRA's commitment to strategic nonviolence.

When the observers inspected the prison between 10:15 and 10:30 PM in preparation for the arrival of the night shift, they found that most of the cell doors in both the minimum and maximum sections were propped open. According to the prisoners, the guards had not even tried to close them. Tension was mounting in the blocks. The observers noted that there was broken glass and "some hotheads" barricading cellblock doors with benches and desks.[448] The prisoners were certain the state police would enter Walpole that night even though the observers, referring to the March 21 date in Waitkevich's memo, tried to convince them otherwise. The prisoners anticipated and prepared for conflict.

By 11:30, tension eased in the max end, the glass was swept up and the barricades removed. Soon after, four observers from the 11 PM to 7 AM shift reported to the prison. It was agreed that the observers from the earlier shift would stay on until 1 AM to be sure that any possibility of disturbance had passed. Howlett noted:

> There is great difficulty interchanging observers in cellblock 10 because the guards there claim to be afraid to open the doors for fear of being rushed. They refused to come to the door to see for themselves that there's nobody within one hundred feet of the door until one of the inmates who seems to have the respect of the guards [by his own notes, this is Dellelo] gives them his personal assurance that there are no inmates nearby.

At 1 AM, with all calm inside, the afternoon shift left the prison proper but remained in the visiting room. One observer remained in 10 Block and three in the general population blocks. A *Herald* reporter was overheard talking about "two million dollars' worth of damage done by inmates to cell doors in maximum."[449] Waitkevich repeated this wild estimate as fact, so the observers decided to investigate. One seasoned observer was sent to inspect the doors in Blocks 2 and 6. The prisoners had rendered the doors inoperative by removing the metal covers over the locking mechanism and disconnecting the wires. In the observer's opinion, one or two days' work by the prisoners themselves could repair the damage. Dellelo, who accompanied the observer, stopped further removal of the panels. The prisoners in 6 Block had only removed two panels. At his direction, they reconnected the wires and replaced the metal covers. Dellelo proceeded to check the hospital, which had been cleared of the majority of prisoners. A closet had been broken into, but no damage had been done.[450]

For the next hour, Dellelo, Hamm, and other NPRA leaders moved about the prison responding to false reports. Guards would call them to central command and ask them to check on reports of destruction in various parts of the prison. At one point, they went so far as to claim that prisoners from 6 Block had entered the observation galleries above the unit.[451] None of the reports were true. Yet, unbeknownst to the prisoners, the rumors were being reported to the administration, accepted as fact, and passed on to the media.

Around 1 AM, Dellelo was confident that all was quiet inside the prison. Yet, at 1:30, Bill Swenson, a prisoner in 1 Block, warned Dellelo that Waitkevich had called the block—Swenson was the person who happened to pick up the phone—to notify the prisoners that the state police were coming in. Grabbing the phone, Dellelo reached Waitkevich, who asserted that "mass destruction" was taking place in the max end of the prison. Dellelo countered that the reports were untrue and invited the superintendent to come in and look for himself. He told Waitkevich that most of the prisoners were asleep, and the rest were "pretty tired."[452]

Waitkevich replied, "Time has run out. It is too late—they are coming in."[453] He warned Dellelo to get everyone back in their cells. When Dellelo asked how much time he had to do so, the superintendent said there was no more time.

The remaining observers did another round and reported that it was quiet inside the prison. There were about "50 prisoners sitting or standing around in the max end and another 50 similarly engaged in minimum."[454] Observers recorded that the prison was "quiet as a morgue."[455] Ed Rodman and state representative Bill Owens arrived at the prison and joined the observers from the afternoon shift who had stayed on in the visitors' waiting room. The two men discussed whether they should enter the prison and decided that they were more valuable on the outside. Both men had received death threats from the guards' union, and since the state police and the guards were armed, it seemed to them the wisest decision. Yet, in the end, both men decided to enter the prison.[456] After it was all over, prisoners repeatedly credited the fact that not one Black prisoner was harmed to the presence of Rodman and Owens.

When Dellelo hung up the phone after his conversation with Waitkevich, he pressed all the prisoners around him into action, sending them out into the blocks to notify prisoners that the state police were indeed coming in. Prisoners throughout the institution were awakened or told to return to their cells. At that time, Dellelo received notice that the main gates separating the maximum end from the minimum end had been closed. If this were true, it would trap some prisoners "out of place," making it impossible for them to return to their cells. A group of prisoners from the max end accompanied him to the gates to investigate.

Around 2 AM, Waitkevich finally informed the group assembled in the waiting room that he could not tolerate the destruction that had taken place and that he had already called in the state police. Still, Boone was not at the prison. Two of the observers, William O'Brien and Eric Howlett, requested that they be allowed to return to the blocks. Waitkevich replied that once security was reestablished and the shakedown completed, the observers would be allowed back inside. He notified the observers that the metal gates separating the max end from the minimum had been shut as a "step in controlling the situation." In reality, this action created a tense and dangerous situation inside the prison because prisoners could not return to their cells—and out of their cells they would be sitting ducks for whatever assaults the state police would, as history has proven again and again, choose to make on them as they reasserted control over the prison. While the observers were pondering this information, guards and state police arrived with guns and ammunition.

As law enforcement surrounded the prison, Howlett reported that a doctor was having difficulty getting into the prison to examine a prisoner who was reportedly injured. In the panic, a prisoner had begun breaking corridor lights near the visiting room with a pitchfork, and Peter Wilson inadvertently cut him as he took it away.[457] The doctor finally succeeded in going in. An hour later, a man was carried out on a stretcher to a waiting ambulance. Later the observers reported hearing five gunshots. Shortly afterward, a fire engine arrived at the main gate.[458]

Within the prison walls, prisoners were attempting to keep themselves and others safe in an increasingly chaotic and dangerous situation. When the gates between the minimum and maximum ends were shut, some prisoners were trapped, as predicted, and unable to return to their cells. The prisoners had the ability to open the gates, which were controlled electronically, but given the threat of state police violence, decided not to. Instead, Dellelo went to the control station and asked the guards to open the gates to allow the 20 to 30 men out of place on each side to return to their units. They denied his request. The guards stated that all the prisoners except those out of place had to return to their cells before the gates would be opened. The men refused to leave as long as their fellow prisoners were trapped on the wrong side of the gates—being caught out of place by armed state police or prison guards without the presence of observers could be fatal. According to the observers and Dellelo, there was a lot of yelling and "pandemonium."[459]

To the prisoners' surprise, the guards began to abandon the prison, even leaving the inner control room.[460] Soon the prisoners and the remaining few observers would be on their own. This signaled the imminent entrance of the state police.

Leaving Hamm and Larry Rooney with one observer at the gate, Dellelo returned to the blocks. He checked all the locking mechanisms as he walked to 6

Block. When he arrived at the block, smoke was pouring from the chaplain's office, which had been set on fire. Jerry Sousa, John Grey, and Artie Morrow were battling the flames.[461] The other prisoners in the block, in an effort to get fresh air into the unit, knocked down a set of doors so they could get to the windows and open them. In a gratuitous move, as the guards withdrew, they fired tear gas into the block. The guards knew the windows in the max end could not be opened. They left the men to suffocate, battling both smoke and tear gas. The prisoners left their cells and huddled close to the few windows, taking turns breathing outside air.

Dellelo received word that Hamm and Rooney had broken through the wall to the dining hall to create safe passage for the remaining observers to get out of the prison.[462] The job was made much easier than expected because the contractors who directed the construction of Walpole had cut costs by building hollow walls between the sections. The walls consisted of two brick walls about 6 inches apart and proved quite easy to breach. Then the men made holes on either side of the metal gate that separated the maximum and minimum ends of the prison, allowing passage between the two ends.[463] The prisoners from the minimum end returned to their cells. The state police were now armed and in the galleries. As Rooney led the white prisoners back to the maximum end, the police opened fire. Rooney was hit.

In the midst of this chaos, Wilson called Dellelo on the hall phone and begged for help in the hospital unit. The men there were worried that the state police would harm the sick prisoners.[464] The prisoner medics also feared the effect that tear gas or the forced entrance of armed state police might have on one recuperating heart patient. As Dellelo led a group to the hospital unit, they too were fired on by the state police and Bruce Manley was hit several times. The prisoners who were returning to the max end told Dellelo that Rooney and Peter Barteloni had also been wounded. When Dellelo asked how badly they were hurt, he was told that there was a lot of blood on the floor.[465] Dellelo stayed with Manley until he was removed on a stretcher to a waiting ambulance. In the end, Wilson was left alone in the hospital unit; somehow he prevented the state police from entering.[466]

After Dellelo received word that Rooney and Barteloni were injured, he rushed toward the central control room, where they were reported to have been shot. From a distance, he saw that the prisoners had been removed and that the floor was indeed covered with blood. As he approached the control room to demand answers, the state police released a warning volley. He retreated to 6 Block, warning everyone he passed that the state police were armed and shooting, and shouting to all of the prisoners to stay in their cells. He spent what little was left of the night in 6 Block.

At 4:15 AM, Waitkevich gave the order for the press and other civilians to leave the prison facility. Up to this time, the allies, press, and prison administration had been clustered in the visitors' waiting room. They moved toward the doors and assembled with Rodman and Owens on the pavement in front of the prison walls. The three observers from the night shift still remained in the prison. When Waitkevich issued his directive, they were asked to leave. Guards who were also exiting the building escorted the observer who had been in 10 Block, while the observer in minimum was escorted out by a group of prisoners led by Hamm. When the second observer came out, reporters surrounded him. Paul Corsetti from the *Herald* asserted, "You said there was a firebomb."

The observer answered, "There wasn't any firebomb!"

The reporter repeated, "I say firebomb."

Irritated, the observer insisted, "But there was no firebomb."[467] Despite the first-hand account available to the *Herald*'s reporters, throughout the night, they were to openly demonstrate that they already had written their story line. Waitkevich was following the same script.

The third observer, Ash Eames, who was in the maximum end, remained inside the prison all night at his own insistence. Armed forces continued to arrive outside the prison. By 6 AM, there were 150 state police, 50 police cars, and 100 standby corrections officers.[468] Smoke was rising from the center of the prison. The fire in the chaplain's office was still burning out of control.

After having delivered the observer from the minimum end to the front of the prison, the Black prisoners returned to 2 Block. Hamm resigned himself to whatever outcome awaited them. Even though Dellelo seemed to have faith that the NPRA could still work things out, the Black prisoners knew that once the state police entered the prison, their "time" was over. Even though it was expected, this was a bitter moment—one made worse, as Hamm explains, by the fact that Boone was the commissioner and he was Black. Even though Boone wasn't calling the shots, the authorities' decision to regain control felt like a personal betrayal.

Unlike the prisoners in the max end, the BANTU leadership did disable all the locks in their block. They prepared for war, taking the lock covers, each weighing over 30 pounds, to the top of the third tier, where they could be most effectively thrown. After they had secured their ability to fight back, they shared a vat of home brew, then closed themselves into their cells—determined to wait out the chaos in as much safety as they could. As Black men who had chosen to challenge the system, they knew they would be the most obvious targets for the police.[469]

Sometime before eight o'clock in the morning, Waitkevich announced over the PA system that the state police were in the prison and that everyone should return to their own cells. He promised that, if they complied, no one would be hurt. All the prisoners, including Dellelo, returned to their cells and closed their own doors manually. A short time later, the state police walked out of the galleries and onto the flats. Dressed in riot gear, they patrolled the corridors. Dellelo could hear some men being taken from their cells; then he heard the beatings begin. After they removed the prisoners, the police entered the empty cells and threw the prisoners' personal belongings out onto the flats, the area in front of the tiers. Then they left the area. The prisoners, exhausted, slept until the afternoon.

As for Hamm, after securing the block, he succumbed to the combination of home brew and exhaustion and fell asleep in the common area of 2 Block. Afraid he'd be set upon in this vulnerable condition, his friends strapped his machete to his chest and helped him into his cell, where he slept until the state police arrived.

They came to his cell first. He remembers awakening when helmet number 451 entered his cell.[470] Hamm had no doubt that this heavily armed policeman intended to kill him. He stood up, dressed in his three-quarter length jacket and jeans, unaware that the machete was strapped on him. He felt it against his chest and his hand moved toward the handle. The officer took one look at this giant Black man, now with the machete drawn and scraping the ceiling; he backed out yelling, "We better leave this one alone." After locking the grate, Helmet 451 clenched his fist, waved it at Hamm and shouted, "We'll be back!" Hamm lowered the machete; it occurred to him that he had never used the machete for anything but carving beef in the commissary.[471]

That night, none of the Black prisoners were beaten or shot. This might be because they had locked themselves in, visibly armed. More likely, it was because Rodman and Owens had entered the minimum end with the state police and then stood on the flats until the police withdrew. The state police had shot guns and rifles; they had already shot three white prisoners. The Black prisoners had openly armed themselves, giving the police a valid reason to shoot. They did not. Rodman stationed himself in 2 Block, while Owens roamed about the prison. Both men remained on the premises for the next two days.

Dellelo was not affected by the cell searches, although a number of men in his block were. Sleeping most of the day, he woke up around four in the afternoon, when Al Lussier, the block representative who was responsible for count, let prisoners out of their cells to clean up the flats.[472]

After dinner, the cells were opened again and the prisoners moved onto the flats to continue their job. The action they took, demonstrating both ownership of and responsibility for their environment, was a direct result of the organizing work the NPRA had done. Unlike during the work stoppages the prisoners had carried out from December 29 to early March, the prisoners now felt that the prison was their space. Even after the state police entered the block, and even though it was the police who'd thrown their possessions onto the flats, they voluntarily went out to clean up their belongings. More important, they gathered up the belongings of the prisoners who had been lugged from the block the evening before and taken to segregation. The NPRA had created pride and a sense of ownership and brotherhood; prisoners were not yet prepared to give that up.

Representative Bill Owens visited the max end somewhere between five and six that evening. Dellelo noticed him in the gallery and motioned for him to come down to the block. Owens was followed by one of the guards, who stood within earshot of their conversation. Owens said he was concerned that the men were out of their cells. Dellelo explained that the prisoners had permission to clean up and would return to their cells when asked. Owens remained uncomfortable. Eyeballing Dellelo and speaking very slowly, he asked, "Oh, there is no trouble?"[473] In hindsight, Dellelo realized that the question should have tipped him off to what was coming next: the prisoners had only been allowed out of their cells to give the state police a pretext to enter the block a second time.

Shortly after Owens left, someone shouted a warning that the state police were coming down the corridor with shotguns. Dellelo walked out of his cell to check the report. He saw the police lining up in the gallery. Using the butts of their shotguns, they broke the glass in the gallery windows and positioned their gun barrels through the broken windows. Dellelo turned slowly, returned to his cell, and closed the grate, locking himself in. State police officers also lined the wall on the flats under the gallery and trained their shotguns on the cells. The prison guards, armed with rifles, marched in formation down the flats. Two or three state police officers took their positions in front of each cell. Two entered Dellelo's cell, one clubbing him in the upper part of his arm; then they cuffed him with plastic cuffs and prepared to remove him from his cell.

But other officers had mistaken the prisoner in the next cell, Mike Stetson, for Dellelo—they both had long hair.[474] The police brought Stetson to the ground, beat him in the face, and pounded his chest. As Dellelo was moved down the tier by two of the state police, two other officers on the flats yelled up, "Hey, there's Dellelo—how come he's still walking?" The men who had been beating Stetson jumped up and ran toward Dellelo. They caught up to him at the top of the stairs. One of the policemen grabbed his hair and smashed his face against the railing. They threw him face-first, hands tied behind his back, down a flight of stairs onto the flats, where they kicked him and dragged him through water and broken glass. They called him names while dragging him through a gauntlet of state police, who stomped on his feet, kicked him, and beat his legs with wooden clubs.

Representative Owens and administrative staffer Walter Anderson witnessed Dellelo's beating on the stairway and saw him tortured on the flats. As he was being pushed, barefoot, through the water and glass, Dellelo overheard Owens demanding his release. Once he was on the other side of the grate, Dellelo requested help from a guard he knew. His arms had been dislocated. At first the guard said he could not help. Eventually, though, he glanced furtively around, checking to make sure they were alone. Then he cut off the plastic cuffs with fingernail clippers and pulled Dellelo's arms back into their sockets.[475] Dellelo was cuffed again and taken to the infirmary for medical attention because his injuries were extensive. While he was recuperating, Anderson stopped by to tell Dellelo that he and Owens had witnessed the beating on the stairs. Anderson urged the NPRA president to sue, offering himself as a witness. Dellelo would reflect that very occasionally, corrupted people affirm their basic humanity.

Dellelo was confined in punitive segregation for the rest of May and into early June. Not surprisingly, he was never charged with an offense. He was isolated both to make sure that his supporters would not see how badly he was injured and to ensure that he could not reorganize the NPRA until the state police had won complete control of the prison and reinstated the guards. The hardcore white leadership of the NPRA was locked down in the maximum end, leaving the majority of BANTU members in minimum.

PICKING UP THE PIECES

Boone had formed the task force to design the transfer of power from the NPRA to the DOC so that it would be done in an orderly fashion. A prison-wide shakedown to remove contraband would have to be part of this process, and it had to be accomplished in such a way that Norfolk County district attorney Burke would not be able to reject its validity. Boone had to prove that he could clear the prison of contraband *and* put his staff in place. A well-organized transition would put Boone back "in the game."

Before the commissioner had left that Friday, he had released notice of conditions of the shakedown out of respect for the prisoners.[476] He wanted to prevent the families from wasting their time by coming up for visits while the prison was shut down. He assumed that the prisoners would understand his predicament and allow the shakedown to take place. He assumed reciprocity. He had gone quite far in meeting their demands, and he trusted they would, at least, show the discipline that they had shown over the previous three months. He trusted that the institution would hang together. He was right in his assessment—of the men. The prison was "quiet as a morgue" just before the guards abandoned it to the police. Again, as in Lorton, Boone was undermined by a "guards' riot." Only this time, he was not able to walk through the back door and ascertain—for himself—that the guards' reports were false.

The Black prisoners knew the guards' return was inevitable. They were not interested in resisting it. They knew they could not. Their goal was personal survival and the survival of BANTU. It was within BANTU that they would continue to develop their agency. They had always seen the NPRA as a vehicle, not as an end.

But the NPRA was the best vehicle for unifying the hardcore white population. These men were older than most of the Black prisoners, and almost all of them were serving life sentences. The NPRA was their only legitimate way out; they were prepared to follow that path as far as they could. But they had also prepared a detour.

> We had discovered a tunnel that led to the main tunnel to the outside. We decided to clear it out so we had clear passage to the outside. If we had succeeded, the hard core would have gone out.
>
> The entry was in the auditorium. We covered the opening with a barrel. One day some of the guys from BANTU were practicing. They had a band. And all of a sudden a bunch of white guys started popping up from the floor behind the barrel. We told them what

was going on. They wanted in. We told them we would take the whole prison out; everyone just had to be quiet. They were. No one blew our cover.

The guards were pissed when they found that tunnel. We were close to taking everyone out. It's the duty of every prisoner to escape if he can. You just can't hurt anybody when you do.[477]

At the end of Dellelo's statement describing the May 18 takeback, written while he was in segregation, a summary composed by the NPRA board after his release was appended.[478] Up to this point, the NPRA had negotiated for workers' rights and ability to lead their lives with dignity and self-determination. Now, the NPRA board, mindful that agreements negotiated with Donnelly that included some of these entitlements had been violently breached, decided to argue for a platform that would protect them from physical abuse and torture, asserting for the first time that they had undeniable human rights.

The prisoners returned to the only written agreement that the NPRA had: that negotiated with Bishop and Anderson, who acted on behalf of the Department of Correction. We will never see the full content of this agreement; the NPRA's papers were deliberately destroyed during the shakedown. Boone's own papers at the Massachusetts State Archive have been so completely purged that only a small file with some draft regulations and an invitation to a barbecue still exists.

That signed agreement was ample evidence that the DOC had accepted the prisoners as "state employees"—despite the denial of the SLRC. Its eradication ensured that future administrations could dismiss the prisoners' claims to agency.

Even though he had created a task force that excluded them, the NPRA knew that Boone had not made the decisions that resulted in the brutal beatings on May 18 and 19. By the time they released their analysis, they had witnessed Boone's futile attempt to pick up the pieces and knew he was trying to salvage the reform initiative. This is perhaps the bitterest aspect of this story. This event, which would eventually be used as pretext to dismiss Boone, was not one within his control. Yet Boone was left alone to justify it and find a way to move forward.

Given Waitkevich's actions on May 18, the prisoners understood he was deliberately trying to touch off a rebellion. When the prisoners' remarkable discipline won out, Waitkevich just decided to act as if the expected rebellion had actually happened. All the while, he refused to communicate directly with the prisoners or to enter the prison to verify the reports he was receiving from guards about its destruction. When he ordered the gates to be closed between the minimum and maximum ends of the prison, he had sowed "panic, and further confusion and rage among the inmates."[479] The prisoners wagered that this act was deliberate. Dellelo offers his opinion:

"Wacky" Walter Waitkevich did not make the call. He was just not that powerful. He got the orders from someone else. It seemed like he had these orders from the beginning. He was a long-time DOC employee. He resented our hold on the prison. He was also like a sacrificial lamb. If things went bad and people died or something, they could just get rid of him. He was never smart enough to realize that.[480]

Waitkevich did call in the state police, but we will never know who ultimately made the decision to deploy them.

The NPRA's analysis then turned to the use of live ammunition in the prison. The leadership charged that the shootings were completely unjustifiable, since the prisoners presented no threat to the guards in the control room. "There was no indication of danger to the lives of either state employees or inmates. The shooting was unwarranted."[481] Waitkevich had assured the men that if they returned to their cells, no one would be hurt. Yet, when the prisoners complied, the police and the guards pulled them from their cells and brutalized them.

At some point during the takeover, all of the NPRA's files were removed from the prison. The only documentation of the NPRA's work and process was what Ryan and Rodman preserved. It is unclear whether the NPRA office was ransacked under the direction of the administration or whether the guards acted on their own behalf. Nonetheless, this wanton destruction, combined with the segregation of NPRA leadership in 9 and 10 Blocks for "'security' not 'punishment' reasons,"[482] had one purpose: to clearly demonstrate that the NPRA no longer possessed power in the institution.

Ed Rodman linked the events that night with the brewing school-desegregation controversy outside the walls.

> The state police had just completed its training in riot control. They came in after the prisoners were already locked into their cells. Many were asleep. This action was in preparation for riots when the schools were desegregated. If you look at how they worked the blocks, they marched in columns, lined both sides of the corridor, like it was a street, worked in pairs with two more as backup, cell by cell, getting control by destruction and violence; the conclusion is inescapable. This was a drill. They were practicing their techniques. Think about it. They were able to practice on live subjects who would have little constitutional rights to redress. It was rich.[483]

Dellelo agreed.

> That's a given. From that point on, we were their guinea pigs. They tried out all their shit on us. One time they even came into 10 Block and lugged every guy. Took 'em out and hog-tied them, destroyed their cells and threw them back in. They paid out fourteen thousand dollars in damages on that one, but that is small change.[484]

One other factor needs to be weighed in assessing the events between May 18 and 19. Boone was upset that Burke was releasing information to the press, and Boone also believed the reports about the laundry and the prostitution rings. He expected the prisoners to behave like law-abiding citizens. When they did not, he had great difficulty reconciling their actions with his vision of prison reform. Ed Rodman remembers discussing this with Boone.

> One time Boone came to me to tell me that he had proof that Dellelo was involved in the scamming. I just looked at him and asked him where he got the "proof" and then asked, "How do you know what is true?" I was never interested in all that. Yes, there probably were scams going on, but look at what was happening. These prisoners and the volunteers were doing something that had never been done before. And Boone really did not see that he and Dellelo were on the same page more than not.[485]

Still, true or not, Burke's reports of prisoner scams, drug use, and possession of weapons were making Boone appear foolish. Given that his job was to be "in control," John O. Boone was offended when he was characterized as the commissioner who controlled the prison at the behest of the prisoners. Thirty years later Boone would reflect,

> Yes, I went to the prisoners and I agreed to work with them. I told them my expectations. I asked them to work with me. I did this because I work from a philosophy of respect. The media turned that into some kind of weakness. That was not what it was.[486]

While demonstrating the simple truth that was at the core of Boone's philosophy—"every person is capable of monumental change"—the NPRA also disrupted racial allegiance through its emphasis on unity among the prisoners. For a brief period, the prisoners agreed that their primary identity was as oppressed workers; all other identities were secondary. Proud of their unity, the men did not see their willingness to redefine their primary identities as a profound threat to the society they wished to rejoin. Yet, civil society depends on these divisions to maintain social control.

11

THE STRUGGLE FOR EXISTENCE

death knell for reform?

*The main reason the whole corrections thing became very
tough wasn't the fact we had some violence, somebody
killed, the fact we had a strike and all that sort of stuff.
It was the day-to-day pressure from the newspapers ...
When you're in public life and you get a few bad headlines it isn't all that much fun, but when you get them day
after day after day and week after week after week, then
it gets rugged and you have to do something about it.*[487]
—Governor Francis Sargent

IMMEDIATELY AFTER ITS BRUTALIZATION OF THE NPRA
leadership, the DOC held a press conference. Superintendent Walter Waitkevich
claimed that 180 state troopers had been called in to put down the "riot" at Walpole. He estimated the damage to the prison at between $800,000 and $900,000.
While Bobby Dellelo lay naked and bleeding in 10 Block as a result of the unpro-
voked assault by state police and guards, Waitkevich praised the NPRA for policing
"inmate vandals," saying, "The NPRA went in and made them stop that (wrecking
cell locks). The NPRA was doing a helluva job and they were supported by level-
headed inmates."[488]

The irony did not end with Waitkevich's public praise. In a gamble to regain public approval for prison reform, Sargent made a startling move that would only serve to further destabilize Boone's leadership. On May 21, while emphasizing his support for Boone, the governor tapped Norfolk County DA George Burke to investigate the state police takeover of the prison, despite Burke's overt support for the guards, and his relentless attacks on John Boone and correctional reform. Sargent had to expect that Burke would use the occasion to blame "Boone's policies" for the riot. In the *Herald* article on the shakedown, Burke was quoted as stating, "The Corrections Department should be indicted in whole for this. They gave control to the inmates and they don't know how to get it back."[489] Boone is only quoted reflecting on how things would have been different had he been present.

After reading Burke's brutal attack on Boone as published in the *Boston Globe,* Sargent released a copy of a letter he wrote to the district attorney.[490] After the fact, the governor cautioned Burke against making "intemperate statements and groundless accusations." Such remarks, he wrote, "only inflame an already volatile situation." Sargent went on, "What concerns me even more is that this style of rhetoric is not unique. Too often in the past your office has been given to this type of highly charged comment." Burke's response was a petty tit for tat: "I haven't seen Gov. Sargent's letter, although it has been handed out to the press. I think the governor is getting very touchy—apparently the truth hurts."[491] Burke went on to explain that he would be requesting ten additional state police detectives to assist him in his investigation. Essentially, the state police department would be investigating itself.[492] As added insult, later that day, the wives of three corrections officers barged into Sargent's office demanding Boone's ouster.

In a lengthy front-page article in the *Boston Globe*, Sargent was quoted chiding the guards and the media, "It's very easy for you and others like you to make a fall guy out of him (Boone) because his skin is black." It wasn't the first time Sargent had called the media and the guards on their racism, nor the last time he lauded Boone's achievements; his position on both was consistent. There is less clarity about his actual support for Boone, however. The same article reported that two months earlier the governor had asked a man Boone had beaten out for the commissioner's job two years earlier if he would be interested in taking it now. Sargent denied the conversation had occurred. And Boone was not yet admitting political defeat. The last word in the *Globe*'s front-page article was given to Boone, who said he was "far from finished. Most people in prison here didn't even have sense enough to steal more than $5,000 [but we insist on] spending more than $10,000 a year to keep each one in prison."

The AHC was back to where it started: outside the prison desperately trying to negotiate its way in. So, in the midst of this chaos, the AHC sent a letter to Boone proposing a May 30 visit to Walpole, with a select group of citizens, including ex-prisoners, to meet with the inmates so they could offer to serve "as advocates for peaceful change within the prison."[493] Rodman assessed Ryan's role in this.

> This is where Phyllis Ryan was magnificent. She was undaunted. She was disciplined. She knew the drill and she did what was necessary. Everyone else was running around looking for the solution and she just focused on the prisoners and how the AHC could be useful to them.[494]

On May 25, John Moriarty, a colonel in the state police, was placed in charge of maintaining security in Walpole. The prison was run as if it were under martial law. Moriarty's first act was to withdraw the recognition of the NPRA.[495] Waitkevich, who worked alongside Moriarty, followed suit the next day. Formally withdrawing the recognition of the NPRA as the "exclusive authorized representative" of Walpole's 566 prisoners, he declared the union election of the previous July to have been rigged.[496] According to a spokesperson at the National Center for Dispute Settlement/American Arbitration Association (NCDS/AAA), Boone, DOC attorney Bob Bell, and Howard Doyle of the guards' union suggested that NCDS/AAA conduct a new and impartial election among the inmates. NCDS was willing to perform this service, but only if the inmate leaders were in agreement, since the proposed NPRA elections were the primary concern of the prisoners, not of the correctional officers, the institutional administrators, department personnel, or anyone else.[497] As Dellelo reported,

> I had been chasing the AAA for over a year. They were busy out at Wounded Knee and couldn't get to us until it was almost too late. I wanted them because I was told they would keep a file of all negotiated agreements in perpetuity. Boy was that a lie. Later, they told me that was not their policy.[498]

When Waitkevich released his memo withdrawing support for the NPRA, 200 prisoners staged a protest inside the prison. This took a tremendous amount of courage. The leadership was locked down, no observers were inside the prison, and state police in riot gear were patrolling the corridors. Ralph Hamm explains how BANTU united the prisoners in the minimum security end of the prison.

> During the initial phase of the state police takeover and the lock-down of the prison, communications between the minimum and maximum sections of the prison were hampered and limited.
>
> For the most part, the bulk of the prisoner population and what remained of the NPRA board of directors that were not beaten and dragged to segregation, conscientiously objected to and refused to cooperate with Colonel Moriarty and his staff.
>
> Down at the maximum end of the prison, where the majority of the white NPRA board members were housed, rumors were being circulated (fueled by the white board members housed in the minimum section) that the Black NPRA members were not taken to segregation because we were in collusion with the state police and the prison administration. These rumors were generated from, and circulated by, what I had come to believe as the true agents of the administration and the agent provocateurs. The rumors fed upon the fact that neither I nor the other BANTU members who

were part of the NPRA were taken to segregation like the white executive board members. These rumors did not contain the fact of Reverend Rodman's and Senator Owens' presence in my cellblock when the riot-gear-clad state police squad entered my cell to beat me, nor of how I backed the squad out of my cell with a machete; and I was not in the mood or frame of mind to enlighten them. It was my attitude at the time that none of them could be trusted, and that they could think what they wanted to think. My main concern was for the welfare of my constituency—the membership of BANTU; as well as somehow devising a method to extract the NPRA board members out of the prison segregation and isolation units and back into the prison population. I would deal with the rumor-mongers later.

Initially the prison population was only allowed out of their cells in the minimum section to go to eat in the chow hall. Administration-selected prisoners served the trays of food, under the watchful eyes of four riot-gear-clad state police. Helmeted and gas-masked state police also manned the observation tower in the chow hall that contained the triggers to release the tear gas canisters that were mounted upon the upper walls of the hall at intervals. Resistance in the chow hall seemed a futile gesture at this stage, and would have only led to more beatings and segregation placements. We needed time to think, not react. We needed time to communicate with our external board of directors, as well as our outside community supporters.

When we locked back into our cells we spent a lot of time screaming, banging on cell doors, and singing the protest songs of the day. After about a week, Moriarty had flyers passed out to the prisoners explaining his desire to open up the prison a little at a time ... that we would be allowed to come out of our cells and mingle in the respective blocks to shower and to clean up the cellblocks and cells. Our cooperation was to determine how long we would remain out of our cells.

I was housed in then cellblock #A-3, which was across the corridor from cellblock #A-2. My cellblock housed the majority of BANTU's executive board of directors (myself, Jack Harris, Henry Cribbs, Ronald Penrose, Donald Robinson, James Flowers, Raymond White, James Hall). Our first order of business was to contact our external board members, and figure out where we stood as an organization in the future under the present conditions and what we foresaw as coming down the proverbial pike. I recall that it was at this improvised board meeting that it was voted that the internal board should attempt to transfer to MCI Norfolk. I was staying because I owed allegiance to NPRA and the Walpole prison population. My strategy was simple, and based upon an expression that I had read as having been uttered by the anarchist Bakunin: "I resist because they exist."

I cannot speak upon what was occurring on a daily basis in the maximum section of the prison during this time. However, in the minimum end it was my strategy to allow Moriarty and the state police to believe that they had gained control of the prison. So, some prisoners went on work assignments and we cleaned the cellblocks somewhat. Moriarty was confident that he was now in control. Then two events occurred: 1) I learned that Bobby and the other board members were severely beaten when they were taken to segregation, and 2) the *Boston Herald* printed an editorial or article stating that the prisoners in Walpole were suppressed through intimidation of the ... "well muscled men in their state police uniforms." My ego took over the situation from here.

I organized a small rally to occur in the main corridor of the minimum section of the prison, between the chapel and the exit gates to the main yard. I told those involved that it would be a peaceful demonstration, and that once the state police came through the control gates to the corridor that everyone was to make it back to their housing units. Prisoners were stationed at the cellblock gates to insure that the guard and two state police officers could not lock the gate shut with us in the main corridor. Two squads of riot-gear-clad troopers marched through the inner control doors to the main corridor in front of control. They unlocked the gates, and marched toward the crowd of prisoners swinging their batons (hitting them upon the palms of their gloved hands to create a slapping sound).

As the troopers approached the prisoners they dispersed and made it back to their cellblocks. I stood alone in the corridor, grasping the handle of my homemade machete under my modified trench coat (cut to three-quarters length and hemmed in a prison avocation business months earlier), while the state police marched their squads around me. Once the corridor had been cleared of prisoners, and the troopers returned to inner control and locked the gates to the main corridor, I turned and slowly walked back to my cellblock. My message had been sent and received.

Up until now we had allowed the prison guards to sit at their desks inside of the cellblocks near the front gate, with two uniformed state police standing next to them. The state police had become so confident they no longer wore their riot gear in the blocks. The peaceful protest ushered in a strike, and the strike was the signal to heave the heavy steel panels (approximately six feet long, two feet wide, and an inch thick), that initially covered the locking mechanism over the cell doors over the third tier railings in the direction of the guard's desk and the state police. They ran out of the cellblocks in the minimum section to our jeers and cheers. Next we sent a flyer of our own to Colonel Moriarty: Release Our NPRA Board Members! No Justice, No Peace.[499]

Hamm made his point. Up until then, the state police had assumed that the Black prisoners had no real control of the prison population. When the state police took back the prison, they had locked down what they assumed was the real leadership of the NPRA: Dellelo, Wilson, and the rest of the white leadership. They vastly underestimated Hamm's actual leadership and his capacity to develop strategy and mobilize the white prison population. Rodman says that it was in this brief space when the white leadership was locked down that the "myth of Ralph Hamm"—the fearless, unstoppable, larger-than-life leader—was born.[500] Hamm was never underestimated again; he was kept in Walpole longer than any other NPRA leader and suffered longer in disciplinary segregation. The record of his actions as vice president of the NPRA has been a significant barrier to his parole. To this day, Hamm suffers under the weight of the image forged during the brief ascendancy of the NPRA. Raising his voice can still get him surrounded by security personnel. He remains the only NPRA board member who is still in prison.

WORKER TO WORKER

The protest in the minimum-security end of the prison was followed by two days of meetings between the guards and the prisoners. Surprisingly, it was the guards who took the initiative, requesting Waitkevich's permission to call the meeting. After listening to the opening conversation, Boone, Waitkevich, Robert Bell (head of the DOC's legal department), and Isenberg left. The prisoners and guards met twice over the weekend of May 26. They proposed governing regulations and negotiated the release of the white leadership who were still in lockdown. Neither side commented to the press after the meeting.[501]

Rodman, who attended the meetings, reasoned that the administrators walked out because they did not know where the meetings were headed, and their presence would have signaled agreement; they wanted to be able to challenge the outcome if they needed to. Rodman cites these meetings as the ultimate moment of institutional change: "It wasn't just the NPRA on one side and guards' union on the other; they worked as men to solve a common problem."[502] Rodman believed that the withdrawal of the administration was a sign that the NPRA and the retraining of the guards had been too successful; the coming together of exploited guards with brutalized prisoners was dangerous for the administration. He remembers thinking, "It's over. They are never going to allow this."

With Dellelo still in segregation, Hamm was the lead negotiator. He proved he had internalized Rodman's conflict-resolution training. No longer was he the table-slapper; he proposed solutions. In retrospect, both Rodman and Hamm felt there was real potential to share power among this group of men. Even if there was scant hope for the two unions within the prison to establish common ground, it would be possible for the NPRA to establish respectful relationships with a core group of line staff. As Dellelo reflected, "This never occurred to us, that we could have worked with the guards that way. It should have, but it didn't."[503] Later, John Kerrigan—a lifer who would become the last president of the NPRA—identified this oversight as a tragic flaw in their strategy; they should have seen, seized on, and exploited this possibility.

Whatever the possibility, reality played out quite differently. From this point on, the administration did not negotiate with the NPRA. Instead, they would agree to talks, but each time they would leave the actual negotiating to the line guards. These guards appeared to negotiate in good faith. They would reach agreements with the prisoners, but no one who was at the table had the power to enforce the agreements, since the line guards neither set nor enforced policy. After this first meeting, one guard reported, "It seems the inmates want the officers to sit down with them and draft some rules and regulations for the administration since, as the inmates said, it is really the inmates and the officers whose lives are affected here."[504]

The prisoners and guards successfully negotiated inmate head-count procedures and Boone supported the outcome. I asked Rodman how he came to be in the prison for these negotiations, since the OP had yet to regain its status. He explained that he just never asked permission to reenter. He showed up and waved at the guards in control, who, by this time, were quite accustomed to seeing him, then walked in. Rodman determined he should have access, and obtained it by claiming it. His action modeled self-determination for the Black prisoners in BANTU. Ralph Hamm recognizes this as one of the most important roles Rodman played.

> Ed showed us something we did not know was possible. He stayed focused, did what needed to be done and never asked permission. He also never apologized or backed down when people put pressure on him. He taught us that you really had to think before you acted. That was the prerequisite to self-determination. We watched him every day.[505]

WORKER AGAINST WORKER

During the guard strike, the Black prisoners had begun running the kitchen. They worked hard and took great pride in their work and in the food they served the prisoners. The baker got up every morning at 3 AM to make bread and pastry for the institution. They also saw that their values weren't shared by all. Richard Neary, the head chef and a guard, would punch in, pour himself a cup of coffee, and go play checkers—or worse, leave. This angered the kitchen staff, who readily understood the labor dynamics inherent in their situation. They were the most vocal among the prisoner voices. They argued that dismissing line guards who were bilking the taxpayers by skipping out on work made sense; so would paying the prisoners a minimum wage to do the work instead. On May 27, the prisoners' frustration over their exploitation blew up. Some of the men assaulted Neary as a warning, but not badly enough to require medical attention.[506]

TURNING CADETS INTO GUARDS

The next day, May 28, Boone pulled the cadet trainees out of Walpole to put them through the same training course that all the guards had gone through. The *Globe* took the occasion to run a feature story on the cadet trainees. All were under 30 and most had no experience in corrections. "They have been described as 'the new breed and the mod squad' by the Correction Department, as 'scab labor and strikebreakers' by some correction officers."[507] The *Globe* article featured 25 of the trainees, "who from March 15 until May 4 kept peace inside the cellblocks of Walpole state prison assisted only by supervisory personnel and a handful of regular officers."

Since the cadet trainees reflected Boone's vision of what a "corrections officer" should be, fundamental conflicts between the line staff and the cadet trainees were inescapable. The cadet trainees were pulled from the prison because Robinson, Isenberg, and Boone did not want to lose them; they knew the line staff resented the trainees deeply. This hostility could be worked with when there was only a handful of guards in the prison, but when the entire workforce returned, the animosity had the potential to turn to brutality. They hoped that the cadet trainees could be brought back after their training was complete, with full standing as corrections officers and members of the guards' union.[508]

REDUCING ORDER TO RULES

On May 30, rather than allowing the AHC in to meet with the NPRA, as they'd requested, Waitkevich released a set of interim regulations governing the movement of the prisoners within Walpole. As the NPRA expected, these were indeed constructed to "break" the NPRA. The prison had been locked down since May 19, and Waitkevich informed the prisoners that these new rules were "effective immediately and superseded all previous procedures." There was no attempt to discuss these new rules with the NPRA board. The NPRA no longer had any form of official standing within the prison. The regulations released by Waitkevich were one in a series of barriers they would struggle to overcome in the upcoming weeks.

These regulations had been designed by Boone's task force. The new regulations included the following: Prisoners were prohibited from leaving their blocks unless called out by inner control; block grill doors were to be locked at all times except during meals and for "authorized residents" to pass (it would be over seven months before prisoners were allowed to leave the blocks except for meals); a pass system was instituted—only prisoners with a pass signed by a staff member or corridor officer would be allowed to leave their blocks; and staff were required to submit passes to inner control and prohibited from giving them directly to the prisoners. All telephone requests and inquiries were to go through inner control, effectively cutting the NPRA off from its allies.

Four days after Waitkevich issued the new regulations, the chairman of the NPRA Legal Committee, John T. Dirring, sent a letter to Boone. He recommended the immediate implementation of the *Model Rules and Regulations of Prisoners' Rights and Responsibilities* compiled by the Boston University Center for Criminal Justice under the auspices of the Administrative Law Reform Project.[509] DOC attorneys had worked on the project and consulted with the NPRA Legal Committee in its development. Robert Bell, one of the DOC attorneys involved, remembers:

This project began before John arrived. Although John Boone wrote the introduction, the DOC never did adopt it as a whole. But it was out there and we used it in drafting regulations, like the regulations on furloughs for lifers. I drafted those. I am particularly proud of that.[510]

DOC attorney Arnold Jaffe remembers working with the NPRA Legal Committee on translating these model rules into actual regulations.

We had done a lot of research—we knew what was out there. What we were trying to do was create an inspirational document for the DOC, well, really, for all of the country. This was a major way of creating a new way to respond to prisoners' needs with rights *and* responsibilities. We acknowledged there were two sides to the issue. This document would create a mechanism for prisoners to move to community corrections facilities. It created a framework to qualify prisoners to get out. It was a brave thing to do.

We worked with the NPRA Legal Committee to get feedback on this document. This was the way Boone worked. He believed in getting all the parties together and working things out. This is again a tribute to people leading the DOC. Here are these guys forty years ago saying you can't get to a solution until you have had an opportunity to talk about the needs. How could DOC legal professionals begin to understand what was really needed in the prisoners' bill of rights? All the things were collaborative at that point.

Working for John Boone was the most positive political experience that I ever had. People from all different backgrounds were working together doing something practical. Now! And the fact that it was so unpopular made it more exciting.[511]

THE CITIZENS RETURN

By the beginning of June, the observers had negotiated their way back inside the prison. Their movement was severely curtailed—they were allowed in the corridors but not on the blocks. Their face-to-face contact with the prisoners was severely compromised. Rodman was opposed to the return: "I really did not feel we could do our job. But John Osler and Phyllis Ryan felt we needed to be there as long as possible."[512] On June 7, the AHC released its report outlining the observers' impressions recorded during the first two weeks of the Observer Program back in late March.[513] The report was accompanied by the following set of recommendations:

1. An Advisory Council should be given a mandate by the governor to convene. It should be composed of inmates, officers, staff, administration, citizens and observers. This council would provide a formal structure for discussion and negotiation of important issues by all parties and would have the power to see that all agreed upon negotiations are implemented. This Council should begin its work by

reviewing prior negotiations to ascertain what has not already been implemented.

2.   An election and recognition of a permanent inmate representative body.

3.   A total restoration of access to outside groups.

4.   A call on inmates, guards and Correction Department administrators to rededicate themselves to working together toward true correctional reform in Massachusetts. In this context we think it is crucial that amnesty be granted to inmates who were involved in incidents that were the result of tensions beyond their control that built up in Walpole.

5.   A thorough review and evaluation of programs, staff, and departmental policy coupled with Development of guidelines by the Advisory Council to insure quality rehabilitative services.

6.   An independent observer program accountable to the council and having ombudsman powers.

7.   An all out effort to reduce the population at Walpole by moving the great majority of current residents into work release, community based programs, and training programs at other institutions.

8.   An appointment of a permanent superintendent who is agreeable to all the above points.[514]

The creation of the advisory council would provide a way to sidestep exclusive DOC control of all outside groups and programs. The AHC refused to become a DOC program, but its members were open to working under a council that would include prisoners and ex-prisoners. Despite the obvious need for such a body, however, this advisory council was never convened.

The week after the AHC published its recommendations, Nils Wessel, chair of the Wessel Commission, was in Boston for a speaking engagement. In an interview with the *Boston Globe,* he voiced his disappointment at the failure of the state to implement the recommendations of the commission's 1955 report, and joined with the AHC in supporting the creation of a civilian advisory committee.[515]

In mid-June, the Massachusetts Council on Crime and Corrections (MCCC) went on record supporting the AHC's recommendations and offering to play a substantial role in future policy development.[516] The open letter the MCCC sent to Governor Sargent mirrored earlier AHC letters, except that the MCCC asked for a "Wessel-type" commission to make recommendations for dealing with the "explosive situation." It also recommended a meeting of all private and public agencies and concerned parties to discuss Walpole. It did not mention including prisoners or, specifically, the NPRA in these discussions. But the MCCC letter did emphasize that a key solution was the implementation of Chapter 777, and was cosigned by the external NPRA and the AHC.[517]

MURDER ON THE BLOCKS

On June 12, during John Osler's observer shift at Walpole, Patrick Gonsalves, a prisoner, burned to death in his cell. Rodman pulled the observers from the prison.[518] As soon as Ryan had assembled the reports from the two observers, the Ad Hoc Committee distributed the following release:

> Last night a man's cries for help went unheeded for nearly fifteen minutes before he was burned to death in a maximum security cell at Walpole State Prison.
>
> Two citizen observers stood helplessly by—unable to open the heavy steel doors which separated them from the rows of locked cells and the victim of a tragic fire. The doors which stood between this man and the help that he needed did not have to be locked for the security of the prison. All of the men were already locked in their individual cells. These doors closed off the rooms containing cells from the main corridors of the prison.
>
> No guards were on duty in the area where the fire victim's cries could be heard.
>
> It was only after being alerted by citizen observers that the guards were able to come to the man's assistance. But by then it was too late. For by the time the proper keys could be found and the "security" doors could be unlocked the man's cell burst into flames and the entire cellblock area began to fill with smoke.
>
> Twenty-five other men all locked in their individual cells, had to wait at least five minutes longer before the prison personnel decided to unlock their cells. Four men were carried semiconscious from the fire area by guards and other inmates. Two were given emergency treatment in the prison hospital, one of them suffering from a war injury which had destroyed one of his lungs.
>
> If the outside doors had been open, observers or guards might have prevented the fire from starting. If the guards had been on duty in the walkways overlooking the cells, the victim could have been released from his cell before the fire started and certainly before the explosion of flames which took his life some minutes later.
>
> We call on Commissioner Boone to exercise the responsibility he holds for the safety and security of Walpole and to put an end to the dangerous policies of locking out observers and locking doors, and to guarantee men will never again be locked away from the help they will need in the event of fire, sickness, or other emergency.[519]

The AHC intended to use Gonsalves's death to gain wider access for civilian groups. Ryan considered a wrongful-death suit, and recommended an independent investigation or a blue-ribbon commission. Against Rodman's advice, observers returned to Walpole a few days later. Rodman, who wanted a clean break with the DOC, left the program in the hands of John Osler, who became its spokesperson.

Even though the observers had witnessed the prolonged death of Patrick Gonsalves, they could do nothing more than tell the story the next day.

The *Globe* article on Gonsalves's death noted that the guards were working without a contract. Some guards were still involved in a "slowdown." As Dellelo remembers,

> This was standard operating procedure. When the guards were an-gling for a better deal on the contract, they would basically stop working, except they would issue a ton of disciplinary tickets to show how "dangerous" their job was. After they got their contract, they would drop all the charges and life would go back to normal. This was the wrong time to play this game. We knew what they were up to, but this time things were still so volatile, someone was going to get hurt.[520]

The cadet trainees were off attending the training module. There was no coun-terpoint to the guards, and they were intent on making the prison hell until their contract was signed.

It soon became apparent that the careful calm the NPRA had maintained from March through May was gone. A week later, on June 19, a prisoner was stabbed 30 times by another inmate and flung to his death from the third tier. A little over a week later, John O. Boone would be forced to resign. The moment for radical reform had passed and law enforcement, not reform, became the solitary focus of the DOC.

THE END OF A CAREER

On June 21, Peter Goldmark called Boone in for a meeting and asked for his resigna-tion. Boone refused. Later that day, the commissioner met directly with Governor Sargent, with Goldmark present. Boone recalls:

> When I got to his office, I said, "Governor, this is nonsense." I said, "You know, I'm ready to go any time, getting ready to go, but you said two years, and this is the wrong way to do it...." And I said, "I'll do anything you want me to do. I'll sign the resignation now, and don't announce this, let me work with you trying to get this thing stable. I do this, that, and the other." I had all kinds of options.
>
> And the Governor looked around and said, "Peter, that sounds reason-able to me." And Peter said, "Governor the decision has been made."[521]

Boone didn't get his two years. He could tick off the amount of time he actu-ally had in months, days, and hours. To this day, Boone believes that if he had actu-ally worked two full years, he could have turned the corner with the department.[522] Sargent agreed to continue to pursue prison reform. At the time of his resignation, Boone had a 75 percent name-recognition rate in the state of Massachusetts—more than any elected official.[523]

> That's why I say the governor had to fire me. Every time I opened my mouth I was speaking for him, and he was going down the drain. You see,

I understood all that, all I wanted to do was participate … and help him recruit somebody to press the thing on, because we had done all kinds of things…. It was a good start.[524]

Boone was not told that Colonel John Moriarty, head of the uniformed branch of the Massachusetts State Police, had already been chosen to take his place as interim commissioner. Later that day, Sargent addressed the public in a televised broadcast to announce Boone's resignation.[525]

Despite Sargent's praise, the governor fired Boone because he had become a liability, and he had become a liability, in large part, because he was Black. A group of state employees had indeed succeeded in getting an administrator fired because they did not want to work for a Black man—particularly a Black man who was committed to real, concrete prison reform. Despite the fact that Boone had pulled Walpole back from the brink of open, violent rebellion, despite the fact that from the time that Boone had recognized the NPRA to the time Moriarty took over, there were no murders or suspicious deaths in Walpole—and then there were two—Sargent chose to fire him because he claimed Boone "could no longer maintain a working chain of command."[526] Despite his promises regarding prison reform, Sargent chose to replace Boone with Moriarty, the man who as superintendent was already in the process of turning Walpole back into the very prison Goldmark had set out to close.

Right after Sargent's speech, prisoners at Walpole mounted a small protest. Prepared, Moriarty repressed them and locked the prison down. Over the next week, he reopened the prison and returned much of the liberty to the prisoners.

BOONE: "OUR STRUGGLE MUST NOT HAVE BEEN IN VAIN."

Ryan was blunt and immediate in her response to Sargent's action, calling it "racist, disgraceful, and reactionary."[527] Boone made his own statement, most likely written before Sargent's televised speech.[528] He resigned with grace and with dignity. He allowed that Sargent's move was understandable. He used his moment of response to voice his commitment to correctional reform and his hope that the NPRA and the guards could continue their negotiations.

To continue this effort will be a difficult task in light of the current lock-up at Walpole. Violence has always been a part and parcel of imprisonment, from slavery to Walpole State Prison. Justice, honest decision making and respect for human dignity are the only methods to reduce violence in a prison, or in any community.

But Boone did not support Sargent's decision to place Walpole under police control. He continued:

Personally, I regret the decision of the Governor to put Walpole under the authority of the state police. Correctional work is a specialized assignment, for which the police are not trained. Placing Walpole under the state police is contrary to the directions and policies of the reform program, and could undo much of the progress that has been made. I urge the Governor to restore Walpole to the authority of the Corrections Department as quickly as possible.

Boone recognized the role the NPRA had played and urged them "not to act in any way that would harm the reform efforts in this critical period, not to act in any way in which they personally have an important stake, play such a vital role." He also referred to the work he had done advancing community corrections. Lastly, he thanked his staff, the observers, and the many people "who worked with me effecting correctional reform." His closing statement was a rallying cry to all the allies: "Our struggle must not have been in vain."

However, Boone also took exception to Sargent's characterization that he could not maintain a chain of command. On June 23, the *Boston Globe* ran an article on his reaction. Using the strongest words he would ever use, he blamed the Sargent administration for not getting the legislature to release the funds for training and hiring of management and guards at Walpole. "It is not John Boone who can't get the cooperation of the guards," Boone proclaimed. "It's the administration which can't get the cooperation of the legislature. Both of them are putting each other in the middle, but really there are 575 inmates locked up in hot cells who are in the middle."[529] Boone accused the Legislative Commission on Correction of concentrating all its efforts on violence, instead of dealing with constructive programs, and openly discussed how his hands were tied in dealings with the guards' union.

THE MEDIA BATTLE OVER LEGACY

The day after Sargent's speech, the *Boston Globe* declared Boone a victim of turmoil at Walpole and of Sargent's indecision.[530] The *Herald* publicly took credit for Boone's ouster. Its editors bragged about how they had sent investigative reporters to Virginia and Washington, DC, to gather information about Boone's credentials "immediately" after his hiring in December 1971 and how they had dispatched Tom Sullivan to Walpole to investigate "events that the correction department sought to cover up." Their editorial page revealed, "Guards and state officials including some legislators began to aid these papers by feeding us with information.... Seldom in recent months has there been a week that Boone's resignation or firing was not sought editorially in these papers."[531]

On the other hand, the *Globe* looked for ways to continue to hold Sargent accountable to the goal of prison reform. The paper interviewed Jerome Miller, the former director of the Department of Youth Services, who was now the director of the Illinois Department of Children's and Family Services. Miller, who had closed all of the juvenile prisons during his tenure, making Massachusetts a model for juvenile justice programs, explained that prison reform would never happen within these "Bastille-type institutions. If we had tried to reform those training schools, the same thing would have happened to me.... So long as you have those places (prisons), they turn into battle grounds and devour you." Miller called Boone "the victim and the scapegoat—a great loss to Massachusetts." He went on to declare,

> Prisons are outmoded, violent bureaucracies that don't protect public safety. There's no way to rehabilitate anyone in them. The facility produces violence that calls for more of the facility. It's a self-fulfilling prophecy. Prisons offer themselves as a solution to the very problems they've created. Institutions are set up to make people fail. That's their latent purpose.[532]

Steve Wermeil of the *Globe* continued to put pressure on the Sargent administration by writing daily stories about the aftermath of Boone's resignation. Walpole was locked down. Moriarty said privileges would be reinstituted "for all inmates when they show that they are willing to abide by the rules and regulations of the institution." The furlough program had been suspended. The Observer Program was to be evaluated by Edward Teehan of the state police "to determine whether [the observer program] serves a purpose of the inmates, the Correction Department and the general public."[533] Moriarty wanted to make sure that none of the observers posed security risks and that none were ex-convicts. "We will no longer maintain a system whereby observers report their observations to everyone but the proper authorities."

Joe Higgins, the deputy commissioner who had filled in as commissioner when Boone was out of state, advised the *Globe* that there was always a sick list of 20 guards at Walpole, supposedly "because of accidents and assaults." The guards' union responded, using the *Herald* as its mouthpiece, by admitting there had been a "perpetual sick list of officers"—and predicting the officers would "suddenly become healthy" due to the changes.[534]

One voice was missing from the pages of the newspapers: that of the prisoners. Throughout the summer, Walpole was closed to the media. *Globe* reporters had to tell their story without talking to NPRA leadership. Eventually, the *Globe* would condemn the news blackout at Walpole in an angry editorial: "Communication between prisoners and the press is not some half-baked idea of wild-eyed reformers. It takes its precedents from history, policy, constitutional law and just plain good sense."[535]

RACISM AS BACKDROP TO RACISM

At the same time that Sargent had decided to fire John Boone, he was supporting the desegregation of the Boston schools. Those who wished to maintain a segregated school system had placed an amendment in the state budget that would forbid busing students across district lines. On July 3, 1973, the state supreme court declared this anti-busing amendment unconstitutional. The state legislature responded by passing a bill that would prohibit busing without consent. The Black caucus was the most vocal opponent of this bill. On July 11, when the bill made it to Sargent's desk, he was prompt with a veto.[536] It was apparent that this struggle placing Black children at the center of a debate over equal educational opportunities would be long and bitter. The ugly racism faced by John O. Boone would be directed at Black children who were simply going to school. Only, these children would have bricks, rather than words, hurled their way.

It was within this context that the Black caucus responded to Sargent's announcement. These legislators were careful. Sargent would be running for re-election in a few months, and if the prisons were still in an uproar he would be defeated. They needed Sargent as an ally in the struggle for school desegregation. They also had to go on record declaring their support for Boone and exposing the role that racism and political pressure had played in his dismissal. The caucus called a press conference. Its members were joined by Marvin Harrell, president of the NAACP, who had the first word, declaring that "Sargent's decision was forced upon him through the combined issues of racism and politics." Representative Bill Owens, the prisoners' fiercest advocate in the legislature, described the hours he had spent in the prison, and how he had heard prison guards vow that a "nigger would not run the state's Correction Department." A close friend of the commissioner, Owens denounced Sargent most strongly:

> Instead of supporting the action of his own appointee, Governor Sargent, influenced by the belligerent dogma of the guard union, stopped the commissioner's action. John Boone has done an outstanding job and has tackled corrections in Massachusetts with skill and determination which is unmatched. All too often, it seems, progressive people are placed in important roles only to be criticized, subverted, deserted, and finally eliminated because those responsible political leaders do not have the guts to stand up and support the changes these individuals are making.[537]

Senator Royal L. Bolling fell in behind Owens: "The greatest tragedy of all was the rebellion of the guards, who from the time Boone took over as commissioner, derided him as 'Boone the Coon.'"[538] Each insult to Boone was an insult to every Black leader in the state. The caucus members knew that what people said out loud about Boone was being said about them behind their backs. They knew Boone was qualified, intelligent, and capable. They knew he was fired because a group of state employees refused to work for a Black man—and they got away with it. When Sargent hired Boone, he was very proud to be able to place a Black man in such a prominent position. Once in the position, Boone was not just window dressing. He was a visible challenge to white supremacy. Later that evening, Marvin Shabazz of the NOI commented, "You can't put a Black man's head on a white man's body, because they will cut it off."[539]

After the press conference, Black leadership went to work planning a "John Boone Day." On July 8, community activists publicly honored Boone with a series of open gatherings: at Franklin Park, on the Boston Common, and in Springfield, at American International College. Boone walked onto the Boston Common dressed in a dashiki and carrying an adze—a symbol of power in Nigeria.[540] He used these events to launch the next phase of his work. He cautioned against using community corrections programs "as a reward and consequently as a tool to exploit," and he pledged to assemble a national coalition for prison reform.[541]

> Mutual hatred and disrespect breeds a relationship which is worse than a slave plantation model, in which poor whites received low wages and vicarious satisfaction working blacks in slavery.
>
> Many who would not be slaves and many abolitionists—the John Browns and Nat Turners—died to change this system and a war was fought. At Walpole, low-income white guards are fighting to preserve a system they are accustomed to. No one has died from correctional reform. Correctional reform cleans up prison jungles where death and devastation have prevailed.

Less than two years later he would form the National Coalition to Abolish Prisons, which he still heads today.

The Ad Hoc Committee condemned Sargent for firing Boone, and demanded that he be reinstated. Then it began a summer-long campaign to make sure the gains of the Boone administration were not lost. Its members were relentless in their efforts to salvage prison reform—with their press releases, demonstrations, and determined presence at Walpole.

That summer, Black community leaders came together to form the Greater Boston Defense Organization Against Racist and Political Repression. Among its founding members were Chuck Turner, Mel King, Margaret Burnham, Obalaji Rust, and Nancy Fischer. All were connected to the Ad Hoc Committee, BANTU, or the Observer Program.

THE NPRA AND THE STRUGGLE FOR EXISTENCE

In the eyes of the prisoners and the AHC, John Moriarty had no shame and no limits. After declaring the NPRA agreements null and void, he went on to order the removal of the swings the NPRA had bought and installed for their children to play on during visits. Later, he would further blur the line between the DOC and the state police by interviewing provisional police officers for jobs as guards. These officers stood to lose their policing jobs because of a civil-service ruling on minority hiring. To ensure jobs for them, Moriarty applied to LEAA for funding for 15 positions and projected that he would need to hire 25 more officers to cover summer vacations.[542] Essentially, he used money that Boone had dedicated to diversifying the workforce to create jobs for white police officers who had been displaced because of an enforced, court-mandated affirmative action plan.[543]

With Boone gone, guards started rumors that the DOC was poised to reopen the infamous Bridgewater segregation unit closed by Boone 18 months earlier—and that the NPRA leaders were slated to be transferred there. The guards' threat became a focal point of heated correspondence between Ed Rodman and the lieutenant governor, Donald Dwight. Rodman chastised the administration and the DOC for even considering the proposal. Dwight responded by accusing Rodman of impeding the guards' right to free speech and democratic thought.[544]

On July 5, the NPRA sent Boone an open letter of thanks. Despite their frustrations with Porelle, and what they perceived as Boone's limitations, they knew they were deeply indebted to him. Boone had formally recognized the NPRA and then stood back and let the prisoners show the public that they too could make a difference. He had paid for these actions with his career. The NPRA used this public letter to decry the guard-nurtured atmosphere of chaos inside the prison. Fearful that the guards' unchecked behavior would lead to violent confrontation, the NPRA placed the responsibility for the prison environment squarely on the shoulders of Moriarty and Sargent.

After the NPRA released the letter, they presented Moriarty with a petition signed by 32 inmates in 2 Block outlining 12 steps needed to "get this prison back to functioning normally." Many of the Black prisoners resided in 2 Block, and BANTU most likely authored those 12 steps. Later, under Hamm's leadership, all of these points would be incorporated in the agreement negotiated between the DOC and the NPRA with the assistance of the American Arbitration Association.

1. Release of all men who want to be removed from the seg unit
2. Collective bargaining before something heavy happens
3. Recognition of the NPRA
4. Withdrawal of the state police
5. More rapid handling of the mail
6. Restoration of 6 day a week visiting
7. Cessation of inmate strip searches
8. Cessation of shakedowns of visitors
9. Restoration of inmate programs
10. Restoration of dining room
11. Restoration of canteen use
12. End to the emergency procedures[545]

BRINGING DOWN THE CURTAIN

Things were becoming very difficult for the observers. On July 9, they began to discuss suspending the program.[546] A few days later, the Reverend James Hofacker was ejected from Walpole after speaking with prisoners. Following Hofacker's removal, 11 observers met with the lieutenant governor and suggested replacing the Observer Program with an alternative program that would not answer to the DOC. Dwight, for his part, seemed satisfied with arrangements as they stood.[547] He explained, "We feel the Colonel ought to have full authority (to run the prison when he was put in there)."[548]

After the meeting with Dwight, John Osler called a press conference. The following is the text of the OP's last statement:

> After negotiating for five days with the lieutenant governor's and the governor's offices, the Ad Hoc Committee suspends the four-month-old Observer Program. During the four months of the program, 1,200 civilians entered the prison in eight-hour shifts for a total of 15,000 hours. Five observers were locked in a staff dining room while riot geared officers went into the blocks to return prisoners to their cells. Prisoners asked why the observers did not document the beatings. Guards denied the beatings and said the observers were locked in because they did not want anyone in the way of returning the prisoners to their cells.[549]

Continuing, Osler challenged Moriarty, saying,

> The state police have crippled us as watchdogs for the public by locking us out of the prison living areas and forbidding us even to speak to the inmates. In the last three weeks, while prisoners have suffered from poor food, inadequate medical care, violations of their civil rights and physical abuse, the observers have been effectively gagged and blindfolded. This can only mean the state police have something to hide from the public.

Moriarty offered to allow the observers to speak with the prisoners. Osler was quick to respond, "We would still not really be allowed to observe fully and that would put us in a dishonest position which we cannot be placed in."[550] Sargent praised the Observer Program as having "singular importance in helping to stabilize a tense and complex situation in that institution."[551] In the end, the AHC suspended the Observer Program without terminating it altogether, leaving an opening for eventual return and a strategic threat to the administration.

STILL STRUGGLING BEHIND THE WALL

The return of the guards and the loss of the observers had re-created the conditions the prisoners had confronted in 1971. Yet the prisoners were not the same. With new consciousness and a new set of skills, the NPRA called for a work stoppage at Walpole on July 15. Their press release read:

> The oppressive conditions at Walpole border upon insanity. Epidemic conditions created by filth, human waste on prison walls, germ infected, stagnated air in cellblocks and heaps of trash on the floor all signal the attitude of men who once again are isolated from the public eye.[552]

Steve Wermeil, of the *Boston Globe*, reported:

> One hundred fifty prisoners went on strike. The NPRA claimed that this was the entire work force at Walpole. Rodman speaking on behalf of the Ad Hoc Committee went on record stating that the strike was a protest against the conditions the inmates find themselves in ... the absence of

observers, the presence of state police, failure of the Walpole administration to continue negotiations with inmates, restrictions on visiting and the loss of the furlough program.[553]

By the middle of July, the NPRA had negotiated an agreement for new election procedures. The prisoners released the following letter:

On July 18, 1973 eight members of the NPRA held a meeting with the National Mediation Board in quest of resolving the official status (by election) of the Walpole Chapter of the National Prisoners Reform Association.

The principle objective is to determine by ballot whether the NPRA retains sufficient confidence by the Inmate Body to be legally recognized by the Administration as the representative voice of the Inmate Body. The NPRA was assured that the results of a new election would be recognized by the Administration and that the Governor's office would enter into a Contract to that end so that in the future such a contract would have to be recognized and complied with by all parties.

Representing NPRA—Robert Dellelo, President; Jack Harris, Secretary; Peter Wilson, Co-coordinator; Tiny J. Dirring, Legal Committee Chairman; Sammie Nelson, Legal Committee Vice-Chairman; and Charles McDonald, Board of Directors Member.[554]

Hamm was not listed as a member of the negotiating team although he was present for most of the meetings. During Dellelo's long lockdown, Hamm's own leadership had been established. He had organized the work stoppage on July 15; this gave him and BANTU strong leverage. BANTU members filled four of the six negotiating positions.[555]

The election was to take place with National Labor Relations Board regulation ballot boxes. Initially, Moriarty refused to allow prisoners in 9 and 10 Blocks to vote. The NPRA opposed this restriction, insisting that all men in the institution had a right to vote. When Moriarty agreed only to the participation of those in 9 Block, the NPRA again insisted that each prisoner, regardless of his status, had the right to vote. Their contention was made for practical reasons as well as principled ones; with 10 percent of the prison population, including some NPRA leadership, in 10 Block, NPRA survival depended on their ability to vote.

Moriarty began a careful dance with the prisoners' union. Although the administration did not officially recognize the NPRA, Moriarty requested that the NPRA allow the kitchen crew to go back to work. This action reflected the difficulty of running a prison without prisoners as laborers, and the success of the NPRA labor strategy. But the NPRA was unwilling to allow an institution that was oppressing them to run smoothly. Dellelo explained, "There were three pillars of power within the institution: the prisoners, the guards and the administration. All had the power to destabilize any initiative." But in 1971, the guards were not well organized, relying on the cronyism of the system to take care of their needs, and the administrative leadership had come under scrutiny. These factors, combined with the informal structure of the institution, created an environment where prisoners could organize effectively.[556]

Their response was based on sound principles of labor organizing:

```
[Neither the] Inmate Kitchen Crew nor anyone else
would ... return to work in any capacity unless and un-
til the following grievances of the entire Inmate Body
were resolved in the order listed below:
1. Full restoration of the Citizen Observers Program
   without restrictions.
2. Restoration of the Furlough Program for Walpole.
3. Restoration of the "One-Third Parole Screening Pro-
   grams" at Walpole.
4. Restoration of all previous visiting privileges.
5. Return of all Outside Groups and Functions.
6. Joint Opening of Maximum and Minimum Blocks.
```

Ralph DiMasi, a member of the NPRA board of directors, amplified the NPRA's statement with a 30-day hunger fast. In a letter to the governor, DiMasi wrote that he was tired of the DOC taking away his visits as punishment. He was weary of watching children try to behave during visits when there were no toys for them to play with. He was personally hurt when the guards "intimidated, insulted, and humiliated visitors." He also cited the continued presence of the state police, the corruption of the disciplinary board, and the reinstatement of guards who had brutalized prisoners. Finally, he was undertaking the hunger strike to support "all prisoners who refuse to work in the slave shops."[557] According to Dellelo, DiMasi never received a response.

The circle had come complete. Because BANTU proposed a new framework to the white prisoners, proposed by capable, intelligent, deliberate leaders, DiMasi accepted the truth: he too was a slave as long as he was in prison, and his reduction in status was predicated on the oppression of Black men. This analysis was clearly grounded in the understanding that imprisonment alone was an equalizer. For the time they were in prison, the white prisoners understood that they, too, were chattel. Once they returned to the streets, this was quickly forgotten. And very few of the white prisoners carried over their experience of racial equity to their communities. Later, in the heat of the racialized busing crisis in Boston, a key leader in the NPRA was arrested during a robbery. He was wearing an afro wig. Ed Rodman ruefully noted that this individual seemed not to care whether a Black man paid for his crime.[558]

A RETURN TO GO

Dellelo decided to step down as president once the elections and negotiations were finished. He also decided to step out. Dellelo explains, "I needed a break real bad. A real break. I began to plan my escape. I could not escape while I was president of the NPRA—that would reflect too badly on the prisoners."[559] Dellelo would eventually escape in October of 1973. He had fabricated a fake zip gun and feigned illness. After being removed from the prison van at Pondville Hospital, he overpowered the two transport guards, took their guns, and forced them to drive him to the Blue Hills reservation just outside of Boston, where he cuffed them to a tree and hitchhiked into Mattapan Square. He was out on escape for nearly a year.

On July 28, 1973, administrators and NPRA leaders signed a memorandum allowing an impartially conducted referendum to determine whether the Walpole residents wanted to be represented by the NPRA, or an inmate council instead. As might be expected, the administrators, including Moriarty and Higgins, preferred an inmate council.[560] The election took place later that day. An overwhelming 84 percent of the prisoners voted to reinstate the NPRA as their elected representative.[561] On August 3, the NPRA board was reaffirmed.

From this point on, things moved quickly. From August 4 to 6 the NPRA went through training by the American Arbitration Association (AAA) in preparation for negotiations. Dellelo, who was on the negotiating team, reports it was rough going.

> Well, the AAA tried to train us. They sat us down and they would, like, role play. Okay, it goes like this. You want whatever; the DOC says no. What do you do?
>
> We would say, "We riot!" or "We go on strike!" They wanted to teach us give-and-take, but we did not have time for that shit. If we were asking for something, we needed it. It was non-negotiable. We could work together on the details. I guess we gave them a hard time.[562]

On August 7, collective bargaining began. Predictably, the negotiations were fraught with difficulty. Two weeks later, they had come to a standstill. Forbidden to meet with the press, the NPRA called Phyllis Ryan and dictated the following statement:[563]

> After 15 days of futile attempts to negotiate, it is clear we are being used as pawns in a life and death political game being played with the men at Walpole. We have been forced to function as captives, as negotiators who can never bring back any new gains from the bargaining table and as peace keepers all at the same time. We, the NPRA must now relinquish total responsibility to Governor Sargent.
>
> It is Governor Sargent who is responsible for creating the current crisis at Walpole. We have been in controlled lock-up for 71 days. All activities and

community programs have been suspended. The food is worse than any of us can remember in 15 years. Visitors are subjected to intimate searches even though we are skin searched when we go in and out of the visiting rooms.

Although the taxpayers spent $750,000 for Boston University to formulate a set of rules and regulations which we are willing to accept, the administration refuses to discuss them, rejects them as "too Boonish," and avoids the subject as if they wanted to continue the chaos at the prison.

Thus the past 71 days have not brought order to Walpole. In effect, the administration has decided that if it can't reopen Bridgewater Department Segregation Unit, they will turn Walpole into a DSU. In the present state of emergency now prevailing at the prison we feel the need for citizen observers. We are also calling for an independent unbiased investigation of the damage to state property and of the beatings and stabbings that have occurred in the past two months.[564]

On September 24, the State Labor Relations Commission finally issued its long-withheld opinion ruling against the NPRA. The commission did agree that the prisoners met the definition of employees, and the state of Massachusetts that of employer. The authors explained that, if the decision could have been made based purely on accepted labor definitions and practices, it would have recognized the union. The commission members struggled over the statutory issues that would impact their ability to advocate successfully for the NPRA. Ultimately, they decided that since they had no statutory power over the commissioner of corrections and since the commissioner had complete power over the prisoners, they would be unable to enforce any agreements negotiated by the prisoners. They rationalized that nowhere in state law was a provision that demonstrated the legislative intent that prisoners be accorded the status of "worker" or extended the protections of workers.

The NPRA pressed forward with negotiations despite the ruling, ultimately producing an agreement, signed sometime in October. By the time it was approved, Dellelo had escaped and Hamm was in segregation, so John Kerrigan signed as president of the NPRA. A marked-up copy of the final draft of the agreement, indicating accord on all major points, was found in the files of Arnie Coles, chair of the external NPRA. Given that the actual signed contract is missing from both state and DOC archives, analysis of the historic agreement is based of necessity on this draft.

The agreement was recognized as a bilateral contract enforceable by binding arbitration before the Massachusetts Labor Relations Commission or the National Center for Dispute Settlement (American Arbitration Association). It contained a one-year sunset clause. The NPRA agreed to return to work and agreed that it would not authorize a work stoppage "unless a serious breach of this agreement is committed by the Administration."[565] Despite the fact that the disciplinary code and procedures are the stick that any prison administration uses to control the prison population, the agreement gave responsibility for dispute resolution among prisoners to the NPRA. The NPRA agreed to "insure all inmate grievances and disputes are promptly, fairly and non-violently determined."[566] This power would decrease the ability of the guards to pit the prisoners against each other and then use the disciplinary code to punish them all. The NPRA was not, however, given the power to address disciplinary infractions. So when the administration wanted to exercise its power, it could categorize a grievance or dispute as a disciplinary violation.

In exchange for the NPRA's commitment to maintain discipline among the prisoners, the department agreed that all meals would be served in the dining room; furloughs and educational and work releases would be reinstated within 18 months;[567] prisoners would receive good time for blood donation; the guards' union and the administration would support a piece of legislation that would make lifers eligible for parole after 10 rather than 15 years (a recommendation of the Elam Committee); and community members would once again have access to the prison. The administration also agreed to consider a family-visit or private-visit program.[568]

The body of the agreement spelled out the rights and responsibilities of each of the programs sponsored by the NPRA. The agreement stipulated the DOC's responsibility for the creation of rules and regulations, which were to be distributed to the prisoners for comment by November 1. This was in itself a first: there had never been written regulations at MCI Walpole. Further, the administration agreed to publish the rules in both English and Spanish. Building on the work done with DOC lawyers developing the Model Rules and Regulations, Walpole's new regulations were to fill "a critical need for a system of law within MCI Walpole, a system which provides direction for residents and personnel on the rights and responsibilities of the residents."[569]

The agreement turned out to be only an exercise; ultimately, enforcement proved impossible. Still, Hamm and Kerrigan, alternating as president when the other was in segregation, used the NPRA as a vehicle to push for prison reform for two more years. A second contract was never negotiated.

For all the prisoners involved, the experience of autonomy and self-determination was critical. For 30 years, through dozens of moves, in and out of segregation, Hamm had kept his NPRA pass card allowing him, as president, to move "freely" through Walpole. When I began writing this book, Ralph Hamm sent me the card with a note, "Perhaps this will be of use getting you into prison."

12

THOSE WHO DARED

the promise of abolition

I could be bounded in a nutshell and count myself a
king of infinite space, were it not that I have dreams.
—Hamlet

FROM THE BIRTH OF BANTU AND THE NPRA AT WALPOLE IN
the fall of 1972 and throughout the struggles, victories, and defeats over the spring
and summer of 1973, the Walpole prisoners never used a "rights" framework to articulate their position. Their struggle was about much more than their rights as prisoners or even as human beings. Their struggle was about the way they defined their
relationship with the world they lived in, and how they would negotiate meeting
their needs and honoring their responsibilities within the confines of their captivity.
First, they proclaimed their unity: they were brothers; the fulfillment of each one's
needs rested upon fulfilling the needs of the other. Next, they were laborers: they
had skills to trade in order to meet their needs. They demanded recognition as such,
including fair wages and the creation of a safe working environment where they could
act upon their fundamental entitlement to take care of themselves, their families, and
their community. Last, they were individual human beings: fathers, husbands, sons,
friends, and students.

After the brutal repression of June and July of 1973, the prisoners, stripped of
much of their power, put forth a plan. Immediately following their successful union
election on July 28, they held what was to be their last press conference. They wanted

the public to know that theirs was a bid for much more than self-determination. They wanted to participate in the constructive development of the communities that they came from, the communities they had harmed. They were particularly concerned about the young men who, without some intervention, seemed destined to join them behind the walls of Walpole. Their "Plan of Action," as they called it, presented their vision for a world where there would be ever-diminishing criminal activity. They attached the "Prisoner Bill of Rights" that was drafted by the California Prisoners Union and advanced by the national office of the NPRA.

The NPRA went further—beyond Walpole, beyond prison reform. They advocated for the abolition of prisons and personal liberty for all prisoners to work with society to resolve the problem of crime. Still, the prisoners understood that while incarceration still existed there was a place for advocacy for recognition of the basic needs and basic rights that were too often violated by prison authorities. If prisoners were forced to sink below this minimum standard, their own humanity would be compromised. The "Bill of Rights" was the minimum standard that the Walpole prisoners could live with. In the ensuing 30 years, it has been a struggle merely to attain this minimum standard.

For many of the volunteers, the experiences from March to May of 1973 revealed two surprising things: prisoners could safely determine their own reality, and a prison with no guards that was run democratically by prisoners functioned smoothly and was profoundly productive. This experience offered a new model: prisoner self-determination and humane containment—the model advocated by John O. Boone.

THE PLAN OF ACTION

Most of the prisoners in Walpole had come through Massachusetts's notorious Training Schools. The men at Walpole saw Jerome Miller dismantle these horrific places where, as children, they had been locked in isolation rooms, sometimes chained to beds. Robert Dellello described growing up in these rooms.

> By the time I got out of prison, at the age of 64, I had spent all but 12 years of my life locked up. The worst part was the juvenile system. Only those of us who grew up in these horrible circumstances can really appreciate what Jerry Miller did when he closed those places down. No child should ever have to live through what we lived through. Children—children do not belong locked up. Children do not belong in prison.[570]

Jerome Miller left Massachusetts in 1972 before he could be fired by an irate legislature.[571] The prisoners were eager to protect his legacy.

The first point of the NPRA's Plan of Action addressed the needs of "juvenile offenders." The NPRA described their vision of a halfway house for youth staffed with "competent psychologists, social workers, and others in the social rehabilitation field who would be available to counsel the residents." They recommended that ex-prisoners be included on staff as mentors and counselors.

The NPRA went on to examine the preparation prisoners needed to re-enter society. At its roots, the NPRA was an educational project. Many of the men were illiterate. The NPRA stressed the need for a basic elementary-school curriculum over college or even a high-school program. The prisoners believed firmly in their capacity to complete their educational preparation and articulated the need for an accredited college program. But they insisted that the primary focus of prison education needed to be elementary and high-school education.

Additionally, the NPRA recommended that prisoners serve as assistant teachers, be involved in curriculum development, and be paid at a paraprofessional level. This recommendation arose from within the NPRA Education Committee, which had set up its own classrooms and developed its own curricula under the leadership of Solomon Brown. They learned that men would participate in classes if the classes were relevant to them and if they could relate to their fellow prisoner-teachers. The DOC did not act upon this recommendation, and by 1974 the NPRA would develop the Adult Basic Education Program in Walpole. The prisoners determined the curriculum and co-facilitated the classes with professors from Curry College and volunteers from the American Friends Service Committee.

The prisoners recognized the fundamental tenet of what has become known as "restorative justice." They knew that they had harmed their victims and that the crimes they had committed had harmed their communities. They also knew that, as perpetrators, their own healing was a prerequisite to the health of society at large. They recommended individual counseling to supplement the group counseling and peer counseling that was available at the time. The NPRA explained that many prisoners needed the security of a confidential, therapeutic relationship to grapple with the issues that had brought them to prison. Family counseling was an important part of the healing process, especially if the prisoner was married and had children. The NPRA recognized that counseling might save the family unit, often destroyed by the pressure and shame of incarceration.

The NPRA was first and foremost a prison-based project. Even though the prisoners recognized that prisons themselves were a primary cause of crime, and the NPRA was an abolitionist organization, the leadership knew from experience that prisons were maintained by complex interests. The path away from punishment and toward problem solving could not be left to prison administrators or advocates or community support groups—no matter how dedicated.

Because of the success of their administration of the prison, the NPRA believed they had proven that prisoner leadership and direction is essential to both the reform and abolition of prisons. Space must be created for prisoners to have a role in policy development, classification, job assignments, and discipline. Without acknowledged prisoner self-determination within the carceral system, prisons would multiply. Their form might change—the new prison might be a better environment or it might be much worse. But without prisoner leadership, it would remain a hopelessly punitive structure, and all of society would suffer the ever-expanding effects of that punishment.

The leadership of the NPRA did not believe that they were unique. They believed that, given the opportunity, similar leadership based upon democratic principles, justice, racial equity, and self-determination could emerge in all prisons. They had learned that prisoners, given resources and preparation, understood that, despite the very real racial, class, and organized-crime distinctions, they were all in their situation together. Prisoners innately knew they had one choice: they could be "pigs" or they could be "men."[572] Given the opportunity, they believed prisoners would choose to be men.

The NPRA prisoners' union was a broad-based project. The Walpole members wanted people who were struggling with the issues of crime and punishment to be in close communication with each other. Prison reform was connected to many other social issues, so lines of communication among advocates needed to be constructed so that people could build upon each other's work. They recommended that a national clearinghouse for prison reform be developed at the NPRA national headquarters in Rhode Island.

The NPRA was a cultural project. Given the effects of racism in prison and in the larger society, the NPRA recommended the development of strong cultural programs that would teach prisoners about their own heritages, increasing their self-esteem and pride. They envisioned rich programs, including music and art. They also recommended that prisoners teach each other about the fullness of their various cultural traditions. The Walpole prisoners had learned that understanding increased appreciation and developed a greater sense of brotherhood.

The NPRA was a full employment project. One of the most crucial tasks a prisoner undertakes upon release from prison is that of finding employment. The NPRA recommended that prisoners work with federal and state governments, along with private industry, to develop job-training programs within prisons. A job-placement network would complement the job-training programs. The NPRA was clear: the jobs needed to be decent and pay fair wages, or prisoners would return to crime. This brief recommendation for decent, well-paying jobs for prisoners was written when the whole country was experiencing the high unemployment and skyrocketing prices that became know as "stagflation." Yet, the NPRA was not about to buy into the idea that there were "not enough" jobs for everyone. The fact that society was willing to waste substantial amounts of money keeping them in prison led them to draw their own conclusions. They knew there were enough resources; they simply needed to be apportioned more pragmatically, and for the good of all people.

And ultimately, the NPRA was a project of abolition. Along with its Plan of Action, the NPRA proposed a number of alternatives to prison. Their own experience had led them to conclude that, given the practical supports outlined in the Plan of Action, 70 percent of prisoners in maximum security prisons—and all those in lower-security prisons—could be released immediately to community-based halfway houses without presenting any real danger to the communities involved. They made this recommendation knowing that the population they were discussing was composed of prisoners who were doing their time in maximum security, and thus were dubbed the most dangerous. This was the cornerstone of John O. Boone's philosophy and a perspective shared by Peter Goldmark, Jim Isenberg, and Boone's administration.

THE PRISONER BILL OF RIGHTS: BOTTOM LINES

The Thirteenth Amendment of the US Constitution prohibits slavery and involuntary servitude, with one exception: as a punishment for those convicted of a crime. With the Thirteenth Amendment, the US government restructured the institution of slavery: it went from being a privatized institution to a nationalized one. Slavery was never abolished in the United States. "Ownership" simply changed hands. People who were convicted were subject to forced labor and regulation of every aspect of their lives: they became the property of the state rather than individuals. It is very difficult to discuss constitutional protections for those who have been stripped of their status as citizens. This conflict affected the burgeoning prisoners' rights movement that developed in the wake of the civil rights movement and the prison rebellions of the late '60s and early '70s. The prisoners' rights movement made its centerpiece a prisoners' "Bill of Rights." California adopted a prisoners' bill of rights into law. Despite the statutory guarantees of prisoner rights, California has the largest and most brutal state prison system in the country and the second-largest death row in the world.

The adopted Prisoner Bill of Rights began with a statement of entitlement. Prisoners are entitled to "every constitutional right exercised by the outside population." But the entitlement was qualified: "except for those inherently inconsistent with the operation of the institution." Interpretation of this exception clause has been the undoing of the entire document each time it has been applied. The exception presupposed that the operation of the institution was a good thing and that the institution should operate unhampered in its dual duty of security and punishment. Although the burden of proof regarding the necessity of depriving prisoners' liberties rested with the institution, the prison system has always been adept at convincing both the judiciary and the public of the absolute necessity of deprivation.

The document went on to guarantee public access to and scrutiny of prisons. Prisoners were defined as persons with the right to certain "essentials" for their well-being, modeled after the UN Declaration of Human Rights. Add the exception clause to each of these as you read them.

1. Unrestricted access to the courts and legal counsel
2. Freedom from physical abuse or threat of physical abuse
3. Adequate diet and sanitation, fresh air and exercise, prompt medical and dental care and prescription drugs

4. Maintenance of relationships by frequent meetings and uncensored correspondence
5. Reasonable access to the press
6. Religious freedom
7. Rules and regulations that must be published in written forms and the prohibition of excessive and disproportionate punishments
8. Uncensored access to reading materials
9. Work release at prevailing wages
10. A judicial proceeding for determination of parole
11. Full restoration of civil rights upon release from prison
12. The unrestricted right to petition for redress of grievances

Movements must recognize the dangers of adopting "rights-based" platforms. Once the rights are defined, the movement is always left with the onerous task of obtaining and defending them rather than advancing their broader causes. This restricts creativity and actual problem solving. But many prisoners and advocates, including those in the Walpole NPRA and the AHC, saw in this list of rights an insurance policy. The prisoners rationalized that if the system worked as it should, the NPRA could at least guarantee prisoners the list above. The problem is, the system does not work as it should; it works as it is intended to.

THE DREAM

The NPRA's plan concluded with an exhortation to the public that served as both explanation and invitation. The NPRA explained that it existed within the context of a struggle to claim their status among "men." Since the NPRA had been reelected by the prisoners as their representative in July 1973, and since the organization had survived the repression of the spring, the prisoners proclaimed the struggle for mere existence over. Now, they stated, it was time to begin their work in earnest.

They declared the time was over when prisoners would sit idly by, "like fans at a ball game," while prison administrators determined their fate. The time had come for prisoners to enter the game, as both players and referees. Because of their experience with the Ad Hoc Committee and the Observer Program, they believed that the general public would actually care about the fate of prisoners. They believed that when the public understood how much the punishment cost taxpayers, prisons would be abandoned and replaced with "workable, less expensive alternatives." The prisoners invited the public to support their vision of a just society, thinking the public understood they needed the prisoners' support to end crime. Most ironically, they assumed that the observers were a mirror for the broader society and that the public, like the observers, shared their vision of a just and equitable society.

This was to be a serious miscalculation born out of a unique experience. Even today, Ed Rodman admits that he does not know why the civilian observer program garnered such support during the crucial three months when the Walpole guards were engaged in their strike and slowdown. Perhaps the dramatic actions of the Walpole prisoners in the year following the prison rebellion at Attica simply engaged the public's attention until the next burning issue came along to distract it. In Massachusetts, that issue was the desegregation of the public schools. The prisoners did not recognize that the interest of the civilian observers had begun to wane even before May 18. After the Observer Program was interrupted in June, the shifts became very difficult to fill. Even if the administration had not placed significant barriers in its way, the program would have been forced to scale back. The energy to maintain it had dissipated.

The prisoners, for their part, were calling out, trying to cajole the public into meeting them once more on their ground, urging them to finish the project that they had begun together and to "replace prisons with a different system of correction for lawbreakers." The NPRA closed its last full public statement with the words, "Join our cause."

WHAT WAS TO FOLLOW?

Within a year, the AHC was replaced with the New England Prison Alliance (NEPA), and the Massachusetts prisoners' rights movement was born. NEPA was both a coalition of organizations and a membership organization. Its mission was "to discover positive solutions to the problems that today's prisons present."[573]

The NPRA was in crisis, under extreme internal and external pressures at the same time. Hamm remembers,

> Once Bobby escaped, and the apparent truce that he negotiated between the Irish and Italian factions dissolved, I (an African-American with no love for either side) could not talk to them and expect results.... During this time the guards and prison administration "systematically picked off" the NPRA, block representatives, council board members and prisoner self-help group leaders under the umbrella of NPRA ... for transfers to segregation units and federal facilities, usually on the trumped up charge of conspiring to take hostages and create a work strike, based upon "reliable informant information" that they never had to prove.[574]

In 1974, with NEPA's assistance the prisoners published "the Walpole Prisoners' Statement." It was drafted by two white prisoners. There was no conscious effort to include broad racial and cultural viewpoints in the document. The board of the NPRA had dissolved. Ralph Hamm and John Kerrigan were unable to maintain the unity within the white prisoner population without Robert Dellelo's influence. Hamm, confined to 10 Block for long periods of time, struggled to maintain programs and cohesiveness among Black prisoners. This became his focus as the demographics of Walpole began to change—a result of crime policy directed at the social control of urban, Black, and Latino communities. While NEPA was a large and vital organization, it glossed over the achievements of the NPRA.

A thousand copies of the statement were made on the prison printing press. In its brief history of resistance at Walpole, the NPRA is mentioned only one time: Ralph Hamm, as former president of the NPRA, is thanked for his work. The NPRA's Plan of Action was redacted into a social memorandum and the body of the 90-page document is a collection of legal briefs and complaints written to assure that prisoners' rights were honored. The social memorandum ended with a criticism of lawyers and judges rather than the challenge to "join our cause."

IN THE END

Since 1974, many organizations have wrestled with the problems presented by the criminal justice system. Over thirty years of dedicated work by these groups is ample testimony to the complexity of the issue. Still, there remain many tested remedies that, if implemented, would diminish many of the problems we confront today. The NPRA hit upon many of them in their Plan of Action. But the problems we would solve are really just the symptoms of the actual dilemma: the existence of the carceral system. It won't be easy. The prison industrial complex (PIC) provides the internal structure of modern society.

The PIC is the postmodern equivalent of the industrial revolution. One of the key problems of the modern era is that of surplus people—in other words, people whose existence will not increase the wealth of the elite—no matter how productively they are engaged. In the industrial revolution, peasants were released from the land. Marx called them the *vogelfrei* or "free folk." They were free to travel to market their labor. Today's *vogelfrei* are freed from productive labor itself. Ironically, they represent a loss in value as long as their bodies are free. Once their bodies are captive, once they are chattel of the state, they become both the raw material and the product of the PIC. In the state of Massachusetts, there is one prison employee for every three prisoners. And this does not take into account the jobs of those who service prisons, the employees of the parole and probation departments, law enforcement, the juvenile justice system, or those who in other ways feed the criminal justice system.

Prisons and the other institutions that constitute the punishment system are a structural solution for the problems of an aging economy. If we take the time to analyze who is in prison and why they are there, we are confronted with the following reality: over 50 percent of the prisoners are Black men between the ages of 18 and 28; 80 percent have substance-abuse problems; 60 percent have done nothing violent; close to 60 percent are in prison because they technically violated their parole contract (in other words, they were not convicted of a new crime); most were abused as children; 64 percent are functionally illiterate; almost all are poor; and all will suffer civil disenfranchisement to a greater or lesser extent for the rest of their lives. What do these statistics mean? While well over half of these men and women have not physically harmed another person, all of these people have been harmed themselves. Why are they imprisoned? One cannot escape the conclusion that they are being punished because they exist. Punishing them is profitable. Letting them live and flourish is not.

In rural communities, those who labored on farms and in factories have watched their ability to be self-reliant disappear as multinational corporations have taken over the production of food and goods. The prison, private or state run, has become synonymous with economic development. These communities envision a prison, sitting there—offering them jobs, always hungry, stable, growing. In reality, the prison pushes away all other community-development partnerships. It does not pay taxes; the schools become impoverished, and downtowns disappear. Still, city planners argue that the only way out is the creation of another prison or a larger prison complex. This scene plays itself out across the country as prisons and related industries have become both the warp and the weft of societal fabric.

The PIC does not end at the US border. American penal experts were brought to Iraq to design the prisons that would cage those who would dissent.[575] The depravity of these prisons was exposed by the photographs from Abu Ghraib depicting the brutal and humiliating torture of Iraqi men. The fact that the Iraqi prisons were modeled after US supermaximum prisons and that torture is also a regular occurrence within their US counterparts was barely touched upon by mainstream media. US-based privatized prison corporations are entrenched in Australia and England and are making inroads in Japan and some third world countries. These corporations not only construct and administer actual prisons but provide food for vending machines and cafeterias, medical care, cleaning supplies, technology to enhance security, consultants to evaluate prison systems, and boutique treatment programs for special populations. Some are designated not-for-profit corporations.

It is tempting to look at criminal justice from a narrow perspective. If we do so, we can convince ourselves that what is needed is youth programs, job training, decent-paying jobs, educational programs for prisoners, better-trained prison staff, and so on. In fact, all of these things must be done in order to repair the damage done by the PIC. In reality, even if we accomplish all of these things, the PIC will remain intact. These reforms, even the radical ones, will become the new prison, creating a different set of jobs and a different set of dependencies.

Often, I hear people saying—"If the prison system was really working the way it is supposed to, there would not be any recidivism. Rehabilitation would take place." In fact, the prison system is working exactly as it is supposed to. Prisoners enter prison; a scant few among them will be able to avail themselves of any resources, change their lives, and come back to their communities prepared to engage as productive citizens. Even though over 90 percent of convicted felons will eventually return to their communities, roughly two-thirds of these men and women will return to prison. There are many reasons that they do not make it—paramount among them is that they are not supposed to. Prisoners leave prison with a criminal record. They cannot get a job; they cannot get public housing; they cannot get educational loans. They are not supposed to succeed. If they truly were supposed to take their place in society, much more would be done to prepare them for the roles they are to play and to make sure that there is a place in their communities for them when they are released. But if they took their supposed place, they could not be raw material. They could not be product.

The PIC consists of a tight braid of US government interests, international economic interests, and punishment regimes. Each of these strands locks the others in place. To understand the complexity of the PIC, the braid must be unraveled so that we can understand how each strand works individually, as well as how it connects to the others. To do so, those of us who are concerned about building a just and equitable society where all people can live in peace need to work together, to listen to and learn from each other's analysis. Whether we work to stop war, end racism, or oppose the oppressions of globalization, we need to see the connections in our work and the ways our issues connect to the punishment regime. We must organize across these issues so that our collective interests as "the people" can begin to dismantle the structures that compose the spectrum of security that ranges from the US self-proclaimed role as global police in the war on terror to the private security guard hired by the local pharmacy. We have to stop being the "fans at the ball game." It is time that we recognize that the cause we join is our own. Like the NPRA, we must create a community of resistance and accept leadership from those who have been most oppressed.

A COMMUNITY OF RESISTANCE

This story takes place just as a completely conscious and focused racialized criminal justice policy was emerging across the country. Even though the criminal justice system was created to control Black and immigrant populations, a dramatic shift in policy toward mass incapacitation began in 1968.[576] These policies were developed in reaction to intense internal pressure for broad social change within the United States and the emerging solidarity with Native American, Southeast Asian, Latin American, and African liberation movements. The civil rights movement, the assassination of Black leadership at all levels of that movement, the Chicago Democratic Party convention, and the urban rebellions from deep within the Black communities culminated with the Bobby Seale trial and the occupation of the city of New Haven, Connecticut, by the National Guard in advance of any actual unrest. It was within this context that the US government began issuing reports that again demonized the Black man. The media built upon these reports and created a climate of fear.

Attica is often cited as the beginning of a liberal penal policy rooted in the rehabilitation model. In fact, the opposite is true. As the prisoners in Attica proclaimed themselves men able to control their own destinies and the men in Walpole formed the NPRA, new policies based on overt racial profiling and incapacitation were already being put in place. Fear of the Black militant was capitalized upon following the Attica rebellion and was the backdrop to the Rockefeller drug laws in New York, which became the model for US criminal justice policy. This deliberately constructed racialized punishment policy resulted in the mass incarceration of Black men and women, swelling the prison populations from under 200,000 to more than 2 million men and women in just 30 years.

During the year that the NPRA represented the prisoner population at Walpole, they struggled against the linchpin of the punishment system. They openly recognized that even though the Black and Latino populations were small, they were growing as the white population was decreasing. Walpole prison relied upon a virulently racist societal structure for its existence. Dealing with racism was the first order of business. The Black leadership made it clear that eradicating racism and prison "reform" were intertwined. Unless the white prisoners agreed to stand with the Black prisoners and accept them as leaders, there would be no unity. The NPRA existed because the white leadership made a conscious commitment to actual brotherhood, equality, and equity. Because of BANTU's commitment to Black Consciousness, the prisoners learned that as long as the powerful maintained the privilege to punish—and to punish unto death—that privilege would be exercised against Black prisoners first, and then on the rest of them. Challenging the punishment regime meant and means ending racism. Black and Latino leadership equal to white leadership was not symbolic; it was the core of the project. It was the root of the NPRA's power.[577]

The NPRA was a community of resistance, and this is the key to unraveling the braid. The men of Walpole evaluated their captivity, studied the way that society defined them, and then rejected the whole package. They resisted the role they had been consigned to in society. They created new definitions for themselves and for the institution they inhabited. And then they committed themselves to living in the world that they had created.

The NPRA refused to define themselves as criminals paying for their transgressions. And so, they did not form an inmate council; they did not advocate for prisoners' rights. They formed a labor union. Rather than acceding to the demand that they be only raw material and product, they made it clear that they were also producers, workers who were imprisoned—exploited as slave labor under the law.

In the 19th century, the call for the abolition of slavery swelled across the world. In the 20th century, the prisoners at Walpole joined voices with outside advocates to call again for abolition, the abolition of the legal slavery of prisons.

Today, their question remains: Do we dare join their cause?

LESSONS LEARNED

by robert dellelo

As I READ THIS BOOK AND REFLECT UPON THE PAST, I HAVE JUST turned 66 years of age and have spent over two-thirds of my life in some form of confinement, from the reform schools to state prison. In April of 1964, I entered Walpole State Prison with a natural life sentence and a seventh-grade education. In November of 2003, having overturned my sentence, I left prison with a bachelor's degree, having majored in sociology. While at Walpole, I was the first president of the Prisoner's Union (National Prisoners Reform Association), and chairman of the Inmate Advisory Council that preceded the NPRA. Now, having over 50 years of field experience in the "causes and effects" of confinement, having watched brats turned into killers and having seen sane citizens turned into violent, hard core, insane criminals, all in the name of "corrections," I hold myself out to be an expert in rehabilitation and corrections.

As an expert, the most important lesson I can pass on is that prisons don't work. They are wrong in concept and wrong in application; they are human abominations, manifesting corrupt policies and politics. Prisons are unreformable monster factories, and when we attempt to "reform" them, it is always an exercise in futility; there is no way to make rational sense out of insanity. Today, in Massachusetts and many other places in the country, we are spending more money on "corrections" than we are spending on higher education. However you try to cut it, that's a formula for social disaster.

The crux of the problem is that we have created a parasitical, self-serving, and self-perpetuating prison system. This system is not only detrimental to the individual, but detrimental to society as a whole. For the most part, individuals leave the system less able to maintain their lives with dignity than when they came in. The present system of "corrections" is an abyss, swallowing up taxpayers' money to incapacitate and debilitate prisoners, denying any meaningful rehabilitation, and consequently producing more crime than originally existed, which gives politicians a stand to call for more prisons. And more.

The bigger this monster system becomes the more uncontrollable and unmanageable it is. More people are invested in it. They buy up stock in prison industries. They bid for the right to provide food, uniforms. Some establish correctional officers' academies, and others attend them, with the guarantee of jobs on graduation. So in the end, these systems create financial security for a few, at the great cost of many. This is why, if there were a magical button, that, if pressed, would instantly rehabilitate all prisoners and reduce the Massachusetts recidivism rate to zero, the Massachusetts Department of Correction (DOC) would not press this button.

Look at this. The increase in correctional officers' salaries since 1992: 70 to 77 percent. The average percent increase in all Massachusetts wage earners' salaries since 1992: 42.3 percent. The salaries of Massachusetts correctional officers in 1992, *excluding benefits and overtime*: $35,386 to $40,531. Correctional officers' salaries in 2003, *excluding benefits and overtime*: $59,919 to $71,946. Add to this all the bonds borrowed for building prisons, and all the tax breaks given to the multinational corporations that build them. Not only is this present system becoming bigger and bigger, it is becoming more and more expensive. Now that the military industrial complex has recaptured the bulk of taxpayers' money and is busy supplying the materials they'd diverted to prisons to the war machine again, states cannot afford to keep prisons open. So they do away with all programs and most services, pushing people out with no attempt at rehabilitating them. Society simply cannot afford this—financially, socially, or morally. So, how do we get out of this?

What we need to do is create a correctional system that is self-disintegrating. We need to create a correctional system that's truly dedicated to *correcting the problem.* Any system that is truly dedicated to corrections has to be grounded in theory and practice on the rehabilitation of prisoners. And by rehabilitate, I do not mean return them to the way they were. I mean to *"prepare and assist each such person to assume the responsibilities and exercise the rights of a citizen of the commonwealth."*

Simply put, if we rehabilitate prisoners there will be fewer and fewer prisoners in the system. There will be less and less need for staff, so slots left vacant by retirement, quitting, or death won't have to be filled. With fewer prisoners and staff we will need fewer prisons. And the money being wasted on containment can go back into primary education and other basic services known to reduce poverty and thus crime.

Only the prisoner can make the decision to rehabilitate himself; however, the system must provide the necessary tools for the individual to use to help his rehabilitative effort. We know that rehabilitation works. But there are no longer rehabilitation programs serving the majority of prisoners. Not only has the political will shifted so that people and politicians somehow feel justified in not providing programs, we also don't have people who are trained in how to assist, support, and help direct an individual down a meaningful path of rehabilitation. Yet there are many individuals in the "correctional" system who, in spite of the present system, have turned their lives around; they have rehabilitated themselves. These individuals possess invaluable knowledge and experience, indeed, they are experts trained (through personal experience) in rehabilitation. If their skills were properly honed and applied, these individuals could be employed by the DOC to teach other individuals to rehabilitate themselves.

And what about the people who are never getting out? How many of these individuals are in the system? I would venture to say, far more than you could ever imagine. The present system doesn't "waste" resources on these individuals. They are left to wallow in the prison cesspool. This is a terrible waste of invaluable resources. And why rehabilitate them? If we "invested" in these individuals, trained them as teachers, provided them with ways to obtain vocational skills, got them certified as instructors in carpentry, plumbing, masonry, this would not only give meaning and purpose to these individuals' lives, it would give them the skills they could pass on to other prisoners who could not only make a living wage on the street, but who could also maintain the institutions, at huge savings to the state. And of course, if they were working for real wages, these prisoners would be paying taxes, which would help defray the cost of the correctional system as it was being converted into a self-disintegrating system, in addition to helping to keep their families out of poverty—and prison.

The DOC might not have the will to make this change. But we do. And the fact is that we have the tools in our hands, too. Massachusetts put good laws on the books back in the 1970s. According to Massachusetts's statutory mandate, part of the powers and duties of the commissioner of the Department of Correction is to rehabilitate prisoners. It's right there in the Massachusetts General Law, Chapter 124:

(e)   establish, maintain and administer programs of rehabilitation, *including but not limited to education, training and employment,* of persons committed to the custody of the department, designed as far as practicable to *prepare and assist each such person to assume the responsibilities and exercise the rights of a citizen of the commonwealth;*

(f)   establish a classification of persons committed to the custody of the department *for the purpose of developing a rehabilitation program for each such person.*[578] [my emphasis]

The reform undertaken by the prisoners and their allies in the 1970s was sacrificed to politics. It fell off the political agenda; and this is why reform isolated within the prison cannot work. It is too subject to who is in office and how the hype around prisons affects the rest of their agendas. There are no consequences for those who choose to ignore the good laws that Massachusetts and other states put on the books.

And that's where we come in. We must demonstrate the consequences. States stand to lose tremendous amounts of money by not fulfilling the wandering policies of the National Institute of Corrections—say, the trend toward "gang prevention" that ends up creating gang members where there were none. But the money Massachusetts would lose through the withdrawal of federal funding pales in comparison to the amount of money it would lose if prisoners sued the Department of Correction for withholding the programming that has been defined as theirs under Massachusetts law.

Voting-rights laws were on the books for a long time before people forced them to be honored, one case at a time. The people of Massachusetts began the push for real rehabilitation over three decades ago. We are poised to continue the struggle— we just need individuals who will work in common cause with the prisoners to claim what is on the books. And when we have it—when people in other states see how much safer we all are, how much more money there is for enhancing our lives—they will clamor for it, too.

ENDNOTES

1   Wessel Commission, *Report and Recommendations of the Governor's Committee to Study the Massachusetts Correctional System* (January 25, 1955), p. 11.

2   David Beck, Philip et al., *Massachusetts Department of Corrections: Strategy, Structure and Executive Manpower* (Cambridge, MA: Kennedy School Case Program, 1977), hereinafter the Kennedy School Report, Introduction, p. 23. Norfolk Prison was designed by the renowned sociologist Howard Belding Gill. The Wessel Commission described the intended plan for the prison: "The plant was designed as a self-contained community with facilities for a town hall and other community enterprises on one hand to a town jail on the other." However, the commission went on to state that, by 1955, "The basic concepts of individualized treatment with well-trained and well-educated house officers, the police force, the specialists in community living and other areas have ceased to exist." Boone would later bring in George Bohlinger, who was a protégé of Gill, to run the prison as it was intended.

3   "The Siege of Cherry Hill," *Time Magazine,* January 31, 1955, reprinted on *Time.com.* The DOC actually brought a military tank inside the prison. A wall had to be broken down to fit it in.

4   Wessel Commission, *Message from His Excellency the Governor Submitting Recommendations Relative to Reorganizing the Correctional System of the Commonwealth* (June 9, 1955), hereinafter the Wessel Report, p. 17.

5   Wessel Report, p. 2.

6   Wessel Report, p. 14. John Boone would make the same analysis upon his arrival in 1970.

7   Wessel Report, p. 22. Again, John Boone would be the first administrator to codify regulations for the DOC.

8   Wessel Report, p. 28.

9   Wessel Report, p. 28.

10 In 1971, the Citizens' Committee on Corrections would struggle with many of the same issues. Their recommendations addressed budget allocations and fiscal corruption, and provided a map for guard training and diversification of the workforce. Wessel never mentions the racial issues inherent in maintaining an all-white corrections staff.

11 Wessel Report, p. 33.

12 Wessel Report, p. 33.

13 The creation of a citizens' review board has been a rallying cry of many prison reformers. Such a review board has been mandated in statute in two different forms in Massachusetts, first in 1955 and again in 1972 (Chapter 777). One has never been empanelled. In 2005, a one-year Citizens' Review Board was established to report on the progress of prison reform. The chair resigned in disgust nine months into the project.

14 This connection would be articulated again in a 2004 report on the findings of the Harshbarger Commission, which recommended a move toward presumptive parole. See "Strengthening Public Safety, Increasing Accountability, and Instituting Fiscal Responsibility in the Department of Correction," issued by the Governor's Commission on Corrections Reform, June 30, 2004, at http://www.mass.gov/Eeops/docs/eops/Gov-Commission_Corrections_Reform.pdf.

15 Wessel Report, p. 61.

16 Wessel Report, p. 61.

17 Wessel Report, p. 87.

18 These recommendations were focused on preparing the idle and "criminal" poor for their future as the industrious or working poor.

19 Wessel Report, p. 93. This small daily wage was to become a prominent collective-bargaining issue for the NPRA.

20 Wessel Report, p. 112.

21 Boone and Isenberg exploited this provision in their community corrections strategies.

22 Despite this provision, no regulations had been established when Boone arrived 16 years later.

23 Incapacitation of people through placement in prison began, in earnest, in 1970, after the civil unrest in 1968 and 1969.

24 John Boone, interview, October 4, 2004, Atlanta, GA.

25 Kennedy School Report, Part I, p. 31.

26 When Jerome Miller became director of DYS, he closed all the juvenile lock-ups, known as Training Schools. The men who had once been held in these prisons said that they were training schools for the adult prisons. Miller replaced these lock-ups with community-based programs that kept the young people within their communities and simultaneously addressed the community issues that put the children in danger. See Miller's *Last One Over the Wall: The Massachusetts Experiment in Closing Reform Schools* (Columbus: Ohio State University Press, 1991). Goldmark hoped to do the same with the DOC.

27 Kennedy School Report, Part I, p. 29.

28 John Boone, interview, October 12, 2001, Atlanta, GA.

29 Most of the officers were unionized into locals represented either by AFSCME or the AFL-CIO. The various locals met together on a monthly basis as the Penal Committee of Council 4–AFSCME; Howard Doyle was council president. At the Bridgewater prison complex and at Norfolk State Prison, the guards, unsatisfied with the representation they received from AFSCME, formed an independent union with 600 members. The Walpole Guards Union was originally independent. Under Boone, it became part of Council 4–AFSCME.

30 Kennedy School Report, Part II, p. 8. This problem was also cited in the Harshbarger Commission report issued in 2004 (see n. 14). The power of the guards' unions, combined with their refusal to recognize prisoners as workers with similar rights, remains a key barrier to institutional reform.

31 Bobby Dellelo is referred to in Miller's book, *Last One Over the Wall*. See n. 26.

32 Robert Dellelo, interview, March 20, 2006, Cambridge, MA.

33 Ralph Hamm, phone interview, March 4, 2004.

34 Ralph Hamm, phone interview, March 22, 2007.

35 Robert Dellelo, interview, March 23, 2007, Cambridge, MA.

36 Robert Dellelo, interview, March 23, 2007, Cambridge, MA.

37 Attica Prisoner Charles Horatio Crowley ("Brother Flip") as quoted in "War at Attica: Was There No Other Way," *Time Magazine*, September 27, 1971, p. 18.

38 "War at Attica: Was There No Other Way," *Time Magazine*, September 27, 1971, p. 20.

39 Kennedy School Report, Introduction, p. 7.

40 Citizens' Committee on Corrections, *Corrections 71: A Citizens' Report* (Commonwealth of Massachusetts, November 30, 1971), hereinafter *Corrections 71*, p. 3.

41 F. B. Taylor, "State Jail Probers Decry Emphasis on Punishment," *Boston Globe*, December 3, 1971.

42 *Corrections 71*.

43 Robert Dellelo, interview, March 14, 2004, Cambridge, MA. The commissioner's collapse from extreme fatigue while awaiting the results of the Elam Committee's meeting with the prisoners at Walpole is documented in the Kennedy School Report, Part I, p. 24.

44 Kennedy School Report, Introduction, p. 12.

45 Robert Dellelo, interview, June 12, 2006, Cambridge, MA.

46 Brother of notorious Boston mobster, Stephen "the Rifleman" Flemmi.

47 Robert Dellelo, interview, April 26, 2006, Cambridge, MA. Nalidar, a brand no longer used, was a sleeping pill.

48 William Ryan's book, *Blaming the Victim* (New York: Vintage Books, 1970), dissected "liberal democratic philosophy," and was the first published condemnation of the Moynihan Report, which blamed Black women for the "total breakdown" of their families. See Daniel Patrick Moynihan, *The Negro Family: The Case for National Action* (Washington, DC: US Department of Labor, 1965), known as the Moynihan Report, at http://www.dol.gov/oasam/programs/history/webid-meynihan.htm.

49 When I opened her boxes 30 years later, I was greeted by the almost fresh smell of cigarette smoke.

50 Phyllis Ryan, "Brief Chronology for the Ad Hoc Committee on Prison Reform." Unpublished document created by Ryan, in Bissonette archive, hereinafter Ryan Source 1.

51 Packard Manse to Governor Sargent, telegram, November 22, 1971, Bissonette archive.

52 Packard Manse telegram.

53 Packard Manse telegram.

54 Packard Manse, "600 Citizens Ask Governor To Close 'Medieval Chambers of Horror,'" press release, December 3, 1971.

55 The Inmate Grievance Committee included Leonard Westmoreland, Bobby Dellelo (until he was shipped out in October), George Nassar, Ralph Hamm, Miguel Trinidad, and Daniel Nolan.

56 Editorial, *Boston Herald Traveler*, November 19, 1971, p. 7.

57 *Haines v. Kerner*, 404 U.S. 519 (1972), January 13, 1972. The US Supreme Court directed a federal court to hear a prisoner's evidence that solitary confinement violated his civil rights. The court ruled against the plaintiff in a 7–0 decision. The case was brought by the NAACP Legal Defense Fund on behalf of Francis Haines, 69, who was serving a life sentence.

58 Phyllis Ryan notes on the conversation with Steve Teichner, December 1, 1971, in assembled notebook labeled "Postcard Welfare Citizen's Group," Bissonette archive.

59 Packard Manse, "600 Citizens Ask Governor To Close 'Medieval Chambers of Horror,'" press release, December 3, 1971.

60 Edward Rodman, interview, December 11, 2007, Cambridge, MA.

61 *Corrections 71*, p. 1.

62 See n. 1.

63 *Corrections 71*, p. 5.

64 *Corrections 71*, p. 6.

65 *Corrections 71*, p. 16.

66 Kennedy School Report, Part I, p. 9.

67 Ralph Hamm, phone conversation, February 28, 2006. Reflecting on this recommendation, Hamm acknowledges the problems presented by informality, but explains that the rise of prison bureaucracy has made it much more difficult for prisoners to organize effectively. The formation of a pan-department union for the guards has compounded the problems prisoners confront. As he puts it, "the bigger the bureaucracy, the bigger the corruption."

68 This has become the mantra of every investigative body and appointed commission.

69 That they even had to mention such basic necessities is an indicator of how terrible the conditions were.

70 *Corrections 71,* p. 28.

71 *Corrections 71,* p. 28.

72 Work release, educational release, and furlough were the foundations of John Boone's correctional philosophy.

73 This comment was fundamental in the prisoners' communication to the committee and to all other advocates—"We are the experts on crime. We know why we are here. We know why we will return. We must work together to solve the problem of crime."

74 *Corrections 71,* p. 24. The closing paragraph is a synopsis of the recommendations outlined on pp. 23–24.

75 Kennedy School Report, Part II, p. 11.

76 Kennedy School Report, Part II, p. 11.

77 Prisoners had to serve two-thirds of their sentences before they could become eligible for parole. Sargent advocated reducing this to half their sentences.

78 Sargent's advocacy for inmate councils indicates the success of the organizing at Norfolk prison, undertaken by prisoners, guards, and administration personnel who voluntarily met to decide how the prison should be run, with various committees responsible for different aspects of prison life. It was the leadership of this organizing effort at Norfolk that was "lugged" to the Bridgewater DSU in November 1971.

79 Judith Brody, "State Finds 'Evidence' Boston Violates 14th Amendment," *Boston Globe,* December 22, 1971.

80 Kennedy School Report, Part II, p. 3.

81 After this incident, the Boone family moved to Atlanta.

82 The Reverend Joseph Boone was a luminary in the Southern Christian Leadership Conference (SCLC).

83 John Boone, untitled draft (Colloquium on Correctional Facilities Planning, Sacramento, CA, 1977), Bissonette archive.

84 Colloquium on Correctional Facilities Planning, "Report" (Sacramento, CA, 1977), hereinafter California Colloquium, p. 246.

85 California Colloquium, p. 241.

86 Cultural competency is about implementing deep knowledge of people and groups, mainly in professional work, in order to do that work better. As such, the call for a culturally competent staff reacts in opposition to the call for an ambiguously diverse one. See K. Davis, *Exploring the Intersection Between Cultural Competency and Managed Behavioral Health Care Policy* (Alexandria, VA: National Technical Assistance Center for State Mental Health Planning, 1997).

87 California Colloquium, p. 241.

88 California Colloquium, p. 241.

89 To produce a riot, guards create the conditions for a number of prisoners to either break "rules" or fight with each other. Then, the guards rush in and brutally suppress the provoked riot.

90 California Colloquium, p. 239.

91 John Boone, interview, October 12, 2002, Atlanta, GA.

92 John Boone, interview, October 12, 2002, Atlanta, GA.

93 John Boone repeatedly says that he took the job because he was impressed with the sincerity of Sargent. This is from an interview with John O. Boone, corroborated by Sargent's memory of the conversation recorded in the Kennedy School Report, Part II, pp. 3–4.

94 The 1954 *Brown v. Board of Education* decision forced this change in legislation.

95 California Colloquium, p. 257.

96 John Boone, "3,000 Years and Life: Penal Abolition in Massachusetts" (Critical Resistance South Workshop, New Orleans, LA, 2002).

97 Richard Audet, "Drinan Tells of Abuses in Prisons," *Boston Globe,* December 5, 1971.

98   In many interviews, Boone has stated that he thought in going North, he would be going to the "promised land"—he was shocked to arrive in Boston and find that the schools were not desegregated, when the schools in the South had been forcibly desegregated nearly ten years before.

99   For analysis of the LEAA and its political impact see Christian Parenti, *Lockdown America: Police and Prisons in the Age of Crisis* (Brooklyn, NY: Verso, 1999). Parenti argues that the framework for the modern prison industrial complex was laid in 1965 by Johnson and then used by Nixon to control poor urban populations' actual and potential political dissent.

100 The text of the Act specifically names the "right" to use block grants "to carry out programs of behavioral research designed to provide more accurate information on the causes of crime and the effectiveness of various means of preventing crime, and to evaluate the success of correctional procedures." "Omnibus Crime Control and Safe Streets Act of 1968," Part D, Sec. 402 b, 3, http://www.fcc.gov/Bureaus/OSEC/library/legislative_histories/1615.pdf, p. 7.

101 Boone's appointment of Moore was unwelcomed by the prisoners. Moore was known as "More Gas Moore" because of his role in gassing the prisoners during the Charlestown State Prison rebellion that motivated the convening of the Wessel Commission.

102 Kennedy School Report, Part II, p. 13.

103 By his own report, Boone created this department—in interviews he has asserted that no regulations, reporting, or research existed in Massachusetts prior to his arrival. Government archives in the Massachusetts State House seem to corroborate this.

104 Boone would take advantage of a provision of Chapter 777 allowing for the hiring of ex-prisoners in order to bring him on staff.

105 Arnold Jaffe (DOC lawyer), interview, July 27, 2006, Cambridge, MA.

106 At the same time, George H. Bohlinger was appointed superintendent of Norfolk. Bohlinger was a student of Howard Gill, the originator of the community prison and one of Norfolk's first superintendents. Bohlinger began his administration by living among the Norfolk prisoners for six weeks. Donnelly proved less open to hearing prisoner concerns.

107 Ryan Source 1, including minutes from the beginning of the AHC, Bissonette archive.

108 *The Docket*, April 1973, p. 1. This is the newsletter of the American Civil Liberties Union (ACLU).

109 Notes for a release of parts of a letter sent to Donnelly after he took over as superintendent. Undated.

110 Undated, unreleased press statement issued close to Boone's appointment urging him to go beyond Sargent's six-point plan. The AHC was given to sending very long telegrams—each represented a substantial financial commitment. Rodman has explained this was intentional. If the AHC had to pay for their words, they were more likely to stand behind them.

111 Kennedy School Report, Part II, p. 5. Boone, Sargent, and Goldmark worked to have this bill passed. The bill required a great deal of "talk, compromise, and strategy." In the House, the bill was passed because of support from prison-reform groups and the editorial board of the *Boston Globe*. It was passed by voice vote. The bill was ushered through the Senate by Kevin Harrington and Joseph DeCarlo. However, the bill did not have strong support from the beginning. Sargent was the motivating force behind it. (Good analysis in Part II, p. 10 of Kennedy School Report.)

112 Kennedy School Report, Part I, p. 14. Because Donnelly successfully negotiated after the riots at Soledad prison, he had abundant experience with the recently formed Prisoner's Union in California and did not wish to deal with another vocal group that spanned both sides of the wall, demanding workers' rights and protections for prisoners.

113 Notes for a release of parts of a letter sent to Donnelly after he took over as superintendent. Undated.

114 Ryan Source 1, p. 2.

115 John Boone, interview, October 12, 2002, Atlanta, GA.

116 Kennedy School Report, Part II, p. 5.

117 F. B. Taylor, "Bridgewater Segregation Unit Closed," *Boston Globe*, February 17, 1972.

118 Its strategy was outlined in a document labeled "Minutes Ad Hoc Committee, March 2." This section relies heavily on these notes.

119 AHC, "Statement of The Reverend Edward W. Rodman," press release, February 17, 1972.

120 Arnold Jaffe (DOC lawyer), interview, July 27, 2006, Cambridge, MA.

121 Robert Dellelo, conversation, March 28, 2006, Cambridge, MA. During one of the negotiating sessions during the tenure of the NPRA, Bobby found the actual proposal for this program. He sent it out to Phyllis Ryan.

122 Robert Dellelo, conversation, December 11, 2007, Cambridge, MA.

123 The right to a hearing and to appeal the outcome of that hearing.

124 This is another example of how seriously the Ad Hoc Committee took the issue of prisoner sovereignty.

125 This section is drawn entirely from the legislation eventually passed, entitled *Chapter 777: An Act to Reform Prisons*. Over the years, this act has been amended, but it still underpins legislation governing the Massachusetts DOC.

126 Chapter 777 required legislative approval to close any prison. The legislators had been caught unawares when Jerome Miller closed all the juvenile lockups, and they wanted to prevent a repeat with the adult lockups.

127 These inspections were the responsibility of the public health inspector, Howard Wensley. Wensley took his job very seriously for over 30 years, following up on every prisoner complaint—from lack of toilet paper to asbestos paint at Framingham. During the budget crisis in Massachusetts in 2003, the Department of Public Health was only given enough money to inspect the prisons once. I spoke with Howard Wensley once before he retired in 2005; he discussed his frustration with careful inspections that did not yield any repairs at all. He left a public record of fiscal mismanagement that should be carefully scrutinized.

128 When Governor Weld reintroduced prisoners to "the joys of busting rocks" in 1990, he gutted the research department within the DOC. Now, all important research is done by outside organizations that do not have unfettered access to the department.

129 Governor Herter empanelled the Wessel Commission.

130 *Chapter 777*, p. 728.

131 This language remains unchanged—and unused—by any commissioner since Boone.

132 Retire, quit, or die.

133 The Sargent administration failed to understand how the large number of lifers at Walpole would undermine their intentions. For these prisoners, self-determination could only be exercised within the institution, and they were determined to control their world. They made sure they would not be left out of the project even if it meant destabilizing the project itself.

134 *Chapter 777*, p. 735.

135 Many prison organizing initiatives are undermined by their advocates' inability to understand this.

136 Robert Dellelo, conversation, December 17, 2007, Cambridge, MA.

137 Ralph Hamm, phone interview, April 19, 2006.

138 Ralph Hamm, letter, March 10, 2004. This was the case for Roosevelt Smith and "Giggi" Washington. Hamm reports: "Roosevelt Smith was blown up by a pipe bomb in the prison laundry when black prisoners were prevented from going to work that day. Giggi Washington was stabbed to death when myself and other black prisoners were set up by Leo Bissonnette and taken to Segregation Block 10—out of Giggi's cellblock."

139 Ralph Hamm, letter, March 4, 2004. A footnote from Hamm within the letter reads, "I remember snatching a thick wooden table leg from the hands of a prisoner when he walked up behind Fred Butterworth in an attempt to smash him in the back of the head, while Butterworth was trying to get prisoners released from their cells in the smoke filled Cellblock #7. I felt that I owed Butterworth a favor, as he interceded and stopped then

Supt. Robert Moore and the guards in 1971 from beating me in Isolation Block 9." In 2004, Boone would send a letter supporting Hamm's petition for parole, citing the many times Hamm had interceded during prison uprisings, thus saving many lives.

140 See n. 89 for an explanation of guards' riots.

141 Kennedy School Report, Part II, p. 7.

142 Ryan Source 1, p. 2.

143 *The Docket,* April 1973, p. 1.

144 Ralph Hamm letter, April 4, 2004.

145 Ralph Hamm letter, April 4, 2004.

146 Ralph Hamm, letter, April 2, 2006.

147 Robert Dellelo, interview, April 25, 2006, Cambridge, MA.

148 Family and Friends of Prisoners meeting, April 2000.

149 Robert Dellelo, interview, April 25, 2006, Cambridge, MA.

150 Ralph Hamm, phone interview, February 19, 2004.

151 Hamm said the main reason the prisoners trusted Dellelo to set things straight was because he was the only person who stood up to the Bear and walked away. Phone interview, April 24, 2006. See Dellelo's re-telling of the encounter on p. 31.

152 Robert Dellelo, interview, April 25, 2006, Cambridge, MA.

153 Ralph Hamm, letter, February 21, 2004. "My view of the guns found in Walpole was that Peter Wilson had them brought in to be planted and found to boost his position as an informant, discredit the prison administration and DOC, as well as to vilify the prisoner population. As rumors go, he was the only person that I was informed had a gun, although we had suspicions that the Italians might own one. If a prisoner is not a part of a specific clique in prison, there is no way that he can know with any degree of certainty what another clique possesses or is doing. Even our 21-member board of directors was not on top of everything that was going on.... But if a specific element in the prison didn't want you to know something, then you never found out."

154 Bobby Dellelo told me this story shortly after he was released from prison. Dellelo survived a lifetime in prison with brutal stories to tell but no bitterness that I could discern. The same is true of Ralph Hamm.

155 *Three Thousand Years and Life,* directed by Randall Conrad (1973). Sousa was a block leader and a member of the NPRA board who would eventually take a turn as president in the final months of the organization's tenure.

156 Ralph Hamm, letter, February 21, 2004.

157 The color of the prisoners' shirts and jeans.

158 Kennedy School Report, Part II, p. 15.

159 Robert Dellelo, interview, April 25, 2006, Cambridge, MA.

160 Jerry Taylor, "Boone Declares Walpole Crisis as Strike Looms," *Boston Globe,* March 14, 1973.

161 This is from the Kennedy School Report; the prisons are not specified.

162 Ralph Hamm, phone interview, April 19, 2006.

163 Rodman's ability to move between groups was a key element in his effectiveness. Because of his history within CORE, SNCC, and the Northern Student Movement, he was well known within the Black community. His political allegiance was never questioned. The fact that he was the face of the AHC gave it a kind of credibility it never would have had without him. Rodman was comfortable making people uncomfortable; this made him indispensable.

164 Ed Rodman letter to Robert Donnelly, June 29, 1972. The request for a meeting was like a mantra, repeated over and over with no acknowledgment. Yet, each time Donnelly needed public support, he would call on them. Donnelly officially resigned on July 20, with the resignation to take effect in September.

165 AHC, "Ad Hoc Prison Reform Group Offers Its Services to Prisoners at Walpole," press release, July 5, 1972.

166 Robert Dellelo, interview, April 27, 2006, Cambridge, MA.

167 Jim Isenberg, phone interview, May 5, 2006, Cambridge, MA.

168 Jim Isenberg, phone interview, May 2003.

169 Ken O. Botwright, "Hits Transfer Policy for Norfolk Shootout Burke Blames Boone," *Boston Globe,* August 29, 1972.

170 Sargent quoted in Kennedy School Report, Part II, p. 17.

171 John Boone, interview, October 12, 2002, Atlanta, GA.

172 Editorial, "Only Humane Prisons Are Secure," the *Monitor's View, Christian Science Monitor,* August 8, 1972.

173 The information about the handheld wand was not known at this time.

174 Elma Lewis was recognized as a "living legend." She devoted her life to bringing art and culture into the Black community in Boston. Lewis and her assistant, Barry Gaither, had begun an art program at Walpole in the fall of 1972. This program was pivotal for Ralph Hamm. His own personal transformation had begun with lyrics to songs that he wrote when he was in solitary confinement awaiting trial at the age of 18. These lyrics evolved into poetry. When he wanted to illustrate some of his works, he wandered into Gaither's classes and discovered that he had considerable talent. Hamm recalls: "Art gave me a way to validate the feeling that I was more than what was apparent to the world. I had already had an experience where I knew the presence of God or something that was greater than myself. Art showed me how to make that concrete." Ralph Hamm, phone interview, April 25, 2006.

175 Ken O. Botwright, "Hits Transfer Policy for Norfolk Shootout Burke Blames Boone," *Boston Globe,* August 29, 1972.

176 Ryan Source 1, p. 3.

177 AHC, press release, July 2, 1972.

178 Meaning that the vision of the future without prison was perceived to be immanently possible because of the work of the NPRA.

179 Edward Rodman, interview, February 2004, Cambridge, MA.

180 Robert Dellelo, interview, April 25, 2006, Cambridge, MA.

181 There were only four Latinos in Walpole then. Three were on the board at any given time.

182 John McGrath, interview, February 2004, Cambridge, MA.

183 Robert Dellelo, interview, April 21, 2006, Cambridge, MA.

184 Ralph Hamm, letter, March 16, 2004.

185 Alexander Macmillan, Madeline H. Miceli, and Henry C. Alaria, "In the Matter of Commonwealth of Massachusetts Department of Corrections and Walpole Chapter of the National Prisoners Reform Association, Case No. SLRX=2," September 24, 1973, p. 1, hereinafter SLRX.

186 SLRX, p. 1.

187 Phyllis Ryan, "Remarks of Warren E. Burger Chief Justice of the United States at the 1972 Annual Dinner of the National Conference of Christians and Jews, Bellevue-Strat-ford Hotel, Philadelphia, PA, November 16. 1972," notes in file named "Nov 16 remarks of Burger," Bissonette archive, hereinafter Burger remarks.

188 Graterford is Pennsylvania's maximum security prison.

189 Burger remarks, p. 3.

190 Burger remarks, p. 6.

191 Burger remarks, p. 14.

192 Massachusetts Correctional Association, *Correctional Reform: Illusion and Reality Bulletin No. 22* (November 1972), hereinafter MCA.

193 MCA, p. 1.

194 MCA, p. 4.

195 MCA, p. 5.

196 MCA, p. 9.

197 MCA, p. 13.

198 John Boone, interview, October 12, 2002, Atlanta, GA, corroborated by Kennedy School Report, Part II, p. 29.

199 James Isenberg, interview, May 6, 2006, Cambridge, MA.

200 Kennedy School Report, Part II, p. 29.

201 Hugh Johnson, interview, March 2004. Ralph Hamm and Robert Dellelo concur that there was a shooting incident when Porelle went into the blocks; there is disagreement about whether what he shot was a shotgun or his pistols.

202 Ralph Hamm, letter, March 4, 2004.

203 John Boone, interview, October 10, 1982, Atlanta, GA.

204 Ralph Hamm, letter, posted March 20, 2004.

205 *The Docket,* April 1973, p. 8.

206 Robert Dellelo, interview, April 21, 2006, Cambridge, MA.

207 *Three Thousand Years and Life.*

208 From a collection of notes assembled by Ryan, but taken by Ryan, Coles, Osler, the prisoners, and Norris, unpaginated, hereinafter Ryan Source 3.

209 March 13, in the package of reports from the first three weeks of the OP, Bissonette archive, hereinafter Source 4.

210 Kennedy School Report, Part III, p. 20.

211 *Boston Globe* editorial (date in the clipping is obscured, but it appears to be late February); Kennedy School Report, Part II, p. 20.

212 The *Globe* editorial claimed 200 jobs would be cut.

213 John Boone, phone conversation, October 4, 2004.

214 Tina Williams, interview, May 2005, Cambridge, MA.

215 Ryan Source 1, pp. 3–4.

216 AHC, "We Need *You* On Wednesday, February 14, 10 AM At Gardiner Auditorium, State House," press release, not dated.

217 Phyllis Ryan notes, in Notebook 1, Bissonette archive, hereinafter Ryan Notebook 1.

218 Ryan Notebook 1.

219 Ryan Source 1.

220 AHC, "We Need *You* On Wednesday, February 14, 10 AM At Gardiner Auditorium, State House," press release, not dated.

221 Letter from Wendy [no last name given] to Bobby Dellelo, dated February 5, 1973, but probably written on February 6. Phyllis Ryan notes Representative Owens' attendance.

222 This is a common tactic when prison administrators want to control a situation.

223 Ryan Source 3.

224 Ryan Source 3.

225 Edward Rodman, interview, May 12, 2006, Cambridge, MA.

226 Ryan Source 3. Both Sunny Robinson (of the Prisoner Health Project) and Phyllis Ryan's notes on previous meetings suggested Rodman and Boone should work with a mediator.

227 Ryan Source 3.

228 Chuck Turner, conversation, April 2006, Boston, Massachusetts.

229 Ed Corsetti and Bob Creamer, "Walpole Head Bares Prison Prostitution," *Boston Herald American,* February 9, 1973. The laundry avocation was lucrative. According to the Kennedy School Report, it garnered over $100,000 annually.

230 Robert Dellelo, interview, Cambridge, MA.

231 Ryan Source 3.

232 Ryan Source 3

233 SCLC, "Massachusetts Unit Southern Christian Leadership Conference," press release, February 10, 1973.

234 Sunny Robinson would note that visitors were regularly searched but guards were allowed to enter the prison unhindered by scrutiny.

235 In January 1999, Parkey Grace told me that some prisoners resisted the strip searches by urinating in their underwear and handing the sopping garment to the guard to inspect. Ralph Hamm has corroborated this.

236 Robert Dellelo, interview, June 12, 2006, Cambridge, MA.

237 This becomes very important on May 18, when the guards and state police test these skills in Walpole.

238 According to then-prisoner Jerry Sousa, this system was widely resisted by the prisoners. *Three Thousand Years and Life.*

239 Jerry Sousa, quoted in *Three Thousand Years and Life.*

240 Ralph Hamm, phone interview, December 18, 2007.

241 Ralph Hamm, letter, May 12, 2006.

242 Ralph Hamm, letter, May 12, 2006.

243 Corsini later became the superintendent of Shirley Medium Security Prison. His tenure there was marked by a lot of institutional unrest. Robert Dellelo, interview, June 12, 2006, Cambridge, MA.

244 Ryan Source 3.

245 Kennedy School Report, Part II, p. 30.

246 Robert Dellelo, interview, May 2, 2006, Cambridge, MA.

247 Ralph Hamm, phone interview, April 25, 2006.

248 Backman was the conscience of this group. He dedicated the rest of his life to winning human rights for prisoners.

249 Robert Dellelo, interview, May 1, 2006, Cambridge, MA.

250 Ryan Source 3.

251 Ryan Source 3.

252 Edward Rodman, public hearing testimony, in archive file named "Rod test 2/14/73," Bissonette archive.

253 Frank Donovan, "Backman Charges Neglect at Walpole, Asks for Probe," *Boston Globe,* February 14, 1973.

254 Edward Rodman, public hearing testimony, in archive file named "Rod test 2/14/73," Bissonette archive.

255 The NPRA defined property damage as a nonviolent tactic.

256 Ralph Hamm, phone interview, February 5, 2006. Isenberg and Boone both used the word "intimate" to describe the pain they felt during this time period. All the men involved were attacked publicly. One cartoon showed Governor Sargent, John Boone, and Ed Rodman as monkeys. Sargent had his ears covered with his hands; Boone, his mouth; and Rodman, his eyes.

257 AHC memorandum, "Date and Agenda for Meeting with Commissioner Boone," February 4, Bissonette archive. The agenda is for the meeting planned for February 15.

258 Ralph Hamm, letter, May 12, 2006.

259 *Three Thousand Years and Life.*

260 This block actually housed 40 prisoners, all NOI members. The jobs were envied because the money earned through them could be sent home to families.

261 Points 13 to 16 and 22 to 24 are missing. When I asked Ed Rodman about this, he said the AHC censored the information for two reasons. First, they did not want to paint so terrible a picture that no one would believe it. Second, they did not want the prisoners to look like they were "animals" for fear that the public might abandon them. For example, it is hard to explain throwing shit as "resistance" to the media.

262 NPRA, "Manifesto of Dehumanization," Bissonette archive.

263 Ryan Source 3.

264 Ryan Source 3; "Boone Rodman Civilian Observers" file, Bissonette archive. In an interview on March 4, 2006, Ed Rodman admitted that he never thought Boone would go for the idea of civilian observers, but he believed it was the only solution he could offer that would support the prisoners' self-determination and increase their safety.

265 John Boone, interview, October 12, 2002, Atlanta, GA.

266 Edward Rodman, interview, March 4, 2006, Cambridge, MA.

267 *The Docket,* April 1973, p. 8.

268 Ryan Source 3.

269 Memorandum by Raymond Porelle, "Special Schedule For Monday, February 19, 1973," Bissonette archive.

270 Williams was part of Boone's administrative team.

271 Robert Dellelo, interview, May 2, 2006, Cambridge, MA.

272 Ryan Source 3.

273 Paraphrased from AHC, "Public Release from Commission," press release, February 21, 1973, from Ryan press release files, Bissonette archive.

274 AHC, "Public Release from Commission."

275 Jerry Taylor, "Porelle Charges Walpole Guards Are Gaming Him," *Boston Globe*, February 28, 1973.

276 Robert Dellelo, conversation, February 18, 2006, Cambridge, MA.

277 Jerry Taylor, "Porelle Charges Walpole Guards Are Gaming Him," *Boston Globe*, February 28, 1973.

278 Jerry Taylor, "Guards Accused of 'Games' at Walpole," *Boston Globe*, February 22, 1973.

279 Ralph Hamm, phone interview, February 2004.

280 Ryan Source 3.

281 Robert Dellelo, interview, May 2, 2006, Cambridge, MA.

282 NPRA, "Grievances: By priority, restoration of the institution and its functions prior to the lockup of 12/29/72," Bissonette archive.

283 "Inmates' Priest Protests Walpole Officials' Tactics," *Boston Globe*, February 25, 1973.

284 "Black Caucus Wants Boone to Solve Walpole Problems," *Boston Globe*, February 28, 1973.

285 Tom Donovan, "Midnight Inspection by 50 After Walpole Inmates Rebel," *Boston Herald American*, March 1, 1973.

286 Donovan, "Midnight Inspection."

287 Donovan, "Midnight Inspection."

288 Alan Sheehan, "50 Listen to Inmates at Walpole," *Boston Globe*, March 1, 1973.

289 Sheehan, "50 Listen."

290 NPRA, "List of Grievances," file 3/1/73, Bissonette archive. Corroborated in the Kennedy School Report.

291 Robert Dellelo, interview, July 24, 2006, Cambridge, MA.

292 Kennedy School Report, Part II, p. 30. According to this source, a "coalition within Walpole between some guards and some inmates had succeeded in forcing Porelle out."

293 *Three Thousand Years and Life.*

294 When the Walpole line guards were out on strike, cadet trainees in Jim Isenberg's training program remained on the job; these trainees, the majority of whom were men of color, were not covered in the guards' union contract.

295 The Priests' Senate's Reflections on Prisons and Prisoners, March 2, 1973, Bissonette archive.

296 "Priests Call For Prison Reform," *Boston Herald American*, March 4, 1973. Also referred to in AHC, handwritten draft entitled "March 3, 1973, Press Conference of the NPRA Internal Board at Walpole," Bissonette archive.

297 Jerry Taylor, "State Police Fill In as Guards Walk Out at Walpole Prison," *Boston Globe*, March 16, 1973.

298 "Priests Call For Prison Reform," *Boston Herald American*, March 4, 1973. This language mirrored the language of the 1971 AFSC publication, *Struggle for Justice*. Rodman reports that *Struggle* was a foundational document; all the advocates were aware of and reading it.

299 United Farm Workers.

300 Robert Dellelo, interview, July 24, 2006, Cambridge, MA.

301 Robert Dellelo, interview, February 15, 2006, Cambridge, MA.

302 Ryan Notebook 1.

303 Ryan Source 1, p. 4.

304 In 9 and 10 Blocks, there were two doors behind which the prisoners had been locked. The first was a grill, which allowed air and sound to pass through, and the second was solid steel with a small window and a food slot.

305 The "blood program" took five days of "good" time off prisoners' sentences when they donated blood.

306 Ralph Hamm, phone interview, February 24, 2004.

307 Frank Kelly, untitled description of his experience, p. 7, Bissonette archive.

308 Ralph Hamm, phone interview, May 29, 2006.

309 Ralph Hamm, phone interview, May 29, 2006.

310 Ralph Hamm, letter, April 15, 2007.

311 "Spokesman at Walpole Killer, Robber, Pusher Inmate Leaders," *Boston Herald American,* March 7, 1973. This article is vicious and incorrect in its portrayal of the men.

312 Edward Rodman, conversation, May 29, 2006, Cambridge, MA.

313 Ryan Notebook 1.

314 Robert Healy, "The Real Issue at Walpole," Political Circuit, *Boston Globe,* March 26, 1973.

315 Editorial, *Boston Globe,* March 9, 1973.

316 Edward Rodman, interview, May 29, 2006, Cambridge, MA.

317 Robert Dellelo, interview, June 3, 2006, Cambridge, MA.

318 Stephen Wermeil, "Walpole Superintendent Withdraws Recognition of Inmates' Organization," *Boston Globe,* May 26, 1973.

319 Ralph Hamm, letter, June 17, 2006.

320 Today the concessions at Walpole are run by the Canteen Corporation.

321 Robert Dellelo, interview, June 14, 2006, Cambridge, MA.

322 SLRX, pp. 2–6 (see n. 185). The Mail Group contract was presented by Porelle in his last meeting with the AHC.

323 Edward Rodman, interview, March 2006, Cambridge, MA.

324 Edward Rodman, interview, March 2006, Cambridge, MA.

325 Edward Rodman, interview, May 29, 2006, Cambridge, MA.

326 Ken O. Hartnett, "Inmates Claim Guards Not Doing Job," *Boston Globe,* March 10, 1973.

327 Hartnett, "Inmates Claim."

328 "Issue Now: Length of Walpole Work Agreement," *Boston Herald American,* March 11, 1973. Ryan had noted her distrust of Anderson all along, identifying numerous instances when he made negotiations difficult or appeared to deliberately destabilize the situation in the blocks. Here, again, Anderson was proving her lack of trust was warranted.

329 "Unrest Now Hits NH State Prison," *Boston Herald American,* March 11, 1973.

330 Robert Dellelo, interview, June 3, 2006, Cambridge, MA.

331 Phyllis Ryan notes in file labeled March 12, Bissonette archive.

332 Ralph Hamm, phone interview, May 30, 2006.

333 Herbert H. Hershfang to Francis Sargent, letter, March 14, 1973—accompanied by press release containing the same statement.

334 Tom Sullivan and Bob Creamer, "Walpole Guards Threaten Strike," *Boston Herald American,* March 14, 1973.

335 Sullivan and Creamer, "Walpole Guards."

336 Sullivan and Creamer, "Walpole Guards."

337 Sullivan and Creamer, "Walpole Guards."

338 Ryan Notebook 1.

339 Ryan Notebook 1.

340 *The Docket,* April 1973, p. 8.

341 *Boston Herald American,* March 15, 1973.

342 Kennedy School Report, Part III, p. 4.

343 Kennedy School Report, Part III, p. 4. See long quote on this page that lays out Goldmark's feelings.

344 Kennedy School Report, Part III, pp. 4–5.

345 Jerry Taylor and Ray Richard, "150 Are Suspended Five Days Without Pay: State Police Fill in As Guards Walk Out at Walpole Prison," *Boston Globe,* March 16, 1973.

346 Taylor and Richard, "150 Are Suspended."

347 Editorial, "The Illegal Strike," *Boston Globe,* March 15, 1973.

348 Editorial, "The Illegal Strike," *Boston Globe,* March 15, 1973.

349 Documented in undated notes from Ryan, written after the takeover in May, titled, "Questions for Boone," Bissonette archive.

350 Kennedy School Report, Part III, p. 1. The report states that the guards returned to their posts. In reality all the observers, the prisoners, and Boone and Rodman agreed that the guards did not resume their posts, but stayed on the observation deck of the prison. Many would punch in and leave, returning only to punch out.

351 Robert Dellelo, conversation, December 27, 2007, Cambridge, MA.

352 From Kennedy School Report, Section III, Addendum A.

353 Robert Dellelo, interview, July 24, 2006, Cambridge, MA. Dellelo also pointed out that the guards' unions have more power now than ever. When the prisons became smoke-free, each guard was given a $500 bonus not to smoke in the prison. That cost the taxpay-ers almost $2 million—that was the entire prison education budget in 2004.

354 John Osler, interview, April 27, 2007, Cambridge, MA.

355 Robert Dellelo, interview, September 2005, Cambridge, MA.

356 Ralph Hamm, phone interview, March 2004. John Boone also reported his memory of illiterate prisoners learning to read under the tutelage of Hamm and Brown in his pre-sentation at Critical Resistance South, New Orleans, Louisiana, April 2003.

357 Ralph Hamm, letter, March 20, 2004. Revisions by Hamm by phone on April 28, 2007.

358 Ralph Hamm, letter, postmarked June 17, 2006, with additions from a January 20, 2008 phone conversation.

359 Jerry Taylor, "Walpole Guards Back, Face Retraining," *Boston Evening Globe,* March 21, 1973.

360 Taylor, "Walpole Guards Back."

361 Jonathan Fuerbringer, "Strike Led Walpole Guards into Sargent Hammerlock," *Boston Globe,* March 21, 1973.

362 Fuerbringer, "Strike Led Walpole Guards."

363 Boone said often in interviews that Sargent had sacrificed his political career for prison reform and that he was one of the finest and fairest men he had ever met.

364 Kennedy School Report, Part III, p. 2.

365 Kennedy School Report, Part III, p. 2.

366 Kennedy School Report, Part III, p. 3.

367 This was to happen in the early '80s and eventually build to a near-total destruction of the bill.

368 Frank Donovan, *Boston Globe,* March 24, 1973.

369 Frank Donovan, *Boston Globe,* March 24, 1973.

370 Ryan Notebook 2, Bissonette archive.

371 The description of this event is drawn from observer reports written by Dave Gagne and five other observers: 352, 353, 355, 356, and 362, in the file labeled March 18, Bissonette archive.

372 Al Larkin, "Boone Demands Probe of Walpole Scuffle," *Boston Globe,* March 25, 1973.

373 Ryan Notebook 2, Bissonette archive.

374 Al Larkin, "Boone Demands Probe of Walpole Scuffle," *Boston Globe,* March 25, 1973.

375 While everyone was involved with "doing," Freeman filed, read, reviewed, and wrote. Without his dedication to maintaining "the record," it would have been much more dif-ficult to write this book.

376 This note was important because the cell was not preserved as evidence.

377 Memorandum by John Boone to Walter Waitkevich, March 24, 1973, Bissonette archive.

378 All the information in this description is from a report by Norfolk DA George Burke, dated April 10, 1973, and submitted to Representative Thomas Colo, in Bissonette ar-chive. The report shows how much disorder existed within the department.

379 Kennedy School Report, Part II, p. 26. In several interviews, Boone said that he thought of the Subilosky escape as sabotage.

380 Kennedy School Report, Part II, p. 26.

381 Ralph Hamm, letter, postmarked June 17, 2006.

382 Steven Wermeil, "Dwight Says Inmates Fear Furlough System Might End," *Boston Globe,* April 4, 1973.

383 "Sargent Calls Furloughs Best Prison Reform," *Boston Globe,* April 4, 1973.

384 Walter Anderson, quoted in Burke report. See n. 378.

385 Steven Wermeil, "Burke Lays Blame for Killer's Furlough on Boone, Aide," *Boston Globe,* April 11, 1973. A parallel article in the *Boston Herald American* is broad-ranging in its criticism of Boone—it covers every failure of the furlough program.

386 Ryan Source 3. Robert Dellelo's words were recorded by Phyllis Ryan.

387 NPRA, "Statement from NPRA, Walpole-Chapter," Bissonette archive. States that the prisoners recognize that simply because they are prisoners, their credibility with the public was weak, but that they felt they had a moral obligation to pursue Burke's allegations.

388 Robert Dellelo, interview, June 20, 2005, Cambridge, MA.

389 Editorial, "What About It, Mr. Burke?," *Boston Globe,* April 13, 1973.

390 Steven Wermeil, "Inmates Challenge DA to Shakedown," *Boston Globe*, April 10, 1973.

391 Frank Kelly, "A Confession," unpublished memoir, pp. 32a–b, hereinafter Kelly.

392 Kelly, p. 1.

393 Kelly, p. 1.

394 Kelly, p. 9.

395 Robert Dellelo, interview, February 16, 2006, Cambridge, MA.

396 Observer 10 report, Bissonette archive. Freeman substituted numbers for observer names, capital letters for guards, and lowercase letters for prisoners. The key to the document was not preserved. However, from the extent of description combined with description of the work that number 10 did, most likely it was Rust. Rust and Kelly were the primary note takers in the beginning. According to Ralph Hamm, Rust spent hours interviewing the men in 9 and 10 Blocks.

397 Observer Report, March 8–25, 1973, Bissonette archive.

398 Observer notes, compiled by Dyche Freeman, "March 12 Often Repeated Requests of Prisoners," Bissonette archive.

399 Observer notes, compiled by Dyche Freeman, "Comments of the Observers March 8–25, 1973," Bissonette archive.

400 "With the showers, see they are in the last cell on each floor. This cell has a grill. When a guy went in, they would close the doors on the unit and the solid doors on each cell. No one could see what happened. So, during the lockdown, some brutal beatings took place in the showers. Many guys decided not to take the chance.

   "The guards would shut off water and electricity and then open all the windows to freeze them out. It is amazing that a guard did not get killed with everything that they were doing." Robert Dellelo, interview, July 12, 2006, Cambridge, MA.

401 Observer 11, March 10, 1973, Source 4.

402 Observer 379, undated, Source 4.

403 Observer 13, March 11, 1973, Source 4.

404 Observer 27, March 11, 1973, Source 4.

405 Edward Rodman, interview, July 29, 2006, Cambridge, MA, and interviews of volunteers.

406 Observer 88, March 17, 1973, Source 4.

407 Observer 88, March 15, 1973, Source 4.

408 Observer 117, March 16, 1973, Source 4.

409 Observer 127, March 17, 1973, Source 4.

410 Observer 325, March 24, 1973, Source 4.

411 Observer 195, March 18, 1973, Source 4.

412 Observer 191, March 18, 1973, Source 4.

413 Robert Dellelo, interview, July 24, 2006, Cambridge, MA.

414 Observer 216, March 18, 1973, Source 4.

415 Observer 222, March 18, 1973, Source 4.

416 Observer 150, March 19, 1973, Source 4.

417 Observer 242, March 20, 1973, Source 4.

418 Observer 246, March 20, 1973, Source 4.

419 Observer 282, March 20, 1973, Source 4.

420 Observer 344, March 24, 1973, Source 4.

421 Observer 322, March 24, 1973, Source 4.

422 Observer 348, March 24, 1973, Source 4.

423 Observer 345, March 24, 1973, Source 4.

424 Observer 380, March 21, 1973, Source 4.

425 Ed Childs, conversation, January 2004.

426 Observer 288, March 20, 1973, Source 4.

427 Observer 276, March 21, 1973, Source 4.

428 Unidentified Observer, undated, Source 4.

429 Robert Dellelo, interview, June 27, 2005, Cambridge, MA.

430 Observer 231, March 17, 1973, Source 4, emphasis in the original.

431 Jerry Sousa, quoted in *Three Thousand Years and Life.*

432 Edward Rodman, interview, June 29, 2006, Cambridge, MA.

433 Editorial, "Mass. Inmates Demand Rights: Prison Now has Chapter of Reform Union," *The Times Picayune*, New Orleans, May 5, 1973.

434 John Boone, interview, October 4, 2004, Atlanta, GA.

435 Tom Sullivan and Earl Marchand, "Two Beaten Guards Suspended by Boone," *Boston Herald American,* March 25, 1973.

436 Ralph Hamm, phone interview, May 1, 2007.

437 The description of events that follows relies on contemporaneous reports by Eric Howlett, an observer who worked the afternoon shift that day, and Bobby Dellelo, then president of the NPRA, augmented by recent interviews with Ralph Hamm, Dellelo, and Ed Rodman. Additional information was taken from Phyllis Ryan's notes, prison memos, press statements, and newspaper articles.

438 "Memo to All Employees, All Inmates Re: Lock-In Searches," dated May 18, 1973, Bissonette archive. In pen, a note is added "observers in."

439 Robert Dellelo's statement, in the "National Prisoners Reform Association Report On Walpole Crisis," June 1973, Bissonette archive, hereinafter Dellelo statement.

440 Dellelo statement.

441 Eric Howlett, "Minutes of the Meeting Between NPRA Representatives and W. Waitkevich," appended section labeled "Vignettes," Bissonette archive.

442 Howlett, "Minutes." The section that follows is derived from these careful notes.

443 Howlett, "Minutes."

444 Ralph Hamm, phone interview, May 1, 2007.

445 Howlett, "Minutes," emphasis in original.

446 Howlett, "Minutes," emphasis in original.

447 Eric Howlett, "Schedule of Events at Walpole State Prison on the Evening and Night of May 18, 1973," Bissonette archive.

448 Howlett, "Schedule of Events."

449 Howlett, "Schedule of Events."

450 Bobby Dellelo's report of his memories regarding the lockdown, written while in segregation, p. 2, hereinafter Dellelo report.

451 Dellelo report, p. 2.

452 Dellelo report, p. 2.

453 Dellelo report, p. 2.

454 Howlett, "Schedule of Events."

455 John Roberts, "The Gaming of Walpole," in *The Docket,* June 1973, vol. 3, num. 3, p. 2.

456 Edward Rodman, interview, July 24, 2006, Cambridge, MA.

457 Edward Rodman, press release draft, undated, Bissonette archive.

458 Howlett, "Schedule of Events."

459 Robert Dellelo, interview, June 20, 2005, Cambridge, MA.

460 All observer reports concur on this fact.

461 Dellelo report, p. 3.

462 Ralph Hamm, phone interview, June 2004. This is also referenced in notes taken by Ryan, Howlett, and Rodman, respectively—sometimes one observer is referred to, sometimes two. Hamm used the plural.

463 John Boone, interview, October 12, 2002, Atlanta, GA, and Edward Rodman, interview, March 20, 2004. This information was later exposed in media reports, and included in the documentary *Three Thousand Years and Life*. The prison had not been built to specifications. The 6-inch gap between the walls was to have been filled with poured concrete.

464 *Three Thousand Years and Life*. Wilson was probably trying to secure the medication so that in the aftermath of the takeover, medication would be available to those who were dependent on the drug. The guards did not fill prescriptions when they wanted to destabilize the prison.

465 Dellelo report, p. 4. Ryan's notes refer to ten prisoners being wounded by gunshot.

466 *Three Thousand Years and Life*. Wilson is credited by a witness in the hospital, who watched him deny entry to the unit.

467 Howlett, "Minutes." Word-for-word exchange heard by Rodman, Howlett, and Wermeil from the *Boston Globe* and recorded in the "Vignettes" section of the report.

468 Howlett, "Minutes."

469 Hamm surmised that Dellelo and some of the white prisoners really had believed that they could change the course of events that night. He felt that the Black prisoners, because of their own experience with "the system," came to the conclusion that they had lost and that the most pressing question was how to survive. Phone interview, June 2004.

470 Ralph Hamm, letter, March 20, 2004.

471 Ralph Hamm, phone interview, July 2005.

472 Dellelo report, p. 4.

473 Dellelo report, p. 5.

474 In official reports, the prisoner is identified as Jerry Sousa—but Dellelo is sure it was Stetson.

475 Robert Dellelo, interview, July 24, 2006, Cambridge, MA.

476 John Boone, conversation, October 4, 2004, Atlanta, GA.

477 Robert Dellelo, interview, July 24, 2006, Cambridge, MA.

478 Dellelo report, NPRA summary, not paginated, hereinafter NPRA summary.

479 NPRA summary.

480 Robert Dellelo, interview, July 25, 2006, Cambridge, MA.

481 NPRA summary.

482 NPRA summary.

483 Edward Rodman, interview, April 2004, Cambridge, MA.

484 Robert Dellelo, interview, July 25, 2006, Cambridge, MA.

485 Edward Rodman, interview, January 2005, Cambridge, MA.

486 John Boone, interview, October 12, 2002, Atlanta, GA.

487 Kennedy School Report, Part III, p. 9.

488 Jerry Taylor, "Accord on Walpole Head Count," *Boston Globe,* May 29, 1973.

489 "Governor Names Burke in Walpole Crisis: Sargent's Prober Blames Boone," *Boston Herald American,* May 22, 1973. It is not clear how in the loop Boone was on the decision to take back the prison and accomplish the shakedown. It appears that Waitkevich made the call, perhaps with Higgins. He states that he was not aware that the state police were called in—the question is, who made the decision?

490 Steve Wermeil, "Sargent Tells Burke to Cool His Walpole Comments," *Boston Globe,* May 23, 1973.

491 Wermeil, "Sargent Tells Burke."

492 Wermeil, "Sargent Tells Burke."

493 Letter from Ad Hoc Committee, May 24, 1973. This letter evinces the tension between Boone and the AHC, a breakdown in communication, and the committee's resolve to move forward with supporting prisoner self-determination. Nonetheless, it asserts that the "primary problem in our prisons is that inmates have no clearly defined process to redress their grievances" and draws the connection between this fact and self-destructive behavior.

494 Edward Rodman, interview, February 2004, Cambridge, MA.

495 Taylor, "Accord on Walpole Head Count."

496 Alfred E. Cowles, *A Report Concerning the Involvement of the NCDS in MCI at Walpole July 16, 1973–December 3, 1973* (National Center for Dispute Settlement, January 25, 1974), hereinafter NCDS report.

497 NCDS report.

498 Robert Dellelo, interview, July 24, 2006, Cambridge, MA.

499 Ralph Hamm, letter, March 24, 2007.

500 Ed Rodman, conversation, April 3, 2007, Cambridge, MA.

501 Stephen Wermeil, "Walpole Guards, Inmates Talk Over Their Grievances," *Boston Globe, May 28, 1973*. Rodman remembers this meeting.

502 Edward Rodman, conversation, September 2001, Cambridge, MA.

503 Robert Dellelo, interview, January 16, 2006, Cambridge, MA.

504 Robert Dellelo, interview, January 16, 2006, Cambridge, MA.

505 Ralph Hamm, phone interview, July 24, 2006.

506 *Three Thousand Years and Life.*

507 Stephen Wermeil, "Correction Dept.'s 'Mod Squad' Cadets to Leave Walpole for Formal Training," *Boston Globe,* May 28, 1973.

508 Jim Isenberg, phone interview, April 2006.

509 The Administrative Law Reform Project was directed by Professor Sheldon Krantz, and assisted by Robert Bell, Jonathan Brant, and Michael Magruder.

510 Robert Bell (DOC lawyer), interview, July 28, 2006.

511 Arnold Jaffe (DOC lawyer), interview, July 27, 2006, Cambridge, MA.

512 Edward Rodman, conversation, February 21, 2004, Cambridge, MA.

513 Phyllis Ryan, draft release, June 6, 1973. The release was scheduled for June 7.

514 Ad Hoc Committee, "Ad Hoc Committee Makes Public Its Recommendations for Resolving Crisis at Walpole," press release, June 6, 1973.

515 "Bay State's Prison Plan 18 Years Later," *Boston Globe,* June 10, 1973.

516 Letter from the Massachusetts Council on Crime and Corrections (MCCC) to His Excellency Francis W. Sargent, June 15, 1973.

517 In addition to John D. Carver, executive director of MCCC, the letter was signed by Arnold Coles, NPRA; Joseph Reilly, Massachusetts Catholic Conference; Julia Kaufman, Council for Public Justice; Margot Lindsay, Committee for the Advancement of Criminal Justice; Senator Jack Backman, Committee on Corrections; Henry Mascarello, Massachusetts Correctional Association; Representative Thomas Colo, Committee on Corrections; Reverend Ed Rodman, Ad Hoc Committee on Prison Reform; Brad Pearson, Self Development Group; and J. Bryan Riley, Massachusetts Halfway Houses, Inc.

518 Edward Rodman, interview, March 20, 2004, Cambridge, MA, corroborated by Stephen Wermeil and Ken O. Botwright, "Walpole Strike Goes On; Demand Still Not Public," *Boston Globe,* date unknown.

519 AHC, press release, "Security Without Safety Contributed to Walpole," June 12, 1973.

520 Robert Dellelo, interview, July 24, 2006, Cambridge, MA.

521 Kennedy School Report, Part III, p. 10.

522 John Boone, interview, October 12, 2002, Atlanta, GA.

523 Kennedy School Report, Part III, p. 10.

524 Kennedy School Report, Part III, p. 10.

525 Kennedy School Report, Part III, p. 11.

526 Kennedy School Report, Part III, p. 12.

527 Kennedy School Report, Part III, p. 13.

528 DOC, press release, "Statement By Correction Commissioner John O. Boone," undated.

529 Stephen Wermeil, "Boone Says Sargent Responded to Pressure In Firing Him," *Boston Globe,* June 23, 1973.

530 Jonathan Fuerbringer, "Boone Failure Can Be Traced to Sargent Indecision," *Boston Globe,* June 22, 1973. This article shows how little the concept of classification or the complicated social reality at Walpole prison was understood in the media.

531 George Briggs and Jack Cadigan, "The *Herald American*'s Crusade Led to Ouster," *Boston Herald American*, June 22, 1973.

532 *Boston Globe,* June 23, 1973, article title and author unknown, Bissonette archive.

533 Stephen Wermeil, "Walpole Calm; Higgins Vows More Controls," *Boston Globe,* June 23, 1973.

534 Eddie Corsetti, "State Police Take Walpole Control," *Boston Herald American*, May 23, 1973. Corsetti was the investigative reporter the *Herald* had sent to Virginia and Washington, DC, to dig up dirt on Boone.

535 Editorial, "Prisoner, Press, and Prison," *Boston Globe,* July 21, 1973.

536 Joseph Rosenbloom, "Flynn Backs Bill, Black Caucus Backs Veto," *Boston Globe*, July 11, 1973.

537 Massachusetts Black Caucus, "Statement of Rep. Bill Owens for Massachusetts Black Caucus," June 22, 1973.

538 Bob Keeley and Bob Creamer, "All Walpole Prison Visitors Searched," *Boston Herald American,* June 24, 1973.

539 Robert Bell (DOC lawyer), interview, July 28, 2006. Bell felt this quote was the most appropriate summary of Boone's tenure.

540 Stephen Wermeil, "Boone Accepts Thank-Yous, Anxious Over Penal Future," *Boston Globe*, July 9, 1973.

541 "Boone Pledges National Coalition," *Boston Herald American,* July 9, 1973. The article is accompanied by a photograph of Boone in a dashiki and carrying a Nigerian ceremonial adze.

542 Stephen Wermeil, "Boone Was Undermined by Officials, Inmates Say," *Boston Globe,* July 5, 1973.

543 Wermeil, "Boone Was Undermined."

544 Letter from Donald Dwight, lt. governor, to Edward Rodman, August 28, 1973. This letter basically says, "The jig is up—we have put the liberals—the Massachusetts Council on Crime and Correction—into the space formerly occupied by the Ad Hoc Committee; you are out of the loop. Get used to it."

545 Stephen Wermeil, "Walpole Program May End," *Boston Globe,* July 13, 1973.

546 Stephen Wermeil and Joseph Rosenbloom, "Ad Hoc Committee Suspends Observer Program at Walpole," *Boston Globe,* July 13, 1973.

547 Wermeil and Rosenbloom, "Ad Hoc Committee." It is possible the observers were just exhausted. The observers showing up in these final weeks are only the few dedicated core. In one statement, Osler says that the observer program was suspended until it could regenerate interest.

548 Boone stated that he felt this was the agreement that Moriarty got from the administration—there would be no second-guessing his decisions.

549 Stephen Wermeil and Joseph Rosenbloom, "Ad Hoc Committee." The beatings were reported in the *Globe,* the *Herald,* and the *Christian Science Monitor.*

550 "Walpole Observers Upset, Quit," *Boston Evening Globe,* July 13, 1973.

551 Robert M. Press, "Observers Leave Walpole, Inside-prison Activities Restricted," *Christian Science Monitor,* July 13, 1973.

552 NPRA, "July 8 Report by Key Black and White Inmate Leaders," in Source 3 files.

553 Stephen Wermeil and Ken O. Botwright, "Walpole Strike Goes On; Demands Still Not Public," *Boston Globe*, July 18, 1973.

554 NPRA Legal Committee, letter, July 19, 1973.

555 Ralph Hamm, phone interview, July 3, 2007.

556 Ralph Hamm, phone interview, February 28, 2006. Hamm explains that the rise of prison bureaucracy has made it much more difficult for prisoners to organize effectively. The formation of a pan-department union for the guards has compounded the problems prisoners confront. As he puts it, "The bigger the bureaucracy, the bigger the corruption."

557 Memorandum by Ralph DiMasi, Board of Directors, NPRA, to Governor Francis Sargent, "Fasting for Thirty Days," July 23, 1973, 12 AM.

558 Edward Rodman, conversation, June 12, 2007, Cambridge, MA.

559 Robert Dellelo, conversation, July 1, 2006, Cambridge, MA.

560 NCDS report. See n. 496.

561 *Three Thousand Years and Life.*

562 Robert Dellelo, interview, February 2004, Cambridge, MA.

563 John Kerrigan was named the new president of the NPRA after the election, so that Dellelo would be able to leave the prison.

564 NPRA, press release, "Walpole NPRA Releases Statement about Stalemated Negotiations," August 29, 1973.

565 The agreement forged in the September negotiation and signed in October, titled and hereinafter "Agreement," p. 2.

566 Agreement, p. 3.

567 Coles's note in the margin reads, "If he's good enough for work-ed, he don't belong in Walpole."

568 There is no evidence that this program was ever actually considered.

569 Agreement, p. 8.

570 Robert Dellelo, interview, July 25, 2006, Cambridge, MA.

571 Jerome Miller chronicles this story in *Last One Over the Wall* (see n. 26). It is currently out of print.

572 Jerry Sousa, quoted in *Three Thousand Years and Life.*

573 *NEPA NEWS* advertisement. NEPA was formed in Franconia, New Hampshire, in April of 1973.

574 Ralph Hamm, letter, February 21, 2004.

575 Larry Dubois, the Massachusetts commissioner of corrections who presided over the creation of the Departmental Disciplinary Unit, Massachusetts's only sensory-deprivation unit, was among the first prison administrators invited to consult on the creation of the Iraqi jails.

576 See Gary B. Nash, *Forging Freedom: The Formation of Philadelphia's Black Community, 1720–1840* (Cambridge, MA: Harvard University Press, 1988), and Noel Ignatiev, *How the Irish Became White* (New York: Routledge, 1995). More than 30 percent of the population of the Walnut Street Jail, the first penitentiary founded by Quakers in Philadelphia, were Black. How many free Black men were in Philadelphia in the 1790s? Perhaps all of them were incarcerated.

577 The board consisted of nine white, nine Black, and three Latino prisoners. There were only three Latino prisoners at Walpole. They were all on the board at one time or another.

578 *Massachusetts General Law*, Part 1, Title 18, Chapter 124, Section 1, http://www.mass.gov/legis/laws/mgl/124-1.htm.

INDEX

ABOUT THE AUTHOR

JAMIE BISSONETTE COORDINATES THE CRIMINAL JUSTICE Program for the American Friends Service Committee in the New England Region. Her current work focuses on developing the National Center for Healing and Transformative Justice. This center will support the criminal justice work of Native people and communities of color. Because of her work on Native civil rights, she works with prisoners, their families, and their communities in the struggle for dignity and self-determination, focusing on sovereignty rather than rights and entitlements. The people she has worked with have taught her that every community has the shared wisdom to solve its own problems. She focuses on juvenile justice and issues of prevention because the protection and education of our children is vital to our future.

SOUTH END PRESS

SOUTH END PRESS IS AN INDEPENDENT, COLLECTIVELY RUN book publisher with more than 250 titles in print. Since our founding in 1977, we have tried to meet the needs of readers who are exploring, or are already committed to, the politics of radical social change. We publish books that encourage critical thinking and constructive action on the key political, cultural, social, economic, and ecological issues shaping life in the United States and in the world. We hope to provide a forum for a wide variety of democratic social movements, and provide an alternative to the products of corporate publishing.

From its inception, the Press has organized itself as an egalitarian collective with decision-making arranged to share as equally as possible the rewards and stresses of running the business. Each collective member is responsible for core editorial and administrative tasks, and all collective members earn the same base salary. South End has also made a practice of inverting the pervasive racial and gender hierarchies in traditional publishing houses; our collective has been majority women since the mid-1980s, and has included at least 50 percent people of color since the mid-1990s.

Our author list—which includes Andrea Smith, bell hooks, Arundhati Roy, Noam Chomsky, Winona LaDuke, Manning Marable, Ward Churchill, Cherríe Moraga, and Howard Zinn—reflects the Press's commitment to publish on diverse issues from diverse perspectives. For more information on the books we publish and ways to become involved with the Press through our street team and internship program, or to make a financial contribution to help us continue this work, please visit us online at www.southendpress.org.

COMMUNITY SUPPORTED PUBLISHING (CSP)

Community Supported Agriculture shares (CSAs) have been helping to make independent, healthy farming sustainable. Now there is CSP, so you can celebrate the bounty of the book harvest! By joining the South End Press CSP, you ensure a steady crop of books guaranteed to change your world. As a member, you receive one of the new varieties or a choice heirloom selection free each month and a 10 percent discount on everything else. Subscriptions start at $20/month. Please email southend@southendpress.org for more details.

Check out the *When the Prisoners Ran Walpole* page on South End Press's website for links to the archival material used to research this book, and to *3000 Years and Life,* the documentary film made about parts of the Walpole prisoners' struggle.

www.southendpress.org/2007/items/87705